THE NECESSITIES OF WAR
A Study of Thucydides' Pessimism

THE
NECESSITIES
OF WAR
A STUDY OF
THUCYDIDES' PESSIMISM

PETER R. POUNCEY

1980
COLUMBIA UNIVERSITY PRESS
NEW YORK

The author and publisher gratefully acknowledge the generous support given
them by the National Endowment for the Humanities and the Stanwood Cockey
Lodge Foundation of Columbia University.

Library of Congress Cataloging in Publication Data

Pouncey, Peter R
The necessities of war.

Bibliography: p.
Includes index.
1. Thucydides.   De bello Peloponnesiaco.   2. Greece
—History—Peloponnesian War, 431–404 B. C.   I. Title.
DF229.T6P68   938'.0072024   80-16887
ISBN 0-231-04994-3

Columbia University Press
New York   Guildford, Surrey

Copyright © 1980 Columbia University Press
Printed in the United States of America

FOR MY PARENTS

CONTENTS

PREFACE

This book is an attempt to reach the mind of Thucydides, as historian and writer, through a reading of his text. As the title indicates, the accent falls heavily on his pessimism—perhaps the strongest first impression, along with his intelligence, that he leaves with his reader. But other qualities, attitudes, categories of thought come into play, as he works his transformation of the confused experience of events in wartime into an ordered history with lasting lessons for posterity. By the time he sets his record down, he has moved the genre of history from many of its earlier assumptions.

Thucydides is a difficult author to see *whole*, as one who wrote a doctoral dissertation on a piece of him can testify. It is not merely a matter of the personal reticence—one always senses his guiding intelligence behind the selection of material, the insistence of the narrative on certain kinds of episodes and on certain points within episodes, the thematic patterns of argument across speeches and debates. Nor is it simply that Thucydides' dramatic sense enjoys confronting the reader with surprising judgments and reversals: the Plague follows the Funeral Oration, Agis' hesitation is stressed before his army wins its decisive victory at Mantinea, Nicias' virtue is praised as an epitaph after his military ineptitude in Sicily dooms his army and himself. The real difficulty in locating the whole of Thucydides lies in the fact that there is genuine ambivalence in the man, especially on questions connected with the pursuit of power, and the abuses to which its exercise can lead. Reticent but also self-aware, he makes room in his history for arguments that speak to each side of this ambivalence. But I do not believe that he ever fully resolved it, and the interpreter must resist the inclination to impose solutions on him, though, as we shall see, the search for them can reward us by limiting possibilities. On the whole, we are probably wiser to take the author's mask of detachment not so much as a sign of evasion, as an indication that questions of morality and evaluative judgments are not his chief concern.

We strike closer to the center of Thucydides' preoccupations if we ask the question "Why is this happening?" rather than "Is this right or wrong?". It is legitimate for a historian to try to explain the causes of the events he describes, and when it comes to explanations Thucydides leaves no shortage of principles to guide us. Indeed, the careful reader may be disconcerted by the way in which the details of the narrative and the attitudes and arguments of the speeches, which comment on the narrative, often seem directed, both in their selection and their development, by some implicit premise. General principles and large definitions stand like policemen at the elbow of events, and steer them into fairly narrow, "typical" patterns. The universal always seems about to intrude on the particular, and the historian, for all his conspicuous self-effacement, tends to become the *éminence grise* of his history. Should he be doing this, when his announced methodology is simply to record events "individually, as they happened, by summers and winters" (2.1; cf. 5.26.1)?

The fact is that we find him doing it all through the work until we reach the eighth book, where the large principles appear to be in abeyance, there are no more speeches, few set pieces, little collective activity, no large currents or direction to the war, but instead complicated activity by scattered individuals. In contrast with what has preceded it, the eighth book reads as though the history has finally got away from the author; we go from total control to something apparently directionless. Why does this happen? In all the long bibliography on Thucydides I know of no adequate explanation for the anomalous shift of technique in the eighth book.

This essay attempts to provide one, and to show that there is intellectual coherence running throughout Thucydides' work, including the eighth book. The first point to note is that the historian is as much interested in *explaining* what happens as he is in *narrating* it; the same intensity which drives him to give the minutest details of an event in which he is interested (the besieged at Plataea counting the number of bricks in the wall that imprisons them) drives him also to look for more comprehensive and indeed ultimate explanations for everything that happens. This accounts for our impression of the general overshadowing the particular. It is not that Thucydides avoids particular explanations for particular events, but that the reader senses all the time that they have their place in a larger system. Thus the Athenians agree to an alliance with Corcyra because they consider war with the Peloponnese inevitable, and they do not want their enemy to have the large Corcyrean fleet; and also because Corcyra offers a convenient way station en route to Italy and Sicily. These are particular explanations but they can be distilled further into their essential ingredients—the Athenians agree to the alliance in pursuit of security and self-interest, two considerations which are seen to underly the whole Athenian policy of imperialism, and indeed the building of power on both sides.

Thucydides could stop there, but he does not. He uses the same system of explanation to trace the development of society from the first human interactions to his own day, and then again to project into the future the validity of his history and its lessons, "for all time." The whole of history, past and future alike, is covered by the same assumption and the same explanation. The assumption is that human nature remains relatively constant, and the explanation is that the basic human impulses of aggression, fear, and self-interest direct the course of history at every stage. Human nature is therefore the architectonic concept of Thucydides' *History* and the ultimate explanation of everything that is done. At first sight, this is no more than a large banality, but I will try to show that it is more daring than it seems; I believe that the congestion of Thucydides' narrative at key points is an indication of the amount of reflection it has cost him to elaborate it. One of the principal difficulties with a large single explanation for the long processes of history is that it must account for opposite trends, for both the rise and fall of a society —in this case, for the development of Athens and Sparta to their "peak of preparedness" and also for the disintegration of their worlds.

In its main lines, the progression is envisaged as follows: Fear and self-interest constantly lead people to assert their power and then to secure it. The stronger the power grows, the more easily it absorbs the weak, and the more danger it presents to the weak. There is therefore a tendency for rival power-blocs to grow up polarized against each other, impelled, as always, by fear and self-interest; weaker states have the choice of being absorbed by a stronger one, or of fleeing for protection to another strong power—it is Hobson's choice of a more or less benign absorption. The fear and self-interest that govern the building up of societies on both sides of a polarity will also ultimately bring them to war against each other—they constitute too great a threat, and their conquest too great a temptation, to each other. The turning point has been reached. When both sides are evenly matched and well prepared (i.e. have abundant resources of manpower and money) then the war is likely to be protracted. And the pressures or necessities of war (death, disease, siege, immobility, shortage of food, forced levies, etc.) act to undo the solidarity of a society, first testing its alliances and control of its subjects, and ultimately producing civil conflict (*stasis*) within itself. Fear and self-interest are still the dominant forces, but they are exercised in an ever-narrowing circle; when *stasis* attacks the center, all collective action is seen to be impossible, and the war is of every man for himself, for his personal survival and his personal advantage. Human nature is thus finally tracked to its proper ground in the human individual. Thucydides follows this progression, first invoking the concept of human nature to explain the imperialism of nations ("it is a law of nature that the strong exploit the weak"), later of parties within a state (most notably in the Corcyrean revolution), and finally in the eighth book reducing the scale of his history to the self-centered activities of named individuals. It is a planned progression, and the descent to the particular, and the smaller scale that results from it, proceeds inexorably without moralizing like a minor premise following a major one in a kind of historical dialectic.

I give the bare outlines of the argument here in the interests of clarity. We will see a more qualified version of it in chapter 2, and then follow it in some detail through the text. The main emphasis will fall on Thucydides' first elaboration of the progression in his introduction, the Archaeology (chapter 3), and the preliminaries and early course of the war (chapters 4 and 5), and then on the period of decline and the pessimistic conclusion (chapters 6, 7, 8 and 9). This division of emphasis enables us to follow a variety of themes through the work—the collective movements of both sides, and the roles played by individuals at various stages of the war; but above all it allows us to watch the skillful transition which Thucydides makes from the confident beginnings of the war in both camps, to its decline into an uncontrollable force for disintegration. We shall put most weight on this latter phase, as I believe it reveals most clearly Thucydides' essential pessimism. By pessimism I mean only this—the conviction that human nature carries within itself drives that are destructive of its own achievements, that they are in fact the same drives as those that build historical achievements in the first place, so that in a sense the way up and the way down are one and the same. When applied to human nature, this is the full implication of Pericles' remark in the peroration of his last speech that "all things are born (*pephuke*) to be diminished" (2.64.3). I believe that this is a conviction that was borne in on Thucydides with increasing bitterness as the war and his exile dragged on, and that he involves his readers in the process of its formulation, to bring them to his own disillusionment.

What has been sketched above amounts, I believe, to the intellectual infrastructure of Thucydides' work; it shapes and stresses the narrative even where, as is mostly the case, it remains implicit. To a contemporary sensibility, though it may appreciate the intensity which such a straitened vision lends to the narrative, this extreme reductionism in the cause of history seems crude and simplistic. But we should recall that the scientific and philosophic tradition that Thucydides inherited would look on a "total" explanation as the only adequate one—he would be naturally impelled to a more comprehensive and universal theory. His problem in shaping a new discipline would be analogous to Aristotle's three generations later: "His whole effort is directed to explanation by reference to general laws, so much so that he . . . was already faced with the perennial problem of scientific enquiry: how is scientific knowledge of the individual possible at all, since science only explains by subsuming under laws that operate universally?" (W. K. C. Guthrie, *A History of Greek Philosophy*, 1:41).

I would hope that this book might be useful to the nonspecialist. To that end, all passages of the text are translated, and where Greek words appear for comment they are transliterated (using the method of Arthur Adkins in *Merit and Responsibility: A Study of Greek Values* [Oxford: Oxford University Press, 1960]). References are given in the body of the text to the relevant book, chapter and section of the Oxford Classical Text of Thucydides. (Readers will find that most translations do not subdivide chapters into sections in this way—there is no great inconvenience about this economy, as the chapters are rarely longer than a paragraph.) All names are printed in their English form.

There is the problem of secondary scholarship—a daunting accumulation over the centuries. The habitual mode of scholarly debate in this field is to pay assiduous attention to this secondary tradition: one discusses the original text, and parades the history of scholarship on it. Such methods have produced models of humane erudition, and also some virtuosities of byzantinism; it is also probably true that from time to time simple wrongheadedness has been allowed to hide behind a clutter of learned reference. But intellectually there are two more serious dangers attached to the whole method: it can make the discipline unnaturally introverted, so that it is blind to developments in other fields that could shed fresh light on its own material; and it can make it doubly conservative (some *proper* conservatism is desirable in a discipline that is by definition retrospective), by encouraging one generation to discuss problems defined by its predecessors: one ends up with classical problems in classical scholarship.

Faced with these hazards, I have decided to keep the mainstream of my argument as clear and untrammeled as possible, concentrating on Thucydides' text for support. My errors will be more exposed by this practice, but that is to the good; and if I am in error on any matter, it is not, after all, because of what someone else has written on it. I do not find that scholars have given an adequate account of Thucydides' most fundamental thinking on human nature, history, and war in its various aspects. This essay tries to fill that deficiency. Philological argument will be kept to a minimum; as I have translated every passage cited, it will be clear to critics on what side of various technical fences I have come down. Historical questions of chronology, politics, or strategy will not be discussed except where they are relevant to the main argument. Simple references to other works are provided for those who wish to pursue such questions further. I have also written brief critiques of books that bear more directly on my argument.

It seems a long time since I first confronted Thucydides, and it is a tribute to those who explained him to me or studied him with me, as well as to Thucydides himself, that he has always appeared interesting and impressive, and the more so the further one goes with him. Over more than twenty-five years I have incurred many debts in this connection, and the two most recent ones must be expressly acknowledged. My friends and colleagues James Coulter in my own department and Herbert Deane, Lieber Professor of Political Philosophy at Columbia, read various parts of the manuscript in various drafts, and encouraged and enlightened me in discussions; they share Thucydides' gift of being able to assess evidence with accuracy (*akribeia*), while being fully aware of its larger implications. The book would have been better if the discussions had lasted longer; but the time comes when one must write it down.

THE NECESSITIES OF WAR
A Study of Thucydides' Pessimism

In peacetime and prosperity, both individuals and cities retain a high morale, because they have not yet been trapped by inescapable necessities. But war, which removes the comfort of their daily lives, is a harsh teacher, and adapts the passions of most people to their actual situation.

Thucydides, 3.82.2

INTRODUCTION

THUCYDIDES' OWN EXPERIENCE OF THE WAR

There is no firm evidence for the date of Thucydides' birth, but two passages in his book suggest terms for it. It is likely that he had to be thirty to be elected general in 424 (4.104.4), and unlikely that he had reached thirty when the war began in 431; his statement at 5.26.5 that he lived "through the whole of the war at an age (*hēlikiāi*) when he could perceive (what was happening)" protects him from charges of immaturity rather than senility: the nuance is that he was *sufficiently* old to understand, rather than *not too* old. We would have him born, then, between 460 and 454 B.C.[1]

The intellectual and rhetorical currents that run through his work tell us that he was closely familiar with the avant-garde cultural developments of his day.[2] In the second half of the fifth century B.C., Athens became the focus of all such developments, and within Athens many of them converged on the elite circle of which Pericles was the central figure. The fact that opposition to Pericles could express itself through attacks on his associates Anaxagoras, the philosopher (Plutarch *Per.* 32.1 and 3), Pheidias, the sculptor (*ibid.* 31.2–5), Damon, the musician (*ibid.* 4.1–2, cf. 9.2 and Aristotle *Constitution of Athens*, 27.4, where the same figure is called Damonides),[3] and Aspasia, Pericles' cultivated mistress (Plut. *Per.* 32.1 and 3), seems to indicate that the association had a certain exclusiveness to it, and thus presented an identifiable target. It does not require very sophisticated detective work to find Thucydides in this group. Even without the evidence of his writing, with its traces of con-

nection to particular figures, his intelligence, his family relationships
with the legendary Miltiades and Cimon, the fact that his family had
traditionally stood in the opposite political camp, his royal connections
in Thrace, and most especially his control of the gold mines there
(4.105.1), would all combine to make him a singularly attractive catch for
the Periclean circle. Plutarch says that at his peak Pericles "concentrated
within himself Athens and all the matters related to the Athenians, . . .
and the hegemony hedged about with subject peoples, the friendships of
kings, and alliances with the powerful" (Plut. *Per.* 15.1): with such talents for absorption, he would have been unlikely to ignore someone of
Thucydides' stature.

On Thucydides' side, for a man of his intellectual power, with half his
roots and his career in the wilds of northern Greece, the climate at
Athens would be exhilarating. He would attend closely to the making of
decisions which directed and exploited a great empire, and would probably share the self-confidence in a "worthiness to rule," and enjoy the new
spirit of enlightenment in which everything had become, it would
seem, humanly possible. We should recognize that the Funeral Oration
is an effort to show that the Periclean order of things is based not merely
on the political realities of the day, or an imperialistic philosophy, but
also on a cultural view of Athens' role in the world—the school of Hellas
(2.41.1), where the people "love beauty without extravagance and learning without effeteness" (2.40.1). In this school, Pericles is a teacher, and
he gives a lesson (*didaskalian*) to try to convey that "for us the struggle is
not the same as for those who share none of our benefits" (2.42.1). If the
Peloponnesian war on the Spartan side was a war for the liberation of
Hellas, on the Athenian side it could be seen as a war not merely to retain an empire, but to safeguard the Athenian way of life (*epitēdeusis*). In
the construction of the Funeral Oration, there is every effort to make the
argument convincing. The claims of Athens' greatness are advanced "not
as boastful words, but as actual fact" (2.41.2), "with solid evidence and
testimony" (2.41.4)—the evidence being Athenian power and what it has
accomplished.

Thucydides mentions the enthusiasm of youth on both sides for the
coming war, "in their inexperience" (2.8.1): there is no reason to think
that he was immune from it at the outset himself. His opening sentence,
which tells us that he began to write as soon as the war started, because

he expected it would be "great and more significant than all wars which preceded it" contains perhaps a muted note of that enthusiasm. Certainly his championship of Pericles conveys his belief that the decision to go to war was the right one, that it was a war worth fighting, and that it was a war that ought to have been won (see 2.65.13).

But enthusiasm and the Periclean view of Athens' destiny have a short life under the pressures of war. The Funeral Oration, as we shall see, is immediately undercut by its confrontation with the facts of the plague. Thucydides often gives us, with evident approval, in the persons of elder statesmen such as Pericles himself, the Spartan King Archidamus, the Spartan ambassadors suing for peace after the capture of Pylos, or Nicias before the Sicilian expedition, the voice of experience and the long view, and his own voice is habitually seasoned, if not embittered, with the wisdom of hindsight. He is fond of using metaphors of schooling to convey the impact of events and situations that force men to learn from experience. War itself is a "harsh teacher"; though "events may proceed no less stupidly (*amathōs*) than the plans of men" (Pericles in his first speech, 1.140.1), the strongest man is "the one who is schooled in necessities" (Archidamus, 1.84.4). It should not surprise us, then, that Thucydides' point of view shows signs of development in the course of the war: an intelligent man should learn something from the experience and observation of a major upheaval lasting twenty-seven years. And it is part of the urgency of Thucydides' *History* that he wants the reader to learn the same lessons for himself (1.22.4).

In his case, the last twenty of the twenty-seven years of the war were spent in exile. The pivotal event was his failure to save Amphipolis from Brasidas in 424, a failure that transformed him from an active participant into a critical observer. Before that, we only know that he caught the plague and recovered from it (2.48.3); he mentions the sense of euphoria and immunity that such an escape brought with it, encouraging "the foolish hope that one would never be destroyed by any other disease" (2.51.6). But he also indicates—and I believe this challenges any view that he was completely fatalistic about the decline of moral standards around him—that those who recovered from the disease felt a social obligation to those who came down with it:

> But if they came in contact with the sick, they were fatally infected themselves. This was especially true of those who had any decency; for their

sense of proper shame drove them selflessly to visit their friends, when even
the relatives had abandoned the ritual lament for the dying, undone by the
burden of constant grief. But it was those who had themselves escaped the
disease who most pitied the sick and the dying, because of their knowledge of
its progress and their own personal sense of confidence; for no one caught it
twice, or at least badly enough to die of it. (2.51.5–6)[4]

At that stage, it would seem that Thucydides bore a charmed life. His
career was not eclipsed by the death of Pericles. When the Spartan
Brasidas began his rampage in Thrace in 424, Thucydides and his influence in the area were well enough known and respected for him to be
elected general. There cannot have been many of his peers to have arrived at such eminence before him, though in wartime promotions often
reward talent more quickly. Nor can it have been only a matter of local
influence which won him the command; it was to be a military appoint-
ment at a dangerous time, and Thucydides must have shown some degree of military competence prior to this, though presumably in a less
responsible capacity. It is interesting that, apart from the Plague, he has
never indicated to this point that he was a party to any of the incidents
he describes; all he gives us is the moment of his failure.

That it was a failure is, I think, clear. In his *Historical Commentary on
Thucydides*, Gomme makes the best case he can for him, but none of it
seems to take into account the crucial importance of the town of Amphipolis, the cost to Athens in establishing it, the fact that it would be the
most obvious goal for Brasidas in the area. There are various small chronological nuances in the text that seem designed to protect Thucydides:
the place was so badly defended that Brasidas could have taken it as soon
as he crossed the bridge, the evening he arrived, if his men had not been
sidetracked into looting (4.104.2)—in which case there would not have
been time even to send a message for Thucydides; the implication is that
the capture of Amphipolis was a foregone conclusion as soon as Brasidas
made his move. Again, the speedy capitulation of the town is partly attributed to the sense of its citizens that help would be some time in coming (106.1)—in other words Thucydides moved faster than anyone had a
right to expect: he tells us that he did in fact move "at speed" (*kata
tachos*—4.104.5). But as Thucydides was well aware, "in wartime opportunities wait for no man" (1.142.1), a Periclean maxim that is as valid for
defenders as it is for the aggressor.

One of the most interesting features about the narrative of Brasidas' activity in Amphipolis—both his capture and defense of it—is the author's evident admiration for the Spartan. This may well be honest objectivity on Thucydides' part, or it may in part proceed from a desire, if one has to lose, to succumb to a worthy victor. Certainly, the attractiveness of Brasidas would be enhanced for Thucydides by the fact that he finishes off the egregious Cleon; but even in the earliest stages of the war, Thucydides has followed his career with sympathy, always singling him out for comment even in unsuccessful ventures. It is as though he saw in this man of action and good sense a kindred spirit: in the generous terms offered to the Athenians in Amphipolis, we see Brasidas eager to reach a settlement with the place, because of his fear of Thucydides and his influence in the neighborhood (4.105.1). This is as close to personal arrogance as Thucydides will come; at one stroke, it writes off the other Athenian general, Eucles, and whatever defenses he might offer, and establishes the historian as the real threat, whom even a Brasidas must take seriously. In return, Thucydides rewards Brasidas with the only truly romantic, and perhaps epic, death in the work. Having taken over a city rife with internal dissent (104.1), he then defends it against its former masters, and dies in the knowledge that his defense has been successful (5.10.11). The whole people follow him to the grave, pay him honors as a Hero, and declare him the Founder of the city, to whom religious rituals are due (5.11.1). Amphipolis is thus remade for Brasidas. The details of this romance are so precise that one wonders whether Thucydides indulged himself for a moment with what might have been if only he had arrived in time to defend the town himself.

Instead of glory he received twenty years of exile—a steep sentence for an officer, who, whatever his delinquencies, saved one town (Eion) and was only secondarily responsible for the loss of another. But Thucydides' failure would not be measured in the public mind by the degree of his responsibility, but simply by the importance of the town; and on that criterion, it would be hard to forget or forgive his lateness. Apart from Aegospotamoi and the Sicilian debacle, the loss of Amphipolis might well be the worst military setback suffered by Athens in the war; it was certainly the final straw which prompted her to make peace. She never got the town back, despite the terms of the truce, which lists the return of Amphipolis to Athens as the first specific provision, singling it out from other towns in the area (5.18.5). As the loss continued, there would be no agitation to curtail the exile of anyone associated with it.

We do not know what Thucydides did in his exile, apart from writing history, or (with any certainty) where he spent it. The two *Lives* that survive place him variously in Aegina, Italy, and Thrace—we may settle on the last, as the *Life* of Marcellinus gives it with some firmness and seems aware of the other sources (*Vit. Marcellin.* 24–25, 46–47; cf. *Vit.Anon.* 7).[5] Apart from that we have a vacuum of twenty years, and should not fill it with speculation. But some points need to be made. It is clear from the intensity of Thucydides' text that he remained absorbed in the developments of the war from which he was excluded. He was a man of action who applauded strong intitiatives, and whose first chapter indicates some enthusiasm for the vast undertaking the Greek world was embarking on. He could not, apparently, walk away from the events, when his own association with them was finished. Carrying the stigma of failure with him, and reduced from action to words, he still paid close attention to every detail of the war, and he still, it seems, wanted to be part of it. The "exile's eagerness" for return, which Alcibiades mentions (6.92.2), is something he clearly experienced himself; when the oligarchs were in power in 411, he mentions their reforms and then adds, apparently out of the blue, "but they did not recall the exiles because of Alcibiades" (8.70.1). The small parenthesis seems quite irrelevant, until we realize that for Thucydides it meant that his banishment had another seven years to run.

Exile would change some of his perspectives as a historian, if only by confirming some tendencies he had within him at the expense of others. The detached, scientific tone would be enhanced; he was disengaged from the action, and no longer inclined to be an apologist for a particular set of policies: as he says, he was "able to study the actions *on both sides* at leisure and in greater detail" (5.26.5). Second, whatever disenchantment he felt at his personal rejection would only be reinforced by the drift of public events, as the war continued to escape from Athens' control. There is very little *Schadenfreude* in the man (except perhaps over Cleon's comeuppance), but certainly real bitterness at the waste of talent and resources in the long period of Athenian decline; we see it in his comment on Pericles' surplus of resources sustaining the war long beyond any terms he would have set on it (2.65.13). Third (extending this point further), in his search for deeper explanations of the events, the fact of his exile, and perhaps even the circumstances of it, would play upon the pessimistic veins of his personality and philosophy.

I have alluded to a kind of antithesis between the Athenian and Thracian parts of his background—Athens standing for civilization, enlightenment, and the amplitude of a large national vision, Thrace for barbarism, provincialism, and a beleaguered sense of isolation. One has only to state the antithesis in such foursquare terms, to question its validity. But I believe there is plenty of evidence in Thucydides' text that he began with this kind of simplistic distinction, and was only taught by his own bitter experience that it could not be sustained.

One needs no further documentation for the romantic view of Athens than the Funeral Oration; Thracian hostility and barbarism receive less central but equally clear-cut allusions. Very close to the time of Thucydides' birth, the first attempt by Athens to found what was to become Amphipolis was thwarted when the Athenian force was massacred by a Thracian army further inland at Drabescus (1.100.3; 4.102.2). Thucydides gives a precise chronological interval between this and the final settlement of Amphipolis under Hagnon ("in the twenty-ninth year"—4.102.3), and also refers back to another abortive effort by Aristagoras of Miletus in 496 (4.102.2). Thucydides' family was influential in this area, but the precise chronologies are not merely a tribute to the care with which they kept records, but to their continued awareness of Thracian hostility to foreign occupation. I believe that Thucydides' view of the hatred with which the allies regarded Athens, and the prominence of fear as a motive of Athenian policy, had its roots in such long memories. They would be reinforced by the alacrity with which the whole area accepted Brasidas' work of liberation, and also by such episodes as the atrocity at Mycalessus, where Thracian slingers, returning home after missing the boat for Sicily, went berserk and massacred the entire population of a Boeotian village, including livestock (7.29–30): "The Thracian race, like most barbarian peoples, is at its most murderous when its courage is high" (7.29.4). Plutarch tells us that Alcibiades, upon his retirement to Thrace after the battle of Notium, made a fortune by making war against the Thracians "who have no king, . . . and at the same time provided safety to the Greeks in the area from barbarian attack" (Plut. Alc. 36.3).

Clearly, life on the frontier has its hazards. Whether Thucydides had his memory refreshed by spending his exile there, or whether it was attended by personal danger, does not matter; a sense of barely quiescent hostility from one's neighbor would be part of his heritage. And the fact of his exile would kill the romance that Athens lived on a more elevated plane of mutual trust and security. When it came to a review of his own case, it is likely that the personal enmity of Cleon was decisive against him (*Vit. Marcellin.* 46); in the last analysis, people act for themselves with little restraint, whether in Athens or Thrace, and that is reason to fear them.

Pericles in his Funeral Oration called Athens "the School of Hellas" (2.41.1) and posed as a schoolmaster giving a lesson on its virtues. But the deepest, longest-lasting lessons that Thucydides learned came from war, "the harsh teacher" (3.82.2): over twenty-seven years, the iron entered into his soul.

1

ACCURACY (AKRIBEIA) AND THE PATTERN OF EVENTS

METHODOLOGY AND POINT OF VIEW

Arguments over comparative greatness are usually trivial. Thucydides begins his *History* with an attempt to prove that his war was the greatest of all wars involving the Greeks, and in doing so tackles the Trojan War, cutting it down to size by logistical calculations on the figures Homer offers (1.10.4), and removing its romantic aspect by insisting that the other cities followed Agamemnon not because of the oath of Tyndareus, but through fear of his greater power (1.9.1–2). We will discuss this passage in greater detail later, but one's first impression on reading it is that the polemics are petty and perhaps perversely literal-minded—they refuse to take epic on its own terms.

But this is exactly the point. For all his aspersions on the credibility of Homer (1.9.3; 1.10.3), Thucydides treats the theme of the *Iliad* as historical. This is striking and serves to remind us that for Thucydides and his immediate audience the narrative of the past is strongly tied to the conventions of epic.[1] Thucydides is writing close to the events he describes, but all his innovations—and they are far-reaching enough to make him seem peculiarly "modern," and to leave him out of step with the dominant strain of historians for several centuries from his own day[2]—are, I believe, not merely spontaneous emanations from his own troubled spirit, but carefully considered both for their impact on a reader brought up in the epic tradition, and for the problems they set the writer of history.

The step that carries him furthest from epic, and causes him to make the greatest adjustments in his methods of exposition, is his reassessment of the individual's status in making history. In the poetic tradition, a *mūthos* typically concerns individuals and their actions or destiny; even in the grandest themes of epic, and even when gods intervene to force the issue, individuals can fill the stage and earn glory (*kleos*).[3] For Thucydides, the large movements of power, by aggression or alliance, are what make history (are truly "significant" or "worthy of note"—*axiologon*), and his judgment on the realities of the Greek world of his day is that the *locus* of power is found in states and their resources rather than in individuals. We will find this judgment operating immediately in his introduction, the Archaeology.

In the meantime, some rough comparisons of Thucydides with Herodotus will help to make the judgment clear. For Herodotus the status of individuals is unquestionably reduced by their destiny, their (sometimes culpable) ignorance of it, and by various religious checks and balances, but the individual action remains the basic currency of his *History*. The range of exploit has been extended more democratically than the conventions of epic allow—the clever thief is given the King of Egypt's daughter (Hdt. 2.121), and Darius' groom Oebares can determine his master's succession (Hdt. 3.85–7)—but the assumption is still that the individual can shape the course of history. In battles, the most conspicuous scenes of collective action, the legacy of epic dictates the practice of recording the names of the individuals who particularly distinguished themselves in the fighting (Marathon, 6.114; Thermopylae, 7.224 and 226; Salamis, 8.93; Plataea, 9.71 ff.). The epic refrain of the *klea andrōn* (the glory of heroes) finds its echo in Herodotus' opening sentence, where he tells us that he is writing "lest the great and remarkable deeds performed by the Greeks and the barbarians should go uncelebrated (*a-klea*)."[4] We should remember that the Muse of History, Clio, is shared with epic, and by her very name (etymologically connected with *kleos*) puts this preoccupation at the center of the genre.

Thucydides works a kind of inversion of the epic assumptions which Herodotus had upheld in his work. It is not that he depopulates history of individuals—even for him politicians must advocate policies, and generals form strategies and lead armies. But hard reflection about the accumulations of power has convinced him that *collective* action, with the full weight of public resources behind it, equipped his generation for the greatest of wars between the Greeks, and that this will be true of all significant history—the greater the resources and the more complete the solidarity behind an enterprise, the more truly "historic" it is likely to be. The status of the individual is necessarily adjusted by this principle. A good statesman is now one who thinks for the whole, who forms national policies appropriate for national needs and resources, and who uses his rhetorical gifts to persuade the people of what is in their national interests. For Thucydides, the real test of the great statesman, as of the great general, is how he keeps his people together under pressure. Just as Phormio rallies his small force when he sees it "forming groups" in its fear (2.88.1), and Brasidas preserves "order and discipline" among his troops when he finds that they have been abandoned by Perdiccas in the wilds of Thrace (4.126.6), so Pericles rallies the Athenian people, though demoralized by the plague, behind his plan (2.65.1–2), and Hermocrates secures national unity in the face of the threat of an Athenian invasion (4.65.1; see his appeal for unity at 4.61.1–2). All of this requires a kind of selflessness, almost an anonymity, which is rare in an epic hero. It is also rare in Thucydides. As is made clear of Pericles' successors generically, unselfish statesmanship runs against the dominant pattern; the trend of individual assertion in Thucydides' *History*, especially as it progresses, is selfish. Individuals grasp for primacy, and so cater to the whims of the people. Whatever titles they carry, they thus abdicate from the direction of affairs and let themselves be led; as the competition for supremacy within the state intensifies, they produce *stasis*, and so end up destroying their city and themselves with it (2.65.7 and 65.10–12; cf. 8.89.3). The pressures of war, of plague, of *stasis*, of defeat are too great for the average individual to surmount. There is, then, for Thucydides, little in individual behavior worth celebrating.[5]

We will follow this negative trend in some detail later. It is enough to observe here that it amounts to a considerable reorientation of the genre. With the subordination of individual exploits, whether anecdotal or exalted, to collective action, history seems comparatively jejune; in the terms of Longinus' distinction, Thucydides by his shift of emphasis seems at first to have forfeited both the *pathos* of the *Iliad*, and the *ēthos* of the *Odyssey:* [6] Herodotus, though he tends perhaps to the latter, could avail himself of both. Without these, what is left to hold the reader? One can see some defensiveness on Thucydides' part in his remark that "the lack of *mūthos* will perhaps make this account appear less entertaining to listen to" (1.22.4).

Instead of entertainment, Thucydides offers *akribeia*—the record of truth arduously compiled. There is a certain parallelism between the making of history and the writing of history: just as the individual action is unlikely to be significant, so the individual *report* of an action is unlikely to be accurate, but must be corrected or reinforced by alternative versions (1.22.2–3). But artistically a history needs more than a labored exactitude: the problem facing Thucydides is how to make a history of often anonymous events, accurately compiled "as they happened, by summers and winters," amount to a unity that is interesting and compelling. The division of the chronology into summers and winters seems to have compounded the problem for him, fragmenting the action even further; Dionysius of Halicarnassus tells us that he was the first to do this and pronounces the innovation unhelpful (Dion. Hal. *Thuc.* 9).[7] But despite these difficulties there is a strong impression of unity, at least on a first reading; as Hobbes wrote, "For as much as his purpose being to write of the Peloponnesian War, this way he hath incorporated all the parts thereof into one body, so that there is unity in the whole, and the several narratives are conceived as parts of that."[8] How is this achieved?

Basically, unity is achieved by a variety of techniques that link a particular event with others in a pattern, often out of strict temporal sequence, or lend it a force or resonance that carries beyond the actual circumstances, so that the history as a whole is given a kind of intentional direction beyond the merely chronological. There seems, then, to be a tension between the *akribeia* of an episode (all the precise details of what actually happens), and the historian's interpretative intention, which imposes the pattern and points the direction from one episode to another. I would see this as a *creative* tension, perhaps essential for the transformation of any list or chronicle of events into true history; clearly both aspects have to be convincing for the account to win acceptance, though they may appeal to different quarters for their validity. In Thucydides' case, *akribeia* appeals directly to the evidence, and the "direction" or "pattern of events" rather to the reader's own experience, for confirmation.

This is a general statement of a problem and its solution which no doubt could be applied to the work of other historians; particular examples of Thucydides' various "binding" techniques, briefly noted here, will give the statement some *akribeia*, and enable us to see the functions the techniques serve in various contexts.

1. The crucial point to note is the *regular use of speech and narrative to complement each other*[9]: the reader is constantly struck by echoes of what he has read before, even before he can place them exactly in narrative or speech. The notion of a calculated complementariness between speech and narrative requires some defense, especially in view of the apparent opposition between them.[10] At root one might say that the opposition proceeds from the ubiquitous *logos/ergon* distinction (where usually the "theory" is refuted by the "fact"—e.g., "In theory a democracy, but in fact rule by the First Man"—2.65.9). Words can change their meanings (3.82.4), whereas actions have determinate effects and can be considered "hard" data. The antipathy between words and actions is carried into the speeches of some of the most reputable speakers: the moderate King Archidamus, for example, says that the Spartans "do not, by an excessive cleverness in useless things, find fault in elegant words with their enemies' preparations, while failing to match them adequately in deeds" (1.84.3); and Pericles begins his Funeral Oration by protesting a convention that requires that the virtues of many, which were displayed in deed, should be dependent for credibility on one man, speaking well or ill (2.35.1).[11]

But clearly an orator will not carry the inadequacy of words too far, nor will a historian. Pericles later in the same speech says that the Athenians "do not consider *words* an obstacle to action; the damage lies rather in not being instructed by discussion in preparation for the action one will have to take" (2.40.2). And even the Spartans acknowledge the usefulness of words in similar terms at a critical juncture of the war, in a speech which Thucydides clearly endorses: "It is our custom not to use many words where few suffice, but to use more where there is an opportunity, by some relevant verbal instruction, to obtain a necessary action" (4.17.2).

The fact is that Thucydides uses more formal speeches than any of his predecessors (Marcellin. *Vita Thuc.* 38), but I can only think of one that is deliberately "wasted" and offers no positive information, but simply invites the reader's scorn for the fatuity of its content—the speech of the Syracusan demagogue Athenagoras on the news of the Athenian expedition (6.36–40; with heavy irony, Thucydides describes him, as he has his bête noire Cleon, as "most persuasive"—6.35.2). The topos of the inadequacy of words vis-à-vis action may reflect to some extent his own personal frustration at being removed from the action and reduced to writing about it; "words are the weapons of the frustrated."[12] But in part, I believe, the opposition is purposely engineered to produce a counterpoint of different tones inside the book. Various voices, including that of the narrator, combine to provide an internal system of evidence within the work, one account confirming, explaining, or occasionally deliberately refuting, or ironically playing upon, another.

a) *Confirmation.* A simple case would be the Athenian countercharge at the Congress at Sparta, or by Pericles in his first speech, that the Spartans are as guilty of selfish motives in their foreign policy as the Athenians, having organized their alliance to their own convenience (*ōphelimon*—1.76.1; *sphisin epitēdeiōs*—1.143.2). These are polemical contexts, but the assertion has been confirmed as a point of fact by Thucydides himself in the Archaeology, using the same word as Pericles (1.19).

b) *Explanation.* Speeches can be used to explain subsequent behavior: thus the Corinthian speech at the first Spartan Congress describes, with impressive induction, the national character types of the two protagonists. In sum, the Athenians are quick to action (*oxeis*) and the Spartans are slow (1.70 passim; *bradutēs*—1.71.4). This gives the reader a key to some of the decisions and actions that the two sides will take, or fail to take, in the war; it is valid throughout the work. Towards the end of the last book, after the Spartans have failed to follow up their advantage in Euboea, the narrator's voice makes the point anew, using the same words: "For they were extraordinarily different in temperament, one side *oxeis* and the other *bradeis*" (8.96.5).

c) *Ironic confirmation.* Cleon lectures the Athenians about the irresponsibility of democracy in its operations, accusing them of attending the assembly like theatergoers looking to be entertained (3.37.1; 38.2–7). We soon find Cleon at the center of a debate in the Assembly in which his description is confirmed, and at which everyone behaves badly: Cleon offers irresponsible challenges over Pylos (4.27.5), Nicias irresponsibly steps down from his command (4.28.3), and the *dēmos*, enjoying Cleon's embarrassment, irresponsibly enforces the challenge (4.28.3 and 5).[13]

2. *"Running" arguments sustained in speeches.* Sometimes one speech clearly answers another in a different debate and context.

a) Before the war begins, the long-term strategies available to the two sides are discussed on three separate occasions. Archidamus, at the first Congress at Sparta, warns his people that it will be a new kind of war, which will find the Spartans short of funds, ships, and naval experience (1.80–81). The Corinthians, at the second Congress, answer this with mention of loans from Delphi and Olympia to build ships and entice mercenaries (1.121.3). Pericles, in his first speech, though he has not been present at either of the previous debates, confirms Archidamus' misgivings and argues that such loans will not make much difference, because nautical competence is not bought but only mastered by long experience (1.142.4–143.2).[14]

b) *Arguments on imperialism.* The Athenian speech at Sparta, the Mytilenean debate, the Melian Dialogue and Euphemus' speech at Camarina all discuss Athens' relationships with her allies. The arguments harden as they go along, abandoning justifications based on Athenian performance in the Persian wars (1.73–74; but cf. 5.89 for the Athenians at Melos; and 6.82–83.2, where Euphemus first advances the argument, and then appears to qualify it with post-Melian skepticism) and claims to praise based on moderation.

We should note that in both examples there is still a close relationship between the speeches and the facts of the narrative. Not only will Pericles' claims of strategic advantage for Athens be confirmed in the early phases of the war, but there is an explicit deferral in the speech to another occasion "at the time of action" (1.144.2), where actual details of Athenian resources will be given; this account is duly reported in indirect discourse by Thucydides at the time of the first Spartan invasion of Attica (2.13; cf. 2.65.13). As for Athenian imperialism, the hardening of the argument in the speeches marches *pari passu* with the progressive abandonment of restraint in the conduct of the war from the first Congress to Melos.[15]

3. *Narrative themes.* The pattern of events can be most sharply delineated by the narrator's choice of material and emphasis.

a) *Stasis*. The importance of internal revolution as a destructive force in history appears in the Archaeology (1.2.4; 1.18.1), in the first incident of confrontation before the war (Epidamnus—1.24.4), in the actual immediate cause of the war (the Thebans are introduced into Plataea by a dissident faction in the town "for the sake of private power"—2.2.2), in the Corcyrean revolution (3.70–83, ending with an impressive moralistic commentary on social collapse), and finally in Athens, where, throughout the last book, individual maneuvers are followed in detail. We will attend carefully to the role of *stasis* in the work.

b) The *paralogos*. The author's view that a great deal of history lies beyond the individual's control and is made rather by "incalculable" events, is stressed both by the explicit warnings of the more impressive statesmen (Archidamus, 1.82.6; Pericles, 1.140.1), and by shaping of the narrative in particular episodes. Thus Phormio's naval victory against superior numbers is secured from retreat by the use of a merchant vessel which "happened to be moored" in the bay (2.91.3), and the Athenian success at Sphacteria, which Thucydides is anxious to portray as anything but the result of Cleon's intelligence, hinges in part on the accidental burning of the scrub-cover on the lower part of the island (4.29.2–3). On the negative side, we have the massive catastrophe of the plague (2.47 ff.) and Nicias' fatal delay in Syracuse because of an eclipse (7.50.4).[16]

4. *Individuals and Incidents as Archetypes*. So far we have talked of various "cross-threading" devices, which the historian uses to give his work unity and establish patterns; taken together, they serve both to explain and enhance the interest of particular events. But patterns once established can be tedious in their sameness, even if intensely colored. There is, as one would expect, considerable variation of intensity and emphasis in Thucydides' narrative; neither the reader nor history itself could support a constant drumroll of unrelenting significance. Most incidents are allowed to stand on their own, complete in the *akribeia* of their details, fixed in time by a simple reference to the preceding event ("in the same summer," "not long afterwards"), and without further implications for subsequent history or our understanding of it.[17]

But there are events and individuals, sometimes clearly within a particular pattern and sometimes at first view standing on their own, to which Thucydides wants to draw particular attention: weighted with significance, they stand out against the regular progression of the history, and become relatively fixed points of reference within the work, which constantly invite the reader's reflections and comparisons. How is this done? The examples of Plataea and Pericles are illustrative:

a) *Plataea*. The drama of Plataea is told by Thucydides in four separate acts: the attack on the town (2.2–6); blockade and siege (2.71–78); partial escape (3.20–24); and final surrender (3.51–68). The importance of Plataea for Thucydides must reside partially in the fact that it is the location both of the opening incident of this war between the Greeks, and of the last battle of the Persian War, which was also the last time the principal powers in Greece had fought on the same side. It provides the focus for the transition from the history of the past—and from the loyalties and conventions of the past, which by now would wear heroic aspects from the burnishing of personal memories and Herodotus' account—to the harsher realities of his own day. The Spartan King Pausanias had awarded the town a privileged and perhaps religious status, and it seems at first that Archidamus, "the intelligent and moderate" king who must address the new problem, is prepared to honor this with adjustments made for the military situation (2.71–74).

But Archidamus was out of action before the drama is finished and all scruples are removed. After a period of moderate negotiation and reason, the small town is put under siege, and though it tries every possible initiative to break the noose, is forced to surrender; after a perfunctory trial the survivors are put to death and the town is destroyed. The war carries Plataea, in just four years, from favored ally to obliteration. For Sparta, over the same period, the dominant attitude changes from respect for the history and conventions of the past, as shown by Archidamus, to total preoccupation with the advantage of the moment—the profitable alliance with Thebes (3.68.4). The same progression, over a rather more extended period, carries Athens from her profession of moderation at Sparta (1.76.3–4) to her destruction of Melos. Plataea is Athens' oldest ally, and Melos is a Lacedaemonian settlement: at the end, in both cases, we can see that the weak victim has been hurt rather than helped by its powerful connection.

All these reflections are, I think, legitimate indications of the importance that Thucydides attaches to Plataea; they establish strong connections with other events in the work, and with Thucydides' regular system of judgment. But the point to note is that for the most part, apart from the single comment at the end about the "profitable" alliance with Thebes, Thucydides will not make the connections for us by any explicit moralization. His own device is to envelop the reader almost claustrophobically in details about the siege and its progress. In the second act we follow a long series of cat-and-mouse ploys between besieger and besieged—efforts to surmount the opposing wall or to undermine it (2.77). The series of initiatives seems at first almost comical, until we realize that for the besieged it is a life-and-death struggle and one they are bound to lose—the noose will eventually be tightened. There is a moment of reprieve—the partial escape in the third act. Again, we have the painfully exact detail: the Plataeans planning to break out stand on the wall, and count the number of bricks in the opposing wall to calculate the length of a ladder needed to surmount it, and more than one person counts to make sure they get the number correct (*tou alēthous logismou*— 3.20.3); when they make their escape they go with the right foot shoeless to get a better grip in the mud (3.22.2). This unblinking, microscopic view of the action, the compounding of endless physical, almost tangible, details, allows the reader, even at this distance, no escape; our sympathy is enlisted for the small band trapped inside the walls by the armies and the politics of far greater forces; they have the innocence of all victims, and we admire their tireless intelligence for self-preservation and their solidarity (counting the bricks, some carrying the others' shields, creating a diversion during the escape), foredoomed as they are. For the Attic readers of Thucydides' own time, the impact of these episodes would be even greater and more painful, given the long bond between Athens and Plataea, the fact that they had not been able to assist their ally, and the fact that they themselves had firsthand experience of siege.

Such passages show the full power of *akribeia*. The density of the detail slows the pace of the narrative down, so that the reader is literally arrested in his stride and must consider what is involved. And again we see the complementariness of narrative and speech. The larger perspectives of history and Plataea's service in the Persian Wars are appealed to both in the brief Plataean exchanges with Archidamus (2.71.2–3), and in their long speech—the longest in the *History* apart from the Funeral Oration— before the final condemnation (3.53–59). When we look at this speech closely we find that the tone of ineluctable disaster, which was built up in the narrative, is carefully maintained. The Plataeans speak after the

Spartans have asked what good they have done for Sparta and her allies in this war (3.52.4). The question is true to the traditional Spartan temperament in its laconic formulation, if nothing else, but it unashamedly puts self-interest as the only legitimate concern. Faced with this implacable sense of priority, everything the Plataeans have to say is irrelevant. They are talking past their judges for the record, fearful that they have already been judged: "We are afraid, not that you may have judged our merits to be inferior to yours and built your charge on that, but that we are facing a verdict that has already been determined as a favor to others" (3.53.4, cf. 56.6; their concern about Spartan motives is reflected in a procession of comments on self-interest—see especially 3.56.3–7). By the end of the speech, all the moral lessons have been drawn: the narrator's voice which has been used exclusively to describe the action of the siege need never change its tone to moralize about it. The balance between narrative and speech and the emphases of both suffice to plant Plataea strongly in our minds as an archetype of the small power and its fate at the hands of a large one, no matter how strong the former ties between them, when self-interest makes its claim in wartime.

b) *Pericles.* Individuals are also shaped into archetypes, their personal qualities concentrated into the function they play within the state—a function that is seen as typical in the development of history. We will examine Thucydides' careful account of Pericles' career later (chapter 5), but a few basic points of technique should be mentioned here. Pericles' role in the work is seen as that of guardian of Athens' true destiny, protecting her against her enemies, shaping her policies, and defining her ideals. In this case, the portrait is worked out in three speeches, which together form a plateau of high-minded consistency in the work, setting standards against which the decline of his successors can be measured. The three speeches go unanswered, a unique mark of privilege: Pericles is always allowed the last word. As for comparisons, they are here made explicit for us in the long analysis of his career, which Thucydides adds to the last speech (2.65), sealing his endorsement by the test of time down to and including Athens' final defeat. The analysis confirms the claims which Pericles has just made for himself in a speech (2.60.5)—he is powerful in judgment, able to speak his mind, totally incorruptible, and truly patriotic, in the sense that he puts his country's welfare before his own ambition (2.60.5; cf. 2.65.8 and 5).

When we examine these claims in the context of the speech itself, we find that Pericles is not merely listing his own qualifications, but by a slightly elliptical argument is defining the ideal of statesmanship in terms of these qualities and no others: in politics, the stupid man cannot think of the right policy; the clever man, who can think of it but cannot explain it, is no better off than if he had never thought of it; if he is not patriotic he cannot be relied on to give advice in his country's interest; and if he is not incorruptible, whatever his other talents, he puts them all up for sale (2.60.6). This shift from the particular to the general changes our attitude to Pericles, and, if we accept the criteria as valid, to all other political leaders in the work. Our comparisons are now directed not merely to noticing how various successors differ from Pericles, but how they differ from him *on his own terms*, i.e., how they fall down on one of the four basic points. And at the same time, Pericles himself is elevated beyond the status of a politician with certain talents, to embody the ideal of statesmanship. As we shall see, when we come to test all that Thucydides tells us about him against this definition, we find that he wears some of the unrealistic gloss of the ideal—the whole image is too high-minded, the aspirations perhaps too high, and the selflessness and the foresight too complete. Against this, the portrait of Cleon is shaped as a kind of antithetic archetype, the embodiment of the irresponsible, self-serving ambition by which Thucydides characterizes Pericles' successors in general (2.65.7 and 10).

5. *The constancy of human nature*.[18] Human nature is the strongest "binding" concept in Thucydides' work, one with almost an architectonic force. The force lies precisely in this: whatever the idiosyncrasies of a nation's or an individual's circumstances or temperament, human beings will behave pretty much the same in similar circumstances in any age, and under pressure they will behave badly. Just as on Hippocratic assumptions the human constitution is basically the same, so that a hitherto unknown disease, which suddenly decimates the Athenian population, can be expected to occur elsewhere with similar symptoms and results (2.48.3), so under the pressures of war, revolution, or natural calamity, people everywhere will be seen to abandon their social conventions and restraint, and follow the impulses of fear and self-interest, in much the same patterns, but with variations of intensity according to local circumstance (3.82.2).[19] This assumption is first shown in the Archaeology (1.22.4), and then repeated in a variety of polemical and criti-

cal situations. It is the assumption that allows Thucydides to postulate that his work is a classic, a "possession for all time" (*ibid.*), losing none of its relevance or urgency. It is also the assumption that gives *akribeia* its force, making its truth not merely particular (i.e., true of what happened in this time and place) but in a sense universal (what will also happen in similar circumstances at any time in the future).

We will examine Thucydides' concept of human nature at length in this book, but it is useful to make some brief comments here on its content and tone, and on how they affect the *History*. First one might be concerned that Thucydides' concept does nothing useful in the work— that it merely conveys an empty kind of fatalism: to say that it is human nature to do something seems tantamount to the tautology "men do what they do." But this is unfair. Before the war begins, in the Athenian speech at Sparta, he has given such propositions a "middle term," by associating human nature with "the three greatest" forces that motivate it—fear, honor, and self-interest (1.76.2; cf. 1.75.3). As the war proceeds the reader watches the elimination of honor from the list, and sees all human activity increasingly dominated by fear and self-interest.[20] It is striking that human nature is brought out only to account for controversial activity, especially aggression (by the Athenians [1.76.2], by Hermocrates the Syracusan [4.61.5], by Nicias [7.77], by the Athenians again at Melos [5.105.2]); or by Thucydides himself to stress the universality of violence and social disintegration that accompany *stasis* (3.82.2). More positive aspects of human behavior, such as the Athenian spirit of initiative or resilience after setbacks, are seen at the more superficial level of national temperament. The bedrock of human nature is shared by all, whether Spartans at Plataea or Athenians at Melos, and whatever possibilities it has in prosperity, under the constant pressures of war its tendency is to fragment.

Even when it is not being expressed, Thucydides' negative view of human nature points the direction of his history, and points it pessimistically, with suppressed moralism, downhill. We will see that ultimately his view of history, as we have it in his unfinished work, constitutes an almost complete inversion of the spirit of epic, and of history as Herodotus had written it—not only does he severely limit the possibility of any individual *kleos*, but also, it seems, the possibility of any real collective success. As the war proceeds, collective actions are hampered by the self-centered assertiveness of individuals or by their weakness. The implication that this will always be the trend of human affairs in times of pressure, that the collective achievements of the past will always be pulled down in this way, is the significant lesson of the *History*. We start the account of the greatest of all wars involving the Greeks, with both sides "at the peak of every kind of preparedness" (*akmazontes . . . paraskeuēi tēi pasēi*—1.1.1), and the account breaks off with both sides clearly diminished, looking busily for Persian support, and, in the Spartan case at least, prepared to sign away Greek independence in Asia Minor to get it.

For Thucydides, then, to moralize about human nature is to be pessimistic about it. We shall see that there are glimpses of more positive attitudes and possibilities, but the darker view is the one that substantially influences the author's choice of material and of some of the techniques to unify it, and more so as the work proceeds. His program for the book, as set out in the Archaeology, seems so clear-cut in its no-nonsense empiricism that the discovery of larger systems of philosophical thought, pushing characters and events into typical roles within the work, can be disconcerting—as though one had discovered that his history had a hidden agenda. The discovery can be made at various levels. Dionysius of Halicarnassus, for example, is not particularly alive to Thucydides' larger designs, but he is certainly alive to his language; in the famous passage on the Corcyrean revolution (3.70–83) he is full of admiration for the plain narration of events in the civil war between democrats and oligarchs, but disapproves where the narration gives way to the analysis of the universal effects of revolution (3.82.2), language which he calls "involuted, hard to follow and with almost tasteless complications of figures" (Dion. Hal. *Thuc.* 29).[21]

Such shifts of tone and technique can introduce fresh confusions about the genre Thucydides has just redefined. The confusions persist into the present century, as is evident from a comparison of even the titles of Cornford's *Thucydides Mythistoricus*[22] and Cochrane's *Thucydides and the Science of History*. We have learned from Aristotle to see the philosophical as a mark of tragedy rather than of history; Cornford accepts this and elaborates the dramatic influence on Thucydides, both structurally and psychologically (see especially chapter 8, "Mythistoria and the Drama").

Cochrane, on the other hand, sees Thucydides' method as sternly rejecting the validity of a general hypothesis:

> To do otherwise is to violate the first principle of scientific method, as laid
> down by the author of *Ancient Medicine*, and applied by Thucydides to
> sociology—to confuse the "is" with the "ought"—in short, to disguise what
> is really philosophy in the gown of science. For it was against the general
> hypothesis that the author had levelled the full weight of his artillery, seek-
> ing to demolish this citadel as the necessary preliminary to genuine science.
> (p. 32)

Such a passage needs careful qualifications, and Cochrane properly
adds some of them in the course of his book. What the author of *Ancient
Medicine* inveighs against in his first paragraph is not the general theory
per se, but the hypothesis in the sense of a postulate, imposed on the
data rather than extracted from them. Clearly the whole trend of Hippocratic medicine is inductive: the precise symptoms of various case histories have no relevance, nor is there any possibility of prognosis, unless
they are seen as particular manifestations adding up to a recurrent classifiable phenomenon. At a broader level than the case history is the *katas-
tasis* ("constitution," or overall condition whether of the body or the
climate), and behind that is "the relatively stable" *anthropeia phusis*
(human nature, with its varying *dunameis*—powers). The question for us
to answer, then, is whether Thucydides' view of human nature is after
all a bona fide scientific one, arrived at inductively from consideration of
the particular *erga* of his period of history, or whether it is a philosophical hypothesis in Cochrane's pejorative sense, charging actual situations with gnomic meanings and heightened drama. We may sidestep the
question for the moment by remarking that it presents itself, as does the
difference between Cochrane and Cornford, as a sharp antithesis, and
that both proceed from the contemporary assumption that the work we
are studying must be classifiable according to categories or genres that
are firmly and exclusively defined both in their principles and methodol-
ogies.

As I indicated at the beginning of this chapter, I do not believe that
such an assumption is valid for the time at which Thucydides is writing.
I have argued that he makes a considerable reorientation of his genre
away from epic assumptions regarding the status of the individual, but

one cannot say that he has purged himself of poetry altogether. Nor is this regrettable. What makes Thucydides' *History* such a strong piece of writing is precisely the tautness derived from an apparently disinterested narrative, fashioned with scientific economy but carrying within it a powerful charge of passion and dramatic sensibility.

At this point, then, one wants to stress not so much divergence from an inherited tradition as continuity with it, and again comparisons with Herodotus are helpful. For all the buoyancy of Herodotus' tone, the dominant reflection behind it is somber—the unpredictability of human events, the gods' jealousy of human prosperity, "Count no man happy until he is dead"; such a view is not greatly at variance with Thucydides' notions of the *paralogos*, or Pericles' concession that "all things are born to decline" (2.64.3), though with Thucydides man carries his nemesis or *Atē* with him, and does not need help of the gods to ruin himself. Somehow Herodotus is able to use his philosophy to give a sense of exuberance to his narrative, as the sudden reversals of fortune keep the reader constantly alert; unpredictability of fortune is matched by the author's unpredictability in digressions; anything at all can happen, and in Herodotus we come to trust that it usually will. But when we probe the charm of the exposition, and look closely at the way the philosophy is presented, we realize that in several technical aspects Herodotus has anticipated Thucydides.

Herodotus introduces his philosophy at the end of his introductory remarks, and as does Thucydides at the end of the Archaeology (1.22, especially 3–4), combines it with a note on methodology:

> On these matters I am not going to say whether they happened this way or differently, but instead I shall point my finger at the man whom I know first mistreated the Greeks, and then proceed to the later history, paying attention to cities great and small alike. For many of those that were formerly great have become small, and many that are great in my day were once small. So mindful of the fact that human happiness never remains constant, I shall treat both the same. (Hdt. 1.5.3–4)

This states a philosophy and a literary intention clearly and economically. We then embark on the history of Croesus, "the first man to overcome the Greeks and make them pay tribute (Hdt. 1.6.2). . . . Before his reign the Greeks were free" (1.6.3). After this introduction we immediately regress to the beginning of his dynasty with the story of Gyges and Candaules, at the end of which we are told that Gyges' rule is confirmed by Delphi, but only to the fifth generation (1.13.2). Keeping count as we move through Gyges' successors, we are aware when we reach Croesus that he is doomed. This is on the face of it surprising, because he is the most successful of his dynasty, having succeeded in bringing the Greeks to heel, where his father and grandfather in their constant war against Miletus had tried but failed. "Croesus held under his rule all the peoples this side of the Halys, except for the Cilicians and the Lycians" (1.28). It is at this *akmē* that we begin the story of Solon's visit, in which the wealthy king, fishing for congratulations, asks who is the happiest man Solon has ever seen, and is annoyed not to receive even honorable mention behind Tellus the Athenian and Cleobis and Biton the Argives—all of them nonentities who had the rare distinction of dying happy (1.30–31).[23] In the next chapter Solon explains the philosophy behind his choice, but the king is not appeased and dismisses him as a fool (1.33). Thereupon nemesis from the god seized Croesus (1.34.1).

We cannot here do justice to this famous story, which contains so much of Herodotus' skill as a storyteller, but there are several points which ought to be made. It is clear that the story takes the historian's basic philosophy and dramatizes it in a specific human situation, which casts its shadow through the whole work. In Solon we have the archetype of the plain-speaking Wise Man, a member of the official Greek canon of Wise Men,[24] coming with the lessons learned from the simple life of Greece to Asia Minor, when so much of the traffic of wisdom went in the opposite direction. In Croesus we have the archetype of the self-indulgent, deluded king, who will be saved on his pyre by the triple mention of Solon's name (Hdt. 1.86.3), and live to become another Solon to his victor Cyrus, espousing the official philosophy of the inconstancy of fate (1.207.2). "The cycle of human affairs" which he mentions usually has a twist in Herodotus, and in the well-intentioned advice he gives Cyrus to cross the Araxes to engage Tomyris, he dooms him, just as he was himself doomed by crossing the Halys. Looking far ahead in the work, we can see the roles of wise counselor and spoiled king assumed again most strikingly in the persons of Artabanus and Xerxes— the uncle, who had tried to dissuade his brother from yoking the

Bosporus to invade the Scythians, trying again to dissuade the nephew from yoking the Hellespont to invade the Greeks (7.10)—though again there will be a twist.

These embodiments of the voice of reason, always attendant on the plans of great potentates, who usually doom themselves despite the good advice they receive, save Herodotus from using his own narrator's voice for too much explicit moralism. We have seen that Thucydides has used similar techniques in such episodes as the destruction of Plataea, where the Plataean speech is used to point comparisons to a more heroic part, or in the characters of Pericles and Cleon, the faithful servant of Athenian interests contrasted with the selfish manipulator of democracy.

We may call this a dramatic or poetic influence—but what of science? Since Cochrane's book we have looked to Hippocratic medicine for a scientific influence on Thucydides, and correctly. But Cochrane, in the full flush of his discovery, is rather patronizing towards Herodotus; he concedes that "he was well aware of the requirements of a genuinely scientific hypothesis," and gives as examples his rejection of the poetic theory of the "stream of Ocean" and his final paragraph, in which there seems to be some recognition of the theory that "physical conditions determine character."[25] Cochrane continues: "Now if Herodotus had consistently made use of these principles as canons of historical interpretation, instead of introducing the religious or metaphysical principles which he actually employed, he might still have produced a great work."! The trouble is, of course, that Herodotus lacks Cochrane's single-mindedness. It is true that he follows his scientific impulses cavalierly rather than systematically. He will talk of the gorge of the Peneus breaking through to the sea between Olympus and Ossa (Hdt. 7.128.1), and say that it looks clearly to him the work of an earthquake (7.129.4). But this follows, and certainly does not cancel, the attribution of the gorge to Poseidon. "The Thessalians say that Poseidon made the gorge through which the Peneus runs, and they have a point. For whoever thinks that Poseidon shakes the earth, and that faults or divisions in it produced by earthquake are his work, would say, if they saw this, that Poseidon had done it" (7.129.4). There is a note of caution in "the Thessalians say" and "whoever thinks," but the theory is "plausible" (oikota), and certainly not disowned. In such a passage one sees Herodotus standing exactly at the divide between a rationalized and a mythical world, but not uncomfortably.

One could cite many instances where he indulges his vein of scientific inquiry, of which the summer flood of the Nile is perhaps the most notable and impressive. Faced with a natural anomaly, he searches for the answer with real persistence: "When I asked what power the Nile had to reverse the trend of other rivers, I was able to get no information from any of the Egyptians" (Hdt. 1.19.3), "neither priest nor anyone else" (1.19.1). However, he is able to accumulate three theories from *Greek* sources (it is perhaps worth noting that the Greeks show more initiative in giving an account of a foreign phenomenon, than the Egyptians do of their own), and disposes of all of them. The flooding cannot be caused by the etesian winds, because a) the flooding occurs whether the winds are blowing or not and b) they should cause the same effect on all rivers flowing in the same direction (2.20.2–3). It cannot be caused by the stream of Ocean—a "rather less scientific and fantastic" notion (2.21). To introduce such a notion is to "refer the matter to the obscurity of *myth*," which has probably been invented by Homer or one of the poets (2.23). Thirdly the theory that the floods are caused by an influx of melted snow to the south (on the face of it "most plausible") will not make sense "to anyone able to reason," because everything we know about the climate south of Egypt shows that it must be hotter still (warm winds from the south, bird migration, color of human skin, etc.—2.22.3–4).

Having disposed of these theories, Herodotus advances one of his own. The fact that it is clearly wrong should not blind us to its sophistication. What he suggests is an inversion—that the apparent anomaly is in fact the normal state of affairs, and that what needs to be accounted for is the fact that the Nile runs so low in winter. He explains this by evaporation: the sun is driven from its course by winter storms (2.24.1) and, moving further south, lowers the water level with its absorbing heat. The water that is "sucked up" by the sun appears again in the rainfall which the winds from that quarter regularly bring. It is striking that in his account of the sun's movements he refers to it as a god (*theos*—2.24.2), but his explanation at no point awards it what we would consider an essential attribute for a divinity—personal freedom. A modern god would presumably be free to go wherever he wanted. The divine beings of antiquity, however, included sun, stars, and planets, whose divinity was thought to be proved, as Plato said, by the *regularity* of their movements. Herodotus therefore feels the need to ascribe a *cause* for the alteration of the course towards the equator—the sun is pushed off line by winter storms, like a boat or any other object.

Such a passage shows that Herodotus can sustain a line of rational inquiry impressively, marshaling intelligent arguments against rival opinions, sternly rejecting anything that smacks of "myth," and resisting any impulses to import "religious or metaphysical principles" to explain the phenomenon in question. However, I do not intend to suggest that Thucydides learned his science from Herodotus rather than from Hippocrates, Anaxagoras (Marcellin. *Vita Thuc.* 22), or anyone else.[26] The principal lesson that Thucydides could draw from Herodotus is not the methods of science, but the fact that the work of history has a place for such methods, and more importantly that they can enhance the power of dramatic episodes, whose narrative structure in other respects owes a lot to epic or tragedy. We have noted this combination in Thucydides, but Herodotus is also aware of its possibilities, as we can see in the story of Solon and Croesus discussed above: the lesson of the inconstancy of human fortune is tied into a precise calculation of the number of days of a human life; given an average life expectancy of seventy years, and allowing for the regular insertion of intercalary months, we emerge with a total of 26,250 days on which something can go wrong (Hdt. 1.32.2–4). This precise mathematical calculation has the effect of stiffening the folk philosophy to which it leads, and of lending it some *akribeia*.[27] The enormous total of days, "not one (of which) brings events exactly similar to those of the one which preceded it" (1.32.4), establishes by statistics the very ground of unpredictability on which the philosophy bases itself.

There is a pleasant, if "mythical," story in Marcellinus' *Life* (Marcellin. *Vita Thuc.* 54) which tells of the young Thucydides attending with his father a recital by Herodotus of his work, and weeping at what he heard—a surprising reaction, perhaps, to the mellifluous Herodotus, and particularly surprising in Thucydides, who seems steeled against emotional manifestations. At all events, Herodotus noticed him and said to his father: "Olorus, your son's nature is passionate (literally 'rages'—*orgāi*) for knowledge (*mathēmata*)." It is a fine compliment, but it is also prophetic of the exact temper of Thucydides' work—the strong emotional verb and the scientific noun catch precisely the synthesis which his writing will achieve. The prophecy may have come more easily to Herodotus because he could claim to have achieved, at least in certain passages if not systematically, the same synthesis himself. Some would argue that the lack of a comprehensive system allows him to get the best of both worlds. But Thucydides is prepared to pay the cost of a more rigorous and systematic method; and though he may have sacrificed the pleasures of *mūthōdes*, he gains in power and intensity. In short, he redefines the genre, and leaves an impressive work, which, as he knew it would, speaks to us still with a contemporary force.

2

THE PROGRESS OF PESSIMISM
IN THUCYDIDES

THE SKETCH OF AN ARGUMENT

After the Funeral Oration (2.35–46) comes the Plague (2.47–55). Death for a known and honorable cause gives way to random death by a mysterious disease, solemn rites of burial in an ancestral tradition (2.34)[1] to indecent, makeshift expedients (2.52.4), claims to respect for authority and law (2.37.3) to actual lawlessness (2.53), and the most elaborate rhetorical construction to the most detailed clinical narrative.[2] The two passages are brought directly into line against each other on a moralistic axis, the speech asserting the virtues of Athens, and the plague canceling them. Taken together, they display Thucydides' power and versatility as a writer, and make a challenging point of entry into his *History*.

What are we to make of the juxtaposition? If we allow ourselves the benefit of a wider context, we might assume that the author intends to convey the antipathy between facts and words or speeches, the hardness of the one against the unreliable softness of the other, a contrast which is often made in Thucydides and, at a superficial level, can be taken as a sign of his skepticism. The reader, then, would be expected to find the Plague, with the authority of the narrator's voice behind it, the more persuasive and realistic account. Taking the two passages alone, we might assume that the narrator has an interest in discrediting the speaker of the Funeral Oration. But there are difficulties with both these assumptions. Not all the facts in the two passages line up against all the words—

the fact of decent burial, for example, accompanies the words of the Oration. And if we widen our focus to embrace another ten chapters, we find that the speaker Pericles is not, in Thucydides' judgment, diminished by the plague, but rather has his status enhanced by it, emerging at the end of a final uncompromising speech with his consistency intact, in splendid isolation as the "First Man." This judgment is made explicit in Thucydides' summary of his career and comparison of his life with those who followed him (2.65): none of them can measure up to his standards.

The historian's endorsement of Pericles against the test of time gives us a clue to another interpretation of the two passages: Pericles may be speaking for Athens in its prime, the Athens which he has largely created, as Thucydides says at 2.65.5—"under him it became greatest." In this case the Plague would prefigure, by a kind of physical concentration of the principle of decay, the long process of Athenian decline. There are indications in the text that confirm this interpretation: the Athenian force which invaded Megara at the end of the first year of the war is described by Thucydides as "the greatest collective (*hathroon*) armament fielded by Athens, when the city was still in its prime and not yet diseased" (2.31.2). In the peroration of his last speech, Pericles describes this *akmē* challengingly in a long period of balanced superlatives, which contains, buried in its heart, an admission of the possibility of decline (2.64.3). In the Funeral Oration, there is no such admission (rather, constant injunctions to the present generation to live up to the traditions they have inherited), but the very fact that this genre of speech is chosen to "hymn" (2.42.2) the greatness of Athens, instead of, say, the celebration of a victory, is revealing: the Funeral Oration, in its emphasis and organization, may be spoken for Athens herself, as much as for those who died for her.[3]

All this seems clear-cut—too much so. Though the interpretation may be substantially correct, it still seems clouded by the currents of skepticism noted at the beginning; and in its impact on the reader, the transition from greatness to decline is not so clearly signposted; as a result the two passages are not evenly weighted in their juxtaposition. Instead, the blight of the Plague retrospectively infects, as it were, the reader's view of the Funeral Oration, tainting euphoria with its pessimism.

The Plague shows Thucydides' interest in the internal disintegration of a society under pressure.[4] There are three other clear examples of this interest in the work, all of them narrative accounts of considerable intensity—the Corcyrean Revolution (especially the famous concluding paragraphs, 3.82–83), the final stages of the Sicilian expedition, and the Oligarchic Revolution in Athens.

In the case of the Plague, the clinical description of the course of the disease is followed by an equally detailed analysis of the social disintegration that followed it, and the two are explicitly linked as cause and effect at 2.53.1; both aspects may be covered by the statement at the beginning of the whole excursus: "I shall tell how it developed, so that if it ever falls again, anyone who has considered my account will have the benefit of prescience and not be ignorant" (2.48.3). This cautionary admonition to posterity reminds us of the general statement Thucydides makes at the end of the Archaeology, where he says that he is writing "for those who want an accurate account of the past to ponder, in the knowledge that the future will develop along similar lines according to the human pattern" (1.22.4).

The passage on the Corcyrean Revolution closely resembles the Plague in its structure: instead of clinical details, we have specific acts of the two parties and their Peloponnesian or Athenian allies, followed by a more general analysis of the social and moral consequences of the revolution, which affected all alike. Again, we have an explicit reference to a permanent pattern of human behavior, which will produce similar convulsions in similar circumstances: "Many atrocities befell the cities as a result of their revolutions, as happens and will always happen, as long as human nature remains the same, though with variations in intensity and form as different circumstances dictate. In peacetime and prosperity, both individuals and cities retain a high morale, because they have not yet been trapped by inescapable necessities. But war, which removes the comfort of their daily lives, is a harsh teacher, and adapts the passions of most people to their actual situation" (3.82.2). The details of the disintegration at Corcyra follow at length.[5]

It might seem at first unfair to include the final defeat of the Athenian expedition in Sicily in the list of "internal" disintegrations. But Thucydides encourages us to do so, both by his explicit comparison of the army in retreat to a city (7.75.5), and also by his concentration on the predicament of the defeated. The following passage makes it clear:

The Athenians pressed on to the river Assinarus, thinking things would be easier for them if they managed to cross it, because they were under constant pressure from large numbers of cavalry and the rest of the Syracusan force, and also from their low condition and need for water. When they reached the river, they lost all discipline and plunged in, each determined to be the first to get across, with the enemy riding them hard and making the crossing difficult. Crowded together and forced to move in a mass, they fell on top of each other, and trampled each other under foot. Some were killed outright, crushed by their weapons and equipment, and others were enmeshed in it and swept downstream. The Syracusans took their stand on both banks, which were steep, and pelted the Athenians from above, while most of them stood disorganized and greedily drinking in the river-bed. The Peloponnesians came down into the river and started slaughtering them. The water was immediately tainted, but they drank it just the same, though it was fouled with mud and blood; in fact most of them fought with each other to get it. (7.84.2–5)

In the next sentence, Nicias surrenders, Thucydides having carried his army beyond defeat to the point of self-destruction.

In the final passage that stresses this theme we return to political *stasis*, this time closer to home, in Athens, with a full array of named personalities. After the oligarchs have made their revolution, Thucydides describes the state of mind among the democrats:

No one else ever spoke in opposition because of fear, sensing the size of the conspiracy; and if anyone did speak out, he was immediately killed in some convenient way. There was never any search for the killers, nor, if there were suspects, was there any trial. The people kept a kind of shocked silence, and considered they were well off if they avoided violence even when they were keeping quiet. Their estimates of the scope of the conspiracy were exaggerated, but served to intimidate them; and it was impossible to arrive at an accurate figure, because of the size of the city, and the fact that individuals were strangers to each other. For the same reason, it was impossible for anyone with a grievance to lodge a complaint with anyone else: he would either have to tell it to a total stranger, or to someone he knew but did not trust. All the leaders of the democratic party communicated with each other suspiciously, as any of them might be a party to what was going on. And it was true that the conspiracy included people whom one would never have suspected of turning to oligarchy; and this group magnified the suspicion of the rest, and contributed greatly to the oligarchs' security by cementing the democrats' mistrust of each other. (8.66.2–5)

The connection of this passage to the Corcyrean Revolution is clear.

Indeed, I believe there are clear similarities in all four of the passages we are considering. In each of them, Thucydides' interest extends beyond whatever external pressures are applied (a plague, an enemy, a repressive party in power, and, generically, the war), and probes the victims to the point where some inner bond of solidarity or self-control snaps. We find them neglecting their dead and dying (2.51.4–5; 2.52.4; 7.75.3), trampling their own men and fighting them for water (7.84.3 and 5), killing their own sons (3.81.5). Laws, social norms, oaths and loyalties, and even conventional meanings of words, all slip away under pressures. As we have seen, the kind of disintegration which these passages show is tied to a view of human nature, with sometimes an explicit, deterministic tag—"this, or something similar, will always happen in similar circumstances." Needless to say, this is a pessimistic view.

In what follows I intend to explore the relationship between this kind of pessimism and the rest of the work, and most especially the relationship between human nature, the war, and *stasis*. There are some points to make at the outset. The first is that human nature, even in the dark passages we have looked at, does not at first seem exclusively responsible for pushing a society to its extremes. There has to be some other causality, notably some kind of external pressure, which disturbs the regular flow of life, as we saw at 3.82.2. In Thucydides' mind, the war seems to be an all-inclusive force of this kind, covering not merely demoralization and defeat in the Sicilian expedition, but also the plague, and *stasis*, whether at Athens, Corcyra or elsewhere; in the final chapter of his own introduction, the Archaeology, he makes a point of listing these and other kinds of calamities, including drought, famine, earthquake, and eclipse, under the cloak of the war (1.23.1 and 3). This is a striking extension of malign influence: by chronological association, if nothing else, Thucydides seems to have drawn the definition of his war large enough to embrace events which are beyond human control.

Secondly, even during the war, Thucydides does not seem to insist on the absolute determinism of human nature.[6] There are individual exceptions to the general trend of disintegration; Pericles, Brasidas, and Hermocrates all seem to be figures who not only retain their personal integrity, but also hold together the society which they lead. Such characters know what is important in war, and urge, and embody, central values. Thus Pericles speaks for the priority of the general welfare over the individual's and for incorruptibility in statesmen (2.60.3–6), and Thucydides makes it clear that he lived up to his principles (2.65.8); Brasidas speaks for honesty when dealing with prospective allies (4.86), and Thucydides calls him "just and moderate towards the cities" (4.81.2); Hermocrates calls on the Sicilians to "realize that it is *stasis*, which mostly destroys cities and Sicily" (4.61.1) and that therefore they "should be aware of this and come to terms, city with city, and person with person" (61.2), and Thucydides gives him a cardinal role in uniting and saving Sicily. All this is unimpeachable, and clearly conforms to standards that Thucydides approves of but finds diminishing in wartime.

But when we look at these characters more closely, we find that they are not only at home in wartime, and tolerate its climate of aggression, but even foster it: Pericles is described before his first speech as "urging the Athenians into war" (1.127.3), in his second he takes pride in making "every land and every sea accessible to our daring" (2.41.4), and, in his last, in "ruling as Greeks the greatest number of Greeks, and holding out in the greatest wars, whether against individual cities or against all comers" (2.62.3); Thucydides acknowledges that "under him Athens was greatest" (2.65.5).[7] Brasidas, who is described by Thucydides as an "activist in everything" (*drastērion . . . es ta panta*—4.81.1), concedes that overt violence "can justify itself with the strength that fate has given" (4.86.6), and after his death is named as one who was "opposed to the peace, because of the success and honor he won from war" (5.16.1). And Hermocrates, facing the prospect of the Athenian invasion, tells the Sicilians at Gela, "There is every excuse for the Athenians to have these ambitions and intentions: I do not blame those who seek to rule, but rather those who are prepared to give way to them. It is everywhere part of human nature to rule the submissive, but also to guard against an aggressor" (4.61.5).

This assumption, that it is natural for the strong to exploit the weak, is used as a rationalization of imperialism by the Athenians at Sparta (1.76.2–3) and at Melos (5.89; 105.2), and by Nicias at Syracuse (7.77.4). With the exception of the Athenian argument at Melos, which we will discuss, the tenor of all these contexts is moderate. In all cases, human nature is appealed to as a defense for an action or policy, in the same way that one uses the phrase "it is only natural" as an excuse. But the argument is not only a rhetorical recourse for the speeches. In the narrative of the Archaeology, Thucydides presents the history of human aggression in very much the same light: from the dawn of history, aggression is a basic fact of human experience, and accepted as such; as time goes on it is responsible for significant accretions of power, which can be a source of profit and security to those who possess it (1.7.1), and even to those who are subject to it (1.8.3). In the period of tyranny in mainland Greece, the tyrants were so preoccupied with their own safety that they ventured nothing "significant" (axiologon—1.17). Thucydides as a historian might regret the lack of "significant" activity to report; but his tolerance of accumulations of power clearly goes beyond this. His approval of Pericles' policies carries with it a note of pride in the achievement of the Athenian empire.

What we seem to have, then, in Thucydides, is a double track of speculation about human nature, one of tolerance, or even approval, of the will to power when it is consolidated into national unanimity and turns outwards against foreigners, but also a pessimistic awareness that the same drive may set itself more immediate goals and destroy a society by stasis. The aggression in human nature is both responsible for getting things done, and for making them come undone.[8] The difficulty is to keep the two trends apart; human nature is found only in individuals, and if aggression is an essential ingredient in it, there is no guarantee that it will sublimate itself in every case to the plane of national causes. There are good reasons why it should, and Thucydides has both Pericles and Hermocrates argue them at a time of crisis for their cities: as Pericles says, an individual's well-being is tied, at least in time of adversity, to his city's; if the city fails, then his own fortunes are likely to fail with it (2.60.3, cf. Hermocrates 4.61.1). The warning is clear, but so is Thucydides' conviction that in times of war it will not be heeded.

Already in the Archaeology, Thucydides advances his view of stasis as the (perhaps inevitable) reducer of power: talking of the first land barons, he says that "because of the richness of their land, certain individuals attained greater power and produced revolutions (staseis), as a result of which they came to grief" (1.2.4). The few phrases describe a pattern of rise and fall, which seems to have the inevitability of a vicious circle: it also seems to correspond to Thucydides' view of Athenian fortunes over the war. In his final review of Pericles' career, having compared his disinterested statesmanship with the selfish ambition of his successors, he attributes the final Athenian defeat to domestic dissent: "They did not finally surrender until they had been caught up in internal feuds, and so undid themselves" (2.65.12 *fin.*). We shall return to this pivotal passage in a moment.

But we can now see that, so far from being a systematic and consistent theory of human nature, Thucydides' thought contains a tension, and perhaps a contradiction, which is basic to it. Thucydides is himself aware of the tension (the conjunction of the Funeral Oration and Plague is not accidentally elaborated) and explores questions arising from it. What is the nexus between legitimate foreign war and destructive *stasis*? Is there no such thing as an excess of aggression, as long as it is done with national solidarity against someone else? Or is there a connection between the loss of restraint in the conduct of war against strangers, and the self-destructive urge, which turns ambition and aggression against one's own city?[9] I believe that it is questions such as these, and the difficulty he finds with them, that prompt Thucydides to give such prominence to moral debates over Mytilene, Plataea, and especially Melos, where political and strategic considerations are subdued to allow the moral issue to emerge with stark clarity.

But I do not believe that these debates answer the question satisfactorily even for him. His alternative is to track the theories of human nature down to their roots in the human individual, examining basic patterns of behavior and basic motivation, and this he does most completely in the eighth book. But the groundwork for this, like so much else, has been laid early, in the first Spartan Congress before the war. In the Athenian speech there, the motivations of human action are reduced to three principal ones (*megistōn*)—honor, fear, and profit (1.76.2).[10] ("Profit" (*ōphelia*) by this point has already been glossed as "self-interest" (*xumpheronta*)—1.75.5–76.1.) Pericles will appeal to honor (*timē*) as a motive ("out of the greatest dangers, the greatest honors are won"—1.144.3), and call on the Athenians "not to shun the toil or give up the quest for honor," which they win from the empire (2.63.1); Brasidas, as we have just noted, was motivated by "the success and honor which he won from the war" (5.16.1). But there is not much talk of honor in the second half of the *History;* by the eighth book it has vanished from consideration.

But the changes in book VIII are more fundamental than the evaporation of a nobler vein of motivation. There are no speeches, and there is a higher proportion of individual activity, and indeed a larger number of named individuals, than in any other book.[11] We shall attend closely to this latter point because it involves a shift of narrative technique. Nowhere else in the work are personal motives and personal enmities so fully exposed on so wide a front. In the whole of the Archidamian War, it is really only the person of Cleon whose mean and narrow motivation is probed to the same depth. This is significant because, as we have seen, Cleon stands as the archetype for Pericles' successors through the war, whose leadership declines disastrously from the standards he had set. In book VIII the focus on individual activity reduces the scale of the war, and at points the narrative seems crowded by trivial detail into bathos.

These are some of the reasons why the last book has consistently been considered anomalous in the work. But we should not carry the anomaly too far. It is important to realize that it has been forecast in the text at precisely the point where, in Thucydides' judgment, the disintegration of Athens is about to begin—at the death of Pericles (2.65). That long chapter is literally a turning point because it not merely assesses a career that is closed, but contrasts it with a future trend, and the description of the trend is not merely an encapsulation of future events, but an *explanation* of them: it explains why Athens lost the war. Athens lost the war, in Thucydides' opinion, because her leaders pursued personal ambitions (*idias philotimias*) and personal profits (2.65.7), and ultimately undid their city by becoming involved in personal feuds (*diaphoras*—2.65.12). The language here very clearly points towards the climate of *stasis* which is thoroughly explored in book VIII, and in fact is strongly echoed there in the explanation for the failure of the oligarchic revolution (variations on the theme of equality, private ambition—*idias philotimias*, again—and the aspiration to become First Man—8.89.3). Book VIII, therefore, so far from being an anomalous appendage, takes its legitimate place as the final term of a progression, which has been forecast early in the work. Without book VIII the progression would be incomplete; with it, Thucydides' unfinished *History* offers us a fully fledged system of explanation, whether we agree with it or not, for the result of the war, even though the narrative never reaches the end.

Having emphasized the two terms of the progression, it will perhaps be useful for us to retrace its course briefly, noticing some of the key passages en route from one term to the other. We find that the early phases of the Archidamian War are controlled by policies of caution, according to the strategies of the two elder statesmen, Pericles and Archidamus. Both are blamed by their own sides for their conduct of the war (Archidamus for dilatoriness at the outset—2.18.3, and Pericles for not resisting the wasting of Attica—2.22.3, for the hardships of the plague, and for the whole decision to go to war—2.59.2, cf. 2.65.2–3). But we have no reason to doubt the human control of the action, especially in the case of Pericles, who is able to absorb the *paralogos* of the plague with his plan and consistency intact. It is perhaps the very caution of these two pivotal figures, both of them the embodiment of their city's virtues, and their insistence on both the need for preparation and the fact that the course of events frequently proceeds incalculably in spite of it (1.84.3–4 for Archidamus; 1.140.1 *fin.*, 2.13.2–9 for Pericles: Thucydides commends his foresight at 2.65.5–6 and 13), which make it at first a *controlled* war.

But Pericles' career is closed at 2.65, and soon afterwards Archidamus' also (3.1 is the last reference where we find him actively deployed), and we move on to an apparently leaderless era forewarned of trouble ahead. We take note of the appearance of Cleon and Demosthenes—the one a "most violent" politician (*biaiotatos*—3.36.6) who clearly departs from Pericles' moderation, even though he echoes some of his words (see chapter 5 below); the other a general who, with his adventures in Aetolia (3.94 ff.), promotes the geographical expansion of the war, against the Periclean doctrine of containment. At first nothing goes permanently wrong. Cleon is narrowly outvoted in the punishment of the Mytileneans, and Demosthenes rehabilitates himself by annihilation of Ambraciots and Peloponnesians (3.105 ff.). The two figures combine for the fine opportunist triumph at Pylos.

But here we come to a crossroads: in a crucial speech, significantly set before the Athenian victory at Pylos, the Spartans ask for peace at Athens, emphasizing once more the unpredictability of success in war (4.18.4), and urging peace before some irreparable consequence (*ti anēkeston*) seizes them and enforces a perpetual public and private enmity towards Athens (4.20.1). The language looks towards a point where the war *escapes* from human control and imposes its own necessities. In the event, the Athenians ignore the Spartan warning and go on to lose the advantage of Pylos with the defeat at Delium and Brasidas' campaign in

Thrace.[12] But even in this phase, as with the mainstream of the Archidamian War, apart from the Plague and the Corcyrean Revolution, the reader has the sense that its course is determined by human initiatives and responses to opportunities. And when the peace is finally made, Thucydides discusses its causality in terms of individuals and their motivation—the removal of Cleon and Brasidas, who favored war, and the insistence of Nicias and Pleistoanax, who both had their private reasons for wanting peace (5.16.1).

It is from this point that the war begins to assume more obvious control over the lives and decisions of the participants,[13] and the opportunities give ground before the necessities. The darker trend of the narrative is, paradoxically, first indicated by the protagonists' inability to enforce the Peace. It is Thucydides' thesis that the Peace was not a genuine intermission, but that the war continued unbroken (5.26.2). He is at pains to convey the climate of suspicion and the maneuvers for advantage on both sides, which confused traditional alliances and set up a scramble for new ones (5.27 ff.). The insecurity of this period is the insecurity of war. Even when the final showdown of the Battle of Mantinea is staged as a resolution of the uncertainty and restores the balance of power and Sparta's lost reputation, Thucydides emphasizes the precariousness of the situation with a full record of Agis' hesitations in the prelude to the battle, and in its actual conduct (5.54, 55, 60; 71.3): the victory which is won has very little to do with his control of the situation.

The Sicilian expedition makes a self-contained narrative, which rehearses in microcosm the patterns of the History as a whole: it has its own Archaeology (6.1–7), a debate at Camarina in which Euphemus justifies Athenian imperialism with much the same arguments that the Athenians have used at Sparta (6.82–87, cf. 1.73–78), and a progression from early ebullience and partial success, into demoralization and loss of control. In the seventh book, from the point where the besieging wall is intercepted (7.6.4), Nicias' initiatives are exhausted, but Thucydides keeps his long-suffering and defeated spirit in the forefront of the narrative, as he shows him overriding the energetic Demosthenes with his superstitions and delays. In the catatonic atmosphere that Nicias engenders, the Athenian aggressors are transformed into victims, and the Syracusans, who are the actual enemy, recede into the background and become almost oblique agents of Athenian destruction. As we have seen, in the final episode before the surrender, Athenians kill each other by trampling men under foot in the riverbed, and fight each other for water.

In the eighth book, the law of human nature that the strong exploit the weak is, as we have said, finally pursued to its ground in individuals;[14] hitherto we have had it used mostly to account for (largely anonymous) behavior between nations (Athenians at Sparta and at Melos), or between parties (at Corcyra). Now national interests become increasingly ignored, as the focus is narrowed to the struggle of named personalities, struggling for personal survival or advantage against personal enemies, in war and in revolution. The pressures of private expediency emerge strongly in such a character as Phrynichus, who moves from being a committed, even eloquent democrat to being a passionate oligarch, driven by his fear of Alcibiades. The personality of Alcibiades looms large in this book, that of the totally self-interested man, whose single-mindedness gives him the flexibility to make the best of any situation for himself (but see chapter 7). Indeed, self-interest is by now the common ground between all the characters and all the feuds, which are described at various levels on both sides—between the Spartans Pedaritus and Astyochus, the Persians Tissaphernes and Pharnabazus, the Syracusan Hermocrates and the Spartan command, the Athenian fleet at Samos and the government in Athens, and in greatest detail a selection of named oligarchs against the largely anonymous Athenian democracy.[15] The war is by now the natural climate of their feuds, sharpening their insecurity and suspicion, fragmenting the social order into the irreducibles of *stasis*.

As was first discovered after the Peace of Nicias, when the signing of the Peace did not bring peace, the war has a life of its own, and the necessities it imposes on individuals are apparently unrelenting, and cannot be brought to an end by any individual action. There is a great deal in common between the aftermath of the Peace in the fifth book, in which the climate of insecurity sends each state in pursuit of new alliances and thereby intensifies the insecurity, and the aftermath of the Sicilian debacle, in which individuals are desperate to forge connections with one group against another within the state. The difference is largely one of scale.

I believe the importance of the eighth book has so far been neglected.[16] It is clear to me that in this book Thucydides finally settles on a pessimistic view of human nature that is applied not merely in ominous isolated episodes but fairly systematically through the narrative, and shows the basic level at which it operates and the basic tendency it has. The basic level is the human individual, and the basic tendency is towards aggression. Various speakers in the work have complacently conceded this, but Thucydides now seems to insist that at least under circumstances of continued pressure, the primary aggression is applied for oneself, at the expense of any larger claims from any society or institution to which one belongs. Thus pessimism at the end seems to override any of the more positive strands we had noted earlier in the work, and the possibilities of collective action recede. The bonds between human nature and war and *stasis* are now complete.

This comes close to a Hobbesian view of human nature, and in an appendix I shall indicate that the similarities between Thucydides and Hobbes on this point are real and extensive. In particular, I believe that in his formulation of the "condition" of human nature as a state of war, Hobbes could draw, if only subconsciously, on the "universality" of the war which he found described by Thucydides, especially in the eighth book. In Thucydides' perception, the Peloponnesian War, which started as a planned confrontation, with a fixed strategy and with definite limits, at least in Pericles' mind, has been transformed by sheer duration into something permanent, which dictates its own necessities: war is indeed a harsh teacher. The principal difference between Hobbes and Thucydides on this point is the difference between a political theorist and a historian. For Hobbes, the condition of human nature is the condition that is found *before* men are persuaded to enter upon the contract of a commonwealth, to surrender their rights, and to look to a sovereign to protect them from each other. The condition of human nature is thus, in a sense, *pacified* by a properly covenanted commonwealth; and the grimness of the condition is made absolute and systematic, and thereby provides sufficient reason to escape from it, and make the contract. Thucydides' perception proceeds from a series of events which he has witnessed and tries to explain in a society at war; he feels no need to make his view philosophically watertight. Even in the eighth book, it is not applied so deterministically that he cannot take note of occasional bright spots on the scene—the resilience of Athens after the news of the Sicilian defeat, the intelligence of Antiphon, the restraining influence of Alcibiades on the fleet at Samos, the partial victories; yet such moments never connect or build towards anything permanent. For most of the personalities involved in the eighth book, the atmosphere is already anxious with the prospect of personal defeat; and the *History* falls silent without allowing us any glimpse of a final victor.

3

THE ARCHAEOLOGY (1.1–23)

Thucydides' introduction to his work is on the whole least helpful about his methods of composition where it is most explicit about them. His chapter on the composition of the speeches (1.22.1–3) is ambiguous and an important source of scholarly contention to this day. But the excursus as a whole is especially useful because it shows the historian's mind operating not as the witness of contemporary events, but with the evidence of the past, as we have to work with it. In this passage, Thucydides not only narrates an account, but builds an argument, and in so doing allows us to judge his power of inference and test his skepticism. He also shows from the outset the importance he attaches to such factors as fear, foresight, and the drive for power, wealth, and security—essential marks, in his view, of a relatively constant human nature, which affect human action and therefore, ultimately, historical change and stability. Such factors are applied throughout the work, to organize and comment on material; they amount to categories of the historian's thought, and act as unifying principles of his history. Thucydides tells us that he

> . . . began to write as soon as the war began, foreseeing that it would be of some magnitude (*megan*), and in fact more important (*axiologōtaton*) than any preceding war, basing his judgment on the fact that both sides were at a peak of readiness for it in every department, and seeing the whole Greek world taking sides, some at the outset and others making plans to join. It was the greatest (*megistē*) upheaval the Greeks had endured, and it involved a large part of the non-Greek peoples, and in fact most of the civilized world. As for earlier history and the remote past, it is impossible to establish any clarity over the gulf of time; but considering the evidence which I can trust

at this distance, I would judge that things were not done on a large scale, either in war or in other spheres of action. (1.1)

The "greatness" of this war is Thucydides' reason for writing his history, and the defense of its greatness against the comparative insignificance of previous wars is the central theme of the Archaeology. His two serious historical challenges come from the Trojan War ("the *greatest* expedition until that time"—1.10.3) and Xerxes' invasion of Greece ("Of previous undertakings, the greatest was the Persian War"—1.23.1). But their claims are disposed of, in one case by logistical calculation, based on the Homeric catalogue, of the average complement of the ships involved (1.10.4–5) and the inadequancy of supplies (1.11), and in the other by the short duration of the war (four battles in all—1.23.1).

This statistical approach is at first disconcerting to a contemporary ear, and seems more appropriate to a book of records than a history. Such an opening puts his work immediately in the tradition of Herodotus' history of the Persian Wars, with its intention of celebrating "the great and wonderful deeds displayed by the Greeks and barbarians." This kind of amplification (*auxēsis*) may be conventional,[1] but Thucydides does not go far without indicating his divergence from the tradition: he criticizes those who write "to appeal to their audience rather than convey the truth" (1.21.1), and acknowledges that the factual orientation of his work and "avoidance of legend will make it perhaps less appealing to an audience" (1.22.4). There is nothing modest about this concession, however, because, given the constancy of human nature, the accuracy of his account will have a universal and permanent applicability: the "empirical" historian can thus invest every atomic fact with significance, as we saw in chapter 1, and by a large inductive leap can read cautionary lessons to posterity.

But there are further points to be made for Thucydides in the face of his tendency to assume that facts and figures, once clearly and accurately established, dispense with the need for explanation. For Thucydides, the numbers involved in the war are evidence (*tekmēria*) of its importance, and the number of events associated with it in the final chapter of the Archaeology (1.23) are evidence of its catastrophic effects. Enumeration has traditionally been an epic device for conveying stature (the catalogue of ships [*Iliad* 2], details of hekatombs, offerings, etc. [*Il.* 23.163–178; 24.228–237], and it carries over into history (the size of Xerxes' force carefully enumerated in Herodotus [Hdt. 7.59.3 ff.] before its progress through Greece, drinking the rivers dry [Hdt. 7.108.2; cf. 109.2]).[2] Thucydides rejects the poetic use of figures: "No one will go wrong on the matters I have discussed, if he considers the stated *evidence*, instead of trusting to poets' songs with their embellishments to give it size; . . . most things with the passage of time are inflated into the mythical" (1.21.1). The language is critical and austere, but is still not very far removed from Pericles' rhetoric about the greatness of Athens: "We have illustrated our power with great achievements and solid evidence, . . . and we have no need of a Homer to sing our praise" (2.41.4).

Thus Thucydides' claim of greatness for the Peloponnesian War is secured with accuracy (*akribeia*), not merely by assertion, against the claims of even epic wars, by using the evidence the poets themselves provide. He can embark on his history confident that whatever it lacks in entertainment, his theme is substantial, and in fact lasting enough to be a possession for all time (1.22.4. *fin.*). But once he has established his claim about the war against epic and historical challenges, he immediately shows in his final chapter that his perception of it is far removed from the heroic; his emphasis does not fall on the *aristeia*, or "the great and wonderful deeds," of individual heroes, but rather on the universality of suffering the war caused, whether from the devastation of the fighting itself, or the natural calamities and portents which accompanied it (1.23).[3] In fact, the deflation of the heroic is fairly systematic throughout Thucydides' account. People take part in a war, not for the display of their valor, or even to honor an oath or an alliance, but in fear; this is true, whether applied to the Greek force in the Trojan War (1.9.3) or, in Thucydides' judgment, to the Spartans in 431—the real cause of the war was their fear of Athenian power (1.23.6; cf. 1.88). Already we have a note of pessimism injected; the debunking of the Trojan expedition is not merely an exercise of epistemological skepticism (such demythologization is quite appropriate in a historian), but of a kind of moral or psychological pessimism, which strips away romance and reduces motivation to the most basic. This sets the tone of the war, and it will be sounded again for emphasis on the very brink of hostilities, when, after the final collapse of peace negotiations, the Spartan herald Melesippus is escorted by the Athenians back to the border unheard, and, on the point of being dismissed, solemnly intones: "This day will be the beginning of great

evils for the Hellenes" (2.12.3). It is, then, the wholesale disintegration
of Greece, which resulted from the war, that gives it its importance, and
it is his perception of this disintegration that gives Thucydides' history
its intensity, and makes it such a remarkable document.

So far we have discussed the central theme of the Archaeology, the
"greatness" of the Peloponnesian War. But when we analyze the introduction more closely, we see that it has a subsidiary function, which
will later be carried on by the Pentecontaetia (the survey of fifty years of
the growth of Athenian power from the Persian War to the outbreak of
the Peloponnesian War—481–431 B.C.—1.89–118). The Archaeology
argues not merely that the Peloponnesian War was the most important
until that time, but shows how, over the passage of time, power became
concentrated enough to set up a conflict on that scale. This development
stops with the Persian War, leaving the Pentecontaetia to bridge the gap.
We will follow the early, mostly prehistorical phase in detail.

Thucydides describes a cyclical process of rises and falls, prompted by
need, greed or the will for power, with changing and expanding goals
and possibilities. To start with, as there was no commerce, conflict cen-
tered on land, and, as there was no sea-travel, on one's neighbor's land
(1.2.2). Fertile land built power, but it was also more precarious because
it was more coveted (1.2.4). An infertile country had an alternate, more
indirect route to power—because no one wanted it, it remained more
stable, and thereby attracted prominent people who had been ejected in
the struggle for power from more volatile areas. This more modest route
accounted for the rise of Attica (1.2.5–6).

The next stage is reached with Minos, and the opening up of sea-
travel, bringing hitherto inaccessible cities into his orbit, and creating the
possibilities of trade and profit (1.8.3). This development proceeds naturally from the geography of Greece, and Thucydides is advancing it here
in the correct causal sequence, and not merely to allow him to round off
neat correspondences later—"there have been land powers and sea powers: at the time of the Peloponnesian War, Sparta was the greatest land
power, and Athens the greatest sea power" (cf. 1.18.2). Thucydides'
argument, then, in its main lines seems clear, intelligent and unexcep-
tionable.

What makes it interesting are the glosses he puts on the various phases of the progression. The first is the emphasis placed on aggression or the will to power as a prime cause of change. The early settlements had no stability, as people were continually forced to leave their land under pressure from stronger invaders (1.2.1). Because they knew this was likely to happen, they did not put down roots or improve their property. They moved on "easily" (1.2.1), and because they thought they could find their daily subsistence anywhere, they were dislodged "without difficulty" (1.2.2). The easy acceptance of aggression by its victims almost removes its menace, and certainly its moral taint. Violence at its first appearance is part of the natural round of things. This is made even more explicit when we come to piracy, the correlative, of course, of the brigandage on land. Piracy is described as a regular way of life, pursued by quite important people for the ordinary motives of "profit and the support of their dependents" (1.5.1), and Thucydides goes out of his way to make it clear that no disgrace was associated with it: "having no sense of shame about their profession, but holding it as some mark of honor" (ibid.). And he adds, in a rather elaborate sentence, that this is still the case in the wilder parts of Greece, and that the early poets regularly show people asking those who arrive by sea, whether they are pirates, "and in such a way that those who are asked would not disclaim it, and those who want to know would not advance it as an insult" (1.5.2).[4] We are still in the mists of prehistory, but Thucydides would have us believe that life by violence was accepted as a natural and potentially honorable existence. And when Minos cleared the sea of piracy, Thucydides allows him no imputation of public service, but has him act for the same basic motives as the pirates themselves, "so that their revenue would come to him" (1.4). The practice of exploitation for gain or power is, then, a universal one, involving Greek and non-Greek alike (1.5.1–2); and whether it is practiced by the individual pirate looking after his family, or Minos building a maritime empire,[5] the basic motivation is the same, and the victims, large or small, have learned to live with it, or even embrace it: "weaker cities in their desire for gain endured subjection to the stronger" (1.8.3). Historical change takes place along a continuum of aggression, beginning with the first bandit, and rising to the concerted and organized violence of an empire. By extension, therefore, we seem to have sketched out in advance the outlines of a justification of the Athenian empire, and so far there seems to be nothing defensive or ambivalent about it; concentrations of power, after all, constitute the "greatness" of the historian's theme.

But Thucydides still has a point to explain: if life is naturally and permanently conducted on a predatory basis, how does one arrive at sufficient stability to allow progress to be made? We have already seen that the earliest settlements were not settled at all ("what is now called Greece was formerly never securely settled"—1.2.1), because of the constant expectation that invaders would uproot them; they did not trade and they did not cultivate the land systematically beyond what was necessary for daily subsistence (cf. 1.2.2). What converts this state of flux into a regulated and stable existence is wealth (capital, or property beyond that needed for subsistence): "The cities which were founded later, when sea-travel was more accepted, had strong resources and therefore could be built on the actual coast and fortified with walls" (1.7.1). Surplus of property gives something worth staying for, and something to defend, and also the wherewithal to build defenses. It is wealth which builds and safeguards the real concentration of power, as shown by Pelops (1.9.2) and later by his heir Agamemnon (1.9.3). The control wielded over the Trojan expedition was not based on the oath of Tyndareus, but on the fear inspired by Agamemnon's great power (1.9.1 and 3), as we have seen. And yet Thucydides does not see that power as impressive by contemporary standards: the reason it took so long to drive the Trojan War to a conclusion was not shortage of men (*oliganthrōpia*) but shortage of supplies (*achrēmatia*) (1.11.1). Wealth supports power, and shortage of wealth limits power. "Before the Trojan War, because there was no wealth, no important venture was undertaken, and even this, though it is more famous than any previous event, is shown by the facts to have been less significant than its reputation" (1.11.3). As Greece came to set more store by the acquisition of wealth, and became stronger, power concentrated in tyrannies became established, instead of ancestral monarchies hedged with constitutional rights (cf. 1.13.1). But tyrannies are only a phase, and, as we shall see, often a retrograde one, on the road to national power.

Wealth, then, is one of the prerequisites for gaining real power; the other equally important prerequisite is civic stability, so that power can take root. The instability of early Greece has been remarked at the beginning of the Archaeology; but it is emphasized as a factor limiting power throughout the whole excursus. "Even after the Trojan War, Greece was again in flux and in the process of being resettled, so that without stability (*mē hēsuchasasan*) there was no chance of growth" (1.12.1; cf. 1.12.4). The tyrants realized this need for stability, looking out for their own well-being and their families' prosperity, and managed their cities as far as possible on a policy of safety first (1.17). Instability is a principal reason why power falls, or fails to grow, whether an individual's or a state's. In the earliest days, powerful landowners "produced civil disorders from which they came to grief" (1.2.4). Freedom from internal strife was the reason why Athens, though comparatively infertile, attracted prominent people, and thus set out on an unorthodox route to power (1.2.6). The rise of Sparta, on the other hand, after a long period of disorder, was able to begin only after it had achieved a settled constitution (1.18.1).

The concept of disorder (*stasis*), undoing stability and the power that grows from it, is a fundamental one in Thucydides' history. The most famous passage, both for the actual progression of a revolution and for the social consequences that follow from it (3.70–85), is devoted to the civil war at Corcyra, which Thucydides offers as a prototype for subsequent convulsions elsewhere (3.82.1). But most of the eighth book is a political anatomy of the oligarchic revolution at Athens, reducing it in scale, as nowhere else in the *History*, to the actual intrigues of particular individuals. There is a fundamental contrast in Thucydides' thought between "concerted" (*hathrooi*—1.3.4; 1.11.2 twice) ventures with national solidarity, and the fragmentation of *stasis*, which reduces all ventures to the scale of private ambition. The one criticism levied at the tyrants, in a rather lenient treatment, is their concern "for increasing their substance and private household (*idion oikon*) in safety, . . . so that no significant (*axiologon*) venture was undertaken by them. As a result Greece was for a long time prevented from joining in any notable enterprise together (*koinēi*), and each state lived cautiously within itself" (1.17).[6] This seems to be a return to the state of isolationism before sea-travel and trade: "The Greeks, each in their city states, undertook no concerted action until the Trojan War, because of their weakness and isolationism" (1.3.4).

The effects of *stasis* are to break down the spirit of common enterprise and send everyone in pursuit of their own self-interest: as we saw in the last chapter, the successors of Pericles are accused of undermining his public-spirited policies by playing politics "according to their private ambition and private profit" (*idias philotimias kai idia kerdē*), and finally brought the state down by "private differences" (*idias diaphoras*—2.65.7 and 12). Exactly the same point, in very much the same language, is made at the other end of the *History* about the Athenian oligarchs in 411 (8.89.3—again, *idias philotimias*). The concept of *stasis* seems to be the only brake that Thucydides puts on the pursuit of power and profit at this stage, and it is not an ethical constraint, at least at first reading, but a politically pragmatic one: civil disorders historically have prevented a state from progressing to power, or have destroyed it when it has achieved it. By the measures of success, therefore, along the path to national greatness, internal disorder is to be avoided. This says nothing about such concerted action as has the community's consent and leaves it secure: it says nothing about Melos.

We have now charted the principal strata of the Archaeology. Several of the basic strands of thought will be developed and qualified in different situations within the work, and we will follow them there. In the meantime it is worth looking at the overall picture, to see exactly how much has been said so far. The purpose of the Archaeology is first to show the magnitude of the Peloponnesian War, in comparison with less significant conflicts, and secondly to describe the historical process by which concentrations of power could be amassed over the centuries to present an encounter on this scale. The key stages are as follows:

1. In the beginning, communities seek nothing but subsistence from land, because their settlements are constantly threatened.

2. Sea-travel begins, at first with piracy, and later with trade. At this stage economies expand beyond the subsistence level and have room for profit.

3. Profit allows, and demands, a) steps to secure property (building walls around cities), and b) concentrations of power with weaker states being absorbed or controlled. Concerted action involving many states is now possible.

4. With the security of power, there is room for the development of domestic life (put aside arms, etc.).

5. But security can always only be relative. The presence of a large power, capable of absorbing a lesser one, sends other states looking for

an alliance which will support them. Large powers, therefore, become focal rallying points against other large powers; leagues of allies and empires of subjects are formed, motivated by self-interest but also by fear of the other bloc. Thucydides sees the Greek world after the Persian War polarized in this way between the Athenians and Spartans, with a permanent climate of hostility and menace, if not constant warfare, between the two (1.18.2–3).[7]

6. Civil disorder (*stasis*) can threaten or set back the process of expansion or assimilation at any point along its development.[8]

Within these stages we noticed that Thucydides allowed himself to show 1) that the predatory instincts for power and gain were universal (common to Greek and barbarian), and 2) that exploitation was accepted easily, if not embraced, by the victims themselves. This gloss is an interesting sidestep into comment on attitudes, behind the simple cause-and-effect progression of history. But we should be careful about making premature equations between Thucydides' judgments about a distant, uncivilized, and mostly mythical past, and his own attitudes. Cannot ethics be refined as society evolves and becomes more complicated? Thucydides does in fact allow a progressive element, both in the overall way of life and in particular details (1.5.3 through 1.6). Piracy is still practiced in the wilder parts of Greece, and in those parts of the world people still go around armed. "The Athenians were the first to put away their weapons and turn to a relaxed and more lavish (*trupherōteron*) way of life" (1.6.3).

On the other hand, in Thucydides' account such changes in the pattern of life do not appear to be essential transformations, but merely advances at different stages along the same time spectrum: "In many other respects, the ancient Greek way of life corresponded to the present customs among the non-Greeks" (1.6.6).[9] And it is clear that in Thucydides' mind the margin of possible improvement is very limited and subject to reversal: at the end of the Archaeology, having looked into the past, he makes an important projection into the future; in fact, he bases the utility of his history to posterity on the fact that it offers "a clear account of what happened in the past, and is likely to be repeated in similar ways, according to the human pattern, in the future" (1.22.4).

4

COLLECTIVE ACTION TO
THE POINT OF WAR

In the Archaeology, we saw Thucydides operate on the principle that it is concerted action that builds power and prosperity for a civilization. Ships and manpower, and the money that acquires them and controls them, are the essential factors in this development. There were prominent individuals who controlled events in the early phases of Greek history (Agamemnon, Minos), but Thucydides makes it clear in each case where their power lay—Minos was the first to acquire a fleet (1.4.1), and Agamemnon had inherited Pelops' wealth, had the largest fleet, and thus was preeminent in power and could muster an expedition of various nations because of their fear of him (1.9.1–3). It is the scope of the venture, rather than any heroic qualities in its leaders, that makes such an expedition "significant" or "noteworthy" (*axiologon*).

Given this scale of priorities, it is interesting to follow Thucydides' narrative technique as he moves out into the body of his text, and to watch his division of labor between anonymous group activity (nations or parties) and the efforts of named individuals. The first episode he describes involves the Athenian alliance with Corcyra, and is told exclusively in terms of the states and parties involved (1.24–55). The names of commanders are given at various stages (1.29.2; 1.45.2; 1.46.2; 1.47.1; 1.51.4), but their individual decisions and actions are not explicitly recorded.

Epidamnus, a remote town on the Ionic gulf, has a revolution. The *dēmos* ends up in power, but the ousted aristocrats join the neighboring tribes in harassing the town. The democratic government in Epidamnus appeals to the founding city, Corcyra, to help to end hostilities and reconcile the dissident group, but Corcyra rejects the appeal and sides with the rebels. Epidamnus then, with Delphi's approval, hands itself over to the original mother city, Corinth, which makes strong efforts to support the town, because of her own grievance against the arrogance of her colony Corcyra.[1] Corcyra in alarm appeals to Athens, which after two debates grants a defensive alliance, believing that war with the Peloponnese was inevitable, and wanting the Corcyrean navy on her side and the convenient harbor on the route to Italy and Sicily (1.44.1–3).

Stripped of personal activity in this way, the phases of the action are seen to conform to patterns which Thucydides sees as historically typical. The interaction between war and *stasis* is made clear. The *stasis* at Epidamnus was reported to begin as a result of the war made on the town by the surrounding non-Greek tribes (1.24.4). The effect of the *stasis* is to undermine its prosperity (1.24.3–4), and the ripples from it reach out until the two major blocs face off in confrontation on the brink of war. We are reminded of another passage: "Later almost the whole Greek world was convulsed, as points of dispute emerged in each place which prompted the leaders of the *dēmos* to call in the Athenians and the oligarchs the Spartans. Normally in peacetime, they would have had no cause or inclination to call them in, but in wartime the chance of acquiring an alliance and at the same time damaging the opposition made appeals for help on both sides an easy recourse for those who wanted to start a revolution" (3.82.1). In the case of Epidamnus, the pattern is not quite so foursquare: democratic Athens sides with oligarchic Corcyra[2] against democratic Epidamnus, which appeals to oligarchic Corinth. But this simply shows that the motives of self-preservation and self-interest, which impel all parties, whether seeking an alliance or a revolution, can override political predispositions. Thucydides seems to make the episode at Epidamnus a cardinal event, keying a progression that will be played out through the *History*: just as the ripples of war reach out from Epidamnus in this incident and involve Athens, so in the course of the war, the contaminating tide of *stasis* moves from this outpost of the Greek world, to its mother city Corcyra, and finally to Athens herself.[3] But all this lies far ahead; the immediate denouement of the episode gives the first convincing display of Athenian naval supremacy.

The second incident which Thucydides narrates as a contributory cause of the war is the revolt of Potidea (1.56–65). The episode shares some of the features of the Corcyrean events—the problems of keeping an outpost subservient (the first of many such cases afflicting Athens directly), foreign intervention on the spot (in this case Perdiccas) exacerbating the matter, and Corinthian dignity further affronted. But on the whole the contrasts in Thucydides' treatment of the incident stand out more. Although the Potidean revolt and the long siege resulting from it have a more lasting effect on the war, Thucydides treats it much more briefly than the Corcyrean affair, and with much more localized detail, refusing it the force of an archetype.

In this case the individuals play a greater part, beginning with Perdiccas (1.57.2), followed by the rival commanders, Aristeus for Corinth (beginning 1.60.2), Callias for Athens (beginning 1.61.1), and, towards the end of the episode, Phormio (beginning 1.64.2). These are not merely parenthetic figures associated with large-scale activity, but central personalities, whose deliberations and strategies are followed in detail. We can speculate on the reasons for this shift in technique: the personality of Perdiccas, the autocratic and unreliable king of Macedonia whose operations close to his own home ground Thucydides always follows with interest, may have keyed the treatment for the other characters in the episode, though they are certainly prominent in their own right and deserve our attention—Aristeus appears at the point of his death as one of the principal thorns in the Athenian side (2.67.4), and Phormio is the most distinguished admiral of his generation. But I believe myself that the principal reason for the change in technique at this point is a literary one. We are about to attend the longest debate in the work, the first Congress at Sparta, which Thucydides uses for the discussion of large issues. Before such passages it is not unusual for him to use this kind of "nominalist" narrative as a bridge passage, less charged with portentous implications and resonance, and therefore allowing the reader to relax a little before making new demands on his concentration.

When we turn to the Congress, it is clear that Thucydides, having provided the reader with all the details he cares to give about the causes of complaint (*aitiai*) between the two sides, has no intention of wasting a debate with recapitulation. Instead, from the particular details of Potidea, we move to a larger consideration of national issues, set against a background of national character. The first two speakers are anonymous (Corinthians—1.68–71, and Athenians—1.73–78), but even when a split in Spartan opinion drives Thucydides to name the speakers for respective positions (Archidamus—80–85, and Sthenelaidas—86), they maintain their place in the larger scheme: Archidamus, under attack from his Corinthian allies, both embodies and speaks for traditional Spartan virtues and methods of conducting affairs, and Sthenelaidas, whose function is to bring the specific issues (which have not really been discussed) to a specific vote, is himself the stereotype of blunt Spartan sentiment and few words.

It is important to realize what Thucydides is doing in this debate. Having established the principle that he will follow the collective movements of the two sides, and individual actions only insofar as they affect the movements of the whole, he now sets out to provide a study of national character-types, so the reader can see the kind of temperament and climate of opinion from which subsequent actions and decisions will proceed. This sort of national *ēthopoiia* calls for inductive judgment at a high level of sophistication, and is another aspect of his craft which Thucydides may owe to Hippocrates. The Hippocratic assumption is that there is a common human constitution, always amenable to the same treatment, but allowing variations in physique, propensity to certain diseases, and temperament, as the result of differing climates, geographical situations, and diets: "You will find in most cases that the physiques (*eidea*) of men and their characters (*tropous*) follow the nature (*phusei*) of their country" (*Airs, Waters, Places* 24 *fin.*). Thucydides is the first historian to apply this doctrine seriously to the psychology of different nations; Herodotus has an adumbration of it (Cyrus is quoted as saying that "soft men come from soft countries" in the last chapter of the work—Hdt. 9.122.3), but for all the wealth of anthropological lore which he accumulates, he rarely analyzes ethnic temperaments into the attitudes or traits that affect *all* a people's actions—different customs and behavioral patterns are narrated for different localities, but the *mentality* that produces the differences is seldom investigated, and human reactions tend to be universal. This can sometimes have incongruous results; a good example, which struck the Greeks of Herodotus' own day as incongruous (Hdt. 3.80.1; cf. 6.43.3), is the debate between seven Persian noblemen on the relative merits of democracy, oligarchy, and monarchy.

The rational attitudes, the conventional political vocabulary, and the drift of the arguments seem out of place in Persian mouths. The incongruity is delightfully enhanced by the denouement of the debate; after it is decided, apparently in proper Western fashion by a vote (3.83.1), that the constitution will remain monarchic, they decide to pick the king by observing whose horse is the first to neigh at dawn outside the city (3.84.3). As we shall see, Thucydides is again more systematic.

In the debate at Sparta, the Corinthians, speaking first and representing Sparta's allies, try to goad their leader into action with the following explicit comparison:

> And we of all people feel entitled to make criticisms of our neighbors, especially given the enormous differences betwen you and Athens, which you don't seem to recognize. You have never taken stock of the Athenian character or of the fact that the struggle will be fought against people who are totally different from you. They are innovators, quick to conceive an idea, and quick to carry out their intentions. Whereas you are intent on preserving the *status quo*, and fail to follow through in action even on essential matters. Again, they are daring beyond their capacity, take risks against their better judgment, and even in crisis remain confident; whereas your character is inclined to be inhibited, to mistrust your judgment even in certainties, and to think you will never escape from the crisis you are always in. They are impetuous, while you delay; they go abroad, while you stay at home. . . . (1.70.1–4)

When the Athenians speak, they have some points to add about the Spartan character—especially the intransigence with which they alienate allies:

> If you were to destroy us and rule in our place, you would quickly forfeit the good will which has come your way through fear of us—at least if you showed the same behavior you displayed in the short period of your leadership against the Persians. For the customs which you practice cannot be assimilated by others. And besides, as soon as one of you goes abroad, he abandons both his own principles and those of the rest of Greece. (1.77.6)

Thucydides appears to offer confirmation of the Spartan deficiencies in a variety of specific instances. The Athenian taunt that Spartan severity would alienate an empire, soon after it was acquired, is confirmed immediately after the debate with the account of Pausanias' arrogance to the allies (1.95.1; 1.96.1) after the Persian War. It will be further confirmed during the Peloponnesian War by the ineffectiveness of the Spartan colony at Heracleia Trachinia, despite its fine strategic position (3.93), and again by some of the trouble the Spartan admiral Astyochus has with the Peloponnesian fleet (8.84.1–2). In fact, this particular judgment against Sparta would hold up into the fourth century, as long as she had a position of authority to exploit.

Similarly, the Corinthian criticism of the Spartan failure "to follow through in action, . . . mistrusting your judgment, even in certainties" is supported by Thucydides in at least two incidents. An ambitious Peloponnesian scheme, fostered by Brasidas, to sail on the Peiraeus unexpectedly, while it was still unguarded, faltered because "they thought it was too great a risk (and it was said the wind prevented them)" (2.93.4). Thucydides' comment on the epidode is trenchant and supports the Corinthians: "If they had been determined and not hesitated, they would have been successful, and the wind would not have stopped them" (2.94.1). There is a more striking example of a lost opportunity in 411, when the Athenians are still reeling from the effects of the Sicilian disaster, and the Spartans take possession of the whole of Euboea, and are poised for a blockade of the defenseless Peiraeus. But they would not clinch their advantage. Thucydides' comment, even in its language, as we have seen, takes us back to the Corinthian speech:

> This was not the only occasion when the Spartan method of war helped the Athenians enormously; there were many others. For the two sides were very different in character, the Athenians quick (*oxeis*), the Spartans slow (*bradeis*), the Athenians adventurous and the Spartans cautious. The Athenians benefited from this especially as a sea power—a fact proved by the Syracusans, who modeled themselves most closely on them, and fought best against them. (8.96.5)

But if outsiders can list the faults in their allies or enemies, and history confirm them, natives can balance the account with self-praise. Thus when the Corinthians and the Athenians have spoken, the former urging the Spartans into war, and the latter warning them against it, but both criticizing Sparta from their own point of view, Archidamus the King comes forward, "a man with a reputation for intelligence (*xunetos*) and moderation (*sōphrōn*)," and reaffirms the traditional Spartan virtue of *sōphrosunē*:

> We are both good warriors and good counselors because of our well-ordered life—good warriors, because self-respect is closely connected with self-con-

trol, and a strong sense of courage with a strong sense of shame. And we are good counselors because we have not been educated into an intellectual contempt for the laws, but even under pressure have learned too much restraint to disobey them. So instead of being intelligent in an academic way, and finding fine words to blame our enemies' initiatives while meeting them inadequately, we rather consider that the minds of our neighbors work similarly to our own, while the strokes of fate are incalculable for all of us. (1.84.3)

Thus Archidamus continues the vein of national character study, and Thucydides confirms this claim, too, at least indirectly, at 8.24.4, where he ranks the Chians second to the Spartans for being able to combine success with moderation. For an Athenian response to Archidamus' claims, we must wait for the Funeral Oration, where Pericles plays off Archidamus' rather anti-intellectual account of the Spartan education, with its stern regimentation, against the natural, unrehearsed, but intelligent courage of Athens, where discussion is no obstacle to performance (2.39.4 and 2.40.2).

As for the Corinthian comments on the Athenian character, they are quickly confirmed in the narrative of the Pentecontaetia, in such episodes as the defeat of the Corinthians and their allies at Megara, by an Athenian force of "young and old," at the same time that the Athenians have a fleet of 200 ships engaged in Egypt, and another sizable force tied down at Aegina. The unexpectedness of the Athenian resistance is very clear—the Corinthians move towards Megara, "thinking it would be impossible for the Athenians to help the Megarians, while they have large expeditions absent in Aegina and Egypt" (1.105.3). Again, there is a distinct note of pride in the record of the exact length of the interval separating the Athenian defeat by the Spartans at Tanagra, "with heavy slaughter on both sides" (1.108.1), from the decisive victory sixty-one days later at Oenophyta, which brought Boeotia under Athenian control (1.108.3). At the other end of the history, underestimation of Athenian recuperative powers is mentioned and excused by Thucydides, when discussing the Chian revolt after the total loss of the Athenian expedition to Sicily; this is one revolt which he says seemed soundly based in its calculations (a surprising concession), because it appeared likely that Athens would be quickly destroyed: "many people made the same mistake" (8.25.3). If these instances of resilience show the positive side of Athenian "daring beyond their power," we can find the negative side in such ventures as Demosthenes' campaign against the Aetolians, the Delium campaign, and above all the Sicilian expedition (see 6.31.1 and 6; 7.28.3); on balance, the losses, leading to final defeat, clearly outweigh the gains.

There are many other details of national temperament and opinion placed in the debate at Sparta, which Thucydides intends his readers to carry with them into the account of the war itself. The Athenian speech is particularly important for the rest of the work. It is given by anonymous speakers, who receive an unusually long introduction, giving their motives in coming forward and a table of contents for their speech. Thucydides tells us that they were in Sparta "on other business" (1.72.1), and that "they did not intend to answer the charges which the cities had brought" (ibid., cf. 1.73.1). We should not therefore be getting the official, diplomatic account, but perhaps something more authentic and closer to the mainstream of Athenian opinon. However, instead of leaving them to speak for themselves in this instance, he has shaded their intentions with two interesting glosses. The first is the intention of convincing their audience of "the power of their own city" (1.72.1), a point which one might have thought did not need making, in view of Thucydides' insistence that it was fear of Athenian power that drove Sparta to war: in this case, the need to impress the point might almost proceed from the consciousness of an underdog status, which seems disingenuous in view of what we know. The second gloss Thucydides imposes is the speakers' desire to "turn the Spartans by their arguments to a more pacific rather than warlike frame of mind" (1.72.1 fin.); this may seem a basic point, but in the context, when the Spartans are about to be persuaded to take a vote for war, it emphasizes that the Athenians still want peace.

In the speech itself, the speakers are true to their word and do not address any of the specific charges brought against them, but they do make a careful defense of the larger issue of Athenian imperialism, out of which all the charges proceed; and, as we shall see, the arguments they introduce here for the first time will be tested, reworked and at points rejected in later parts of the text. Their argument is tied together by the theme of advantage (ōphelia)—at first a historical survey of the advantages Athens conferred on the Greek world, including Sparta, by her conduct in the Persian War (1.73.2 (twice); 74.1; 74.3), and then the advantages which Athens enjoys from the empire (75.3; 76.1; 76.2): the former entitle her to the latter. Thus by skillful sleight of hand, altruism is converted to self-interest.[4] The speakers argue that there is nothing reprehensible in this change; they did not take the empire, but were given it by their subjects themselves (1.75.2; 76.2), and have now been "overwhelmed" (nikēthentes) by the three great human motivations of honor, fear, and self-interest to hold on to it:

> We have done nothing astonishing, committed no perversion of human nature, if we took an empire when it was offered, and now refuse to let it go, overwhelmed (nikēthentes) by the three great factors of honor, fear and profit. We were not the first to do this. It has always been an established practice that the weaker should be constrained by the stronger. Moreover, we consider ourselves worthy of our role, and you seemed to think so too, until calculations of self-interest prompted you to use the argument of justice, which no one in history ever took seriously enough to deny themselves a profit, when there was a chance of acquiring something by force. The people who really deserve praise are those who, while following their natural instincts to rule others, have more respect for justice than the power at their disposal requires. And we are sure that anyone who inherited our empire would prove our moderation convincingly. (1.76.2–4)

In this crucial passage, we have the first explicit statement of the law of nature, that the strong exploit the weak, which we had observed working itself out in practice in the Archaeology. It is significant that at this first expression by anonymous Athenian speakers, it is claimed as a credit to Athens, "worthy of praise" (76.3),[5] that she does not use this law to her full advantage, but instead practices some justice (she allows her subjects to bring lawsuits against citizens, and sometimes they even win—1.77.1) and moderation. We will follow what happens to this moderation in chapter 6.

So far we have seen that the debate at Sparta looks far beyond the issues for which the Congress met, giving us broadly based indications of the differences between the two sides in character and principle, on which they may be expected to proceed in the war itself. Thucydides himself has given the reader as much detail on the specific issues as he considers relevant, and so has released the speeches for these larger considerations. It remains for the ephor Sthenelaidas, in a brief but belligerent paragraph, to bring the Congress to a specific vote for war, on the basis of what he sees as clear Athenian violations of the truce (*adikia*).[6]

No sooner is the vote taken than Thucydides again broadens the basis of discussion, by explaining it not in terms of the issues, but in terms of the Spartan fear of growing Athenian power, which seems at first sight to bypass the debate we have just attended, just as the debate seemed to bypass the issues leading up to it. But this is not the case. He returns, in fact, to his own assessment of the "real cause of the war, though the least recognized" (*alēthestatē prophasis, aphanestatē de logōi*—1.23.6)—the fear the Spartans have of Athenian power.[7] This carries us down to the most basic level of causality—a national reaction that is prompted not so much by any single incident, but by the large historical development of its rival over generations. We now see that in the debate, the Athenians' defense of their imperialism since the Persian War speaks directly to this deep-seated cause, and in fact answers it by attributing their own behavior to a reciprocal fear:

> As a result of our actual circumstances, we have been forced to develop it (the empire) to this point, impelled chiefly by fear, though also by honor and self-interest. For as most people hated us, and some had already revolted and had to be suppressed, and you yourselves were no longer so well disposed, but rather suspicious and hostile, it no longer seemed safe to run the risk of letting it go, for those who broke away would go over to you. (1.75.3–4)

Thucydides now embarks on a narrative excursus, which is intended to provide the factual background to these arguments. The Pentecontaetia falls into two phases: 1) an account of the immediate aftermath of the war, with precise details of the transfer of the hegemony over the Greeks from Sparta to Athens (1.89–96), and 2) an account of the development of the Athenian empire from the moment they inherit it until the Corcyrean incident (1.97–118). There is a considerable difference in the narrative technique used in the two phases, and, as usual in Thucydides' set pieces, some hidden agenda. The first phase begins with Themistocles' ingenuity in having the fortification of Athens rebuilt in the teeth of Spartan opposition; this has nothing to do with the transition of the hegemony, but establishes in the first incident after the Persian War a basic Spartan fear of Athens, which will grow in time, and in Thucydides' judgment at least, to the full-blown *alēthestatē prophasis* of the Peloponnesian War (see 1.88 for a repetition of the cause given at 1.23.6). The focus in this passage is entirely on the person of Themistocles, who has already appeared twice in the work as providing direction at two crucial moments of Athenian history—in the Archaeology, as the man who converted Athens to a sea power (1.14.2), and in the Athenian speech at Sparta (challengingly to a Spartan audience) as the "most intelligent (*xunetōtaton*) general" in the Persian War (1.74.1). Now the wall-building incident presents the Spartans with the fait accompli of Athenian renaissance, which, in the warm climate of shared victory, they must accept with at least superficial good grace (1.92). But the episode also shows Athenian fear of Sparta: the elaborate diplomatic ruse engineered by Themistocles to get the walls built indicates the Athenian anxiety that Sparta might physically prevent them from rebuilding their defenses. The attitude is one of an upstart power still in awe of the established leader.

From Themistocles, the Athenian victor of Salamis, with his swift perception and action on the new threat from Sparta, we move to Pausanias, the Spartan victor of Plataea, and his alienation of the allied force in its work of liberation after the war. Again, we have several points confirmed from the Athenian speech: 1) Spartans with an empire would quickly make themselves unpopular (1.77.6; cf. 1.95.1 and 3); 2) Spartans in command abroad tend quickly to be corrupted (1.77.6; cf. 1.95.7); and 3) the Athenians did not take their empire by force but at the request of the allies themselves (1.75.2; 76.2; 95.1; 96.1). The two episodes invite comparisons and clearly favor Themistocles—both leaders set off in new directions after the war, Themistocles seeing, and countering, future enmity to Athens from her ally Sparta, and Pausanias making personal terms with his former enemy Persia; Themistocles is farsighted, public spirited and again successful in his plan, while Pausanias' role seems purely negative—probably treacherous—and unpopular at home and with his allies. The intelligent Themistocles secures his ends by diplomatic tactics, while the Spartan Pausanias is described as "violent" (*biaiou*—95.1), and his command as "more like a tyranny than a generalship" (95.3). We shall find the two men again yoked together at the end of their story (1.126–138).

With the transfer of the hegemony achieved, Thucydides turns to the transformation of the League which Athens has inherited into the Athenian empire. This is a new excursus (*ekbolē*–97.2), and the narrative technique changes and again becomes almost completely impersonal, with commanders' names mentioned only parenthetically with their actions. Even Cimon and Pericles are introduced in this fashion (1.98.1 and 111.2 respectively), despite the large role which we know from other sources they played in this development. It becomes even clearer from the emphasis and the structure of the whole passage that Thucydides, like the Athenian speakers at Sparta, is prepared in large measure to take the empire as "given." He shows us remarkably little in the way of territorial acquisitions. Including Sestus from the beginning of the previous section (89.2), only four towns are attacked and incorporated into the empire (Eion, 98.1; Scyrus, 98.2; Carystus, 98.3). All subsequent gains after this initial burst of activity are lost before the end of the excursus; these include Boeotia and Megara (with Nisaea and Pegae), Troezen and Achaea, with substantial losses of manpower at Drabescus (100.3) and in Egypt (109; 110).

Instead of acquisitions, Thucydides shows himself interested in *revolt*. We begin with the revolt of Naxos (98.4), which serves as the prototype of the allies' suppression (99 passim). Revolt is the key factor in their loss of independence (the word occurs in various forms three times in the chapter), and Thucydides unsympathetically suggests that the allies themselves were responsible for their failure, because, by giving up their naval contributions to the League and settling for cash quotas, they left themselves unprepared for war (99.3). The lesson of Naxos is underlined in the next chapter by the revolt of Thasos, a particularly dangerous event for Athens, because we are told Sparta had intended to support the Thasians by invading Attica at the same time, but were prevented by the revolt and entrenchment of their own helot population at Ithome (100.2–100.3). At the other end of the excursus, the revolts of Naxos and Thasos are balanced by the revolts of Samos and Byzantium (115.2–117 *fin.*). Thus the structure of the whole confirms one of the points made by Thucydides in the introduction to this passage, where he says that the Athenians acquired their power "against the barbarian, *against their own allies when they revolted*, and in regular encounters with the Peloponnesians" (97.2).

When we analyze the Pentecontaetia as a whole we find that it has two stages and two styles, and that basically it makes, or rather endorses, two points: both of them are made and reworked in other contexts. The first point is the corroboration of the "true cause" of the Peloponnesian War—the Spartan fear of growing Athenian power, which is illustrated by the attempt to prevent the Athenians from rebuilding their walls, by the intention to help Thasos in revolt, by the rejection of Athenian help at Ithome, by the whole of the first Peloponnesian War, and by the Spartan invasion of Attica in 446, synchronized with the revolts of Euboea and Megara. The second point is the corresponding fear aroused by this hostility in Athens, enforcing the need to retain its recalcitrant empire for fear that it would slip away and join the other side. We have seen this fear expressed in a rhetorical context by the Athenians at Sparta (1.75.3–5); but the grounds for it were already established by Thucydides in the Archaeology, where he indicates the conditions of hostile polarity in the Greek world after the Persian War (1.18.2–3). The patterns are made clear in the Pentecontaetia. The Athenians "alone of the allies" are asked by the Spartans to return home, after sending assistance to Ithome, "for fear lest, if they stayed, they might be persuaded (by the helots) to try something subversive" (102.3). Whatever the disposition of the Athenians towards the helots in Ithome at the time of the incident, they accept them into their alliance upon its conclusion (103.3). In the same chapter, the Megarians leave the Peloponnesian League and join the Athenians (103.4). Those who reject, or are rejected by, one side go over to the other. We shall see the arguments from fear, which proceeds from this polarity, reworked later (chapter 6).

Upon the conclusion of the Pentecontaetia we return to the Peloponnese for a second Congress (1.119): what does it have to add to the first? Formally, it is used to bring the *allies* to a vote for war; the Spartans themselves have voted at 1.87.1–3, but it was made clear at 87.4 that the allies would vote separately. The only recorded action between the two meetings is the consultation of Delphi (118.3). It is possible that at the first Congress there was no quorum of allies present, and that only those who were interested in airing their grievances attended. The only speech recorded at this second convention is naturally given to the Corinthians, the most important of the allies and those most affected by the confrontations already described. From Thucydides' point of view the speech recalls the reader to the issues of the moment after the fifty-year digression, and adds the final cement to a solid Peloponnesian front against Athens. Little by little we inch our way to war.

In terms of content, the Corinthian speech, besides urging the recalcitrant that their interests are at stake, does have fresh information to impart—a consideration of possible strategy open to the Peloponnese in the coming war. In the first Congress, the only strategic considerations put forward on the Spartan side were the negative ones of Archidamus. Strictly speaking, Sthenelaidas, who spoke after him, was in a position to answer these; but Sthenelaidas was the fourth speaker in what had already become the longest recorded debate in the *History;* and to protract his speech further would destroy the obviously intentional contrast between the reflective, moderate king and the reflexive belligerence of the laconic ephor. So it is left for the Corinthians to talk about the prospects of raising loans, building a fleet, and establishing fortresses inside Attica. Pericles will answer them in his first speech; but in the meantime we should note that we have not yet been told the name of a single Athenian who is active in shaping *current* policy.

5

PERICLES

By the end of the second Corinthian speech to the allies, we have a
united Peloponnesian front against Athens. The climate of concerted belligerence, whatever the provocation of Athenian actions and attitudes, is
brought to a vote of war by the Peloponnese *first*, in logical conformity
with the analysis of the "true" cause of the war, Spartan fear of growing
Athenian power. The narrative to this point has concentrated heavily on
national issues and developments, and the speeches have supported this
slant for the most part with statements of national interest, argued
anonymously. Of the seven speeches we have had to date, five have been
anonymous, and the other two, by Archidamus and Sthenelaidas, were
only "named" to argue for, and perhaps embody, two sides of Spartan
opinion.

By this time, we are more than ready for a change of scene to Athens,
to see how all this animosity is received there. The transition is only
gradually made in a series of charges and countercharges conveyed across
the rift of suspicion by shuttles of embassies. Thucydides uses this diplomatic interval to bring Themistocles and Pausanias back to center stage,
this time in connection with the story of Cylon, the first person to attempt to establish a tyranny at Athens (1.126). Thus the clock is put
back in time, the focus narrows once more to personalities, the two
Greek protagonists of the Persian War are again juxtaposed for the
reader's comparison, this time with both *in extremis* because of national
rejection; in this final chapter of their story, Themistocles again seems to
win the comparison, making good his escape to Persia, while Pausanias is
walled in at home. The retrospective trend of the narrative is accom-

panied by a shift in the style to a more diffuse and anecdotal account, smacking dangerously of *mūthōdes*.

There are several puzzling aspects about this long digression (1.126–138):[1] what significance can it have, when it is provoked by a totally specious demand from the Spartans (the expulsion of Pericles), which they themselves knew would never be met (1.127.2)? It would be easy to explain it as a small indulgence by the historian in the pleasure of biography and reconstruction of the past; we saw Thucydides at work before in this vein, in the Archaeology (and also in the wall-building episode—1.89–93), and he clearly enjoys it, especially when he has the opportunity to challenge an accepted version (the oath of Tyndareus— 1.9.1, or the killing of Hipparchus—1.20.2; cf. 6.53–59). But in the present passage, Thucydides does not seem much preoccupied with the correction of previous accounts—the Cylon affair appears in Herodotus with fewer details (5.70–72), and the murder of suppliants attributed to the president of *naucraroi* instead of the archons, but Thucydides does not insist on the differences with any emphasis, and simply seems to tell the story for its own sake. In the episodes that deal with the discrediting of Themistocles and Pausanias, Thucydides takes over where Herodotus leaves off, and we do not have other sources to compare; but, again, the stories seem to be told for their own sakes, without any carping over the details of rival versions. In fact, the neat dovetailing of these two stories with the end of Herodotus' *History* and the relaxed, almost anecdotal tone of the narrative suggest a deliberate, if gentle, parody, as though to show those critics who found his own work less "entertaining" that he was capable of a more readable vein. The details of Themistocles' seeking sanctuary with his enemy, King Admetus of the Molossians, charming his wife and dandling his child on his knee to render himself more pathetic (1.136.3), display his guile in an exactly Herodotean scale and manner, and so do the circumstances of Pausanias' conviction, with the messenger tampering with the seal of the letter to read of his own death sentence (1.132.5). But the fact that the Greek heroes of the Persian War are followed through the aftermath of war to their rejection by the Greeks they had led to victory, defuses the epic tone of Herodotus' climax.[2] The irony of the sequel would appeal to Thucydides, for whom the realities of war and history were grimmer and less edifying; in this graceful passage, projected into the times and manner of Herodotus' own material, he wickedly insinuates a seed of doubt. This is correction of another, and more comprehensive, sort, challenging a view of history.

But there is more to the passage than an exercise in gentle parody or deflation. As we have seen, Themistocles has already appeared three times in the work (in the Archaeology as responsible for the conversion of Athens to a sea power—1.14.2; in the Athenian speech at Sparta as the "most intelligent general" in the Persian Wars—1.74.5; and at the beginning of the Pentecontaetia as responsible for rebuilding the walls of Athens in the teeth of Spartan opposition—1.90–93). No other individual to this point has appeared so frequently. In the final assessment at 1.138.3, his political genius is endorsed in the authentic voice of Thucydides, under the familiar categories of practical intelligence (*xunesis, kratistos gnōnai*) and foresight (*proeōra, tōn mellontōn aristos eikastēs*). There is a distinguishing note on his capacity for improvisation on scant preparation, which does not occur explicitly elsewhere. But in this short character sketch, the first in the book, we seemed to have a series of incidents, from wall-building to acceptance by the Persians, enlarged to a kind of apotheosis of the Athenian character, matching the general description that was given by the Corinthians at Sparta. But the whole triad of figures in this digression are specially marked by Thucydides for eminence in their own time: Cylon is introduced as "an Olympic victor in the old days, of noble family and powerful influence (*dunatos*)" (1.126.3). Pausanias and Themistocles, at the end of the digression, are called "the most brilliant" (*lamprotatous*) of the Greeks of their time (1.138.6). In the next chapter, Pericles is introduced as "the first among the Athenians of that time (*anēr . . . prōtos*) and the most powerful in word and action" (1.139.4). He thus steps forward to give his conclusive judgment on all the preliminaries to the war in the company of distinguished figures from the past. In fact, Pericles is bound up with them even more closely, and is at root the occasion for the whole excursus, because we have been told at the outset that the Spartan demand to drive out the curse incurred in the Cylon affair was directed at him, and intended to embarrass him at Athens (1.127.2): "For he was the most powerful of his contemporaries, and determined Athenian policy; and he opposed the Spartans on all points and did not permit compromise, but was always urging Athens towards the war" (127.3). Thus Pericles brackets the whole interlude, and invites the reader's comparisons with

the other *prōtoi andres* in the same context, especially with the greatest of
them, Themistocles, who gives a distinguished pedigree to his anti-Spartan policies.

We can see, then, that Pericles' speech is given a carefully prepared introduction in the work, with his status against a large historical backdrop
already established by the company he keeps. He comes forward to
speak "once and for all" (*hapax peri hapantōn*) on the matter of the Spartan
grievances, and the unanswered speech that is given to him effectively
concludes the preliminaries to the war for both sides; by the end of it,
Athens is no less committed to the war than Sparta was at the end of the
first Congress. It is conscientious of Thucydides to stress the predisposi-
tion to fight on both sides, when the actual incident that sparked the war
was quite extraneous to both of them.

Pericles' career did not begin with his speech on the eve of war. In fact
it coincides with some thirty years of the Pentecontaetia, and he was as
influential in building the Athenian empire as Thucydides allows he was
in steering it into war. But, as we have seen, the Pentecontaetia has no
room for personalities, once it has left the first incident of tension between Athens and Sparta, the rebuilding of the walls under Themistocles' direction immediately after the Persian War. As is the regular
practice with military commanders, including Cimon, in this passage
Pericles is introduced parenthetically in connection with the expedition
he leads to Sicyon, Achaea, and Oeniadae (1.111.2). This is the only
aggressive command he undertakes in this excursus, and it is the only
point where his career is seen to overlap with Cimon's, who dies in the
next chapter. The rest of Pericles' effort is devoted to defensive work,
restoring the situation after the revolts of Euboea and Megara in 446
(114.1–3) and Samos in 440 (116.1–3 and 117.2). There is no explicit
mention that the transition from Cimon to Pericles signaled a shift in
Athenian imperial policy, reverting to the Themistoclean anti-Pelopon-
nesian stance from that of Cimon's friendship with Sparta.[3] The fact is
that Thucydides does not make it clear that there *was* any such change in
Athenian leadership: the pattern of events and the outbreak of the first
Peloponnesian War make the change of policy clear, but it is not associated with any individuals; it all proceeds from general or national
currents of suspicion or resentment.

But, as we have seen, the material of the Pentecontaetia is presented in such a way that Thucydides is saved from any account of the maneuvers of internal politics. It is clear on his principles that he sees a conflict between the two major Greek powers as inevitable: power engenders fear in others, and two powers engender reciprocal fear in each other, and eventually action against each other to protect themselves. Spartan suspicion of Athens was evident as soon as the menace of Persia receded, and continued through the first Peloponnesian War. Even when Athens makes a five-year truce with the Peloponnesians (112.1), the tension continues: Sparta establishes the Dorians in Delphi, and Athens ousts them and hands it over to the Phocians (112.5). A little later we have the revolt of Boeotia, and then the synchronized revolts of Euboea and Megara in 446/5, coinciding with a Spartan invasion of Attica. Pericles retrieves this situation, and the Thirty Years Truce is made (115.1), but he is soon in action again with the revolts of Samos and Byzantium, during which we again hear (this time from the Corinthians in the debate on the Corcyrean alliance—1.40.5) that the question of helping the Samians was raised by "the other Peloponnesians," presumably including the Spartans. Thus in the first incident and the last of the Pentecontaetia, Spartan enmity to Athens is suggested by Thucydides, even though no action is taken; in the middle of the period there are regular bursts of active hostility and confrontation.

Pericles' role in all this seems modestly conservative: he is more prominently displayed as a general trying to save critical situations, than as an empire-building politician or conquistador. Thucydides has carefully planned the point at which he intends to introduce him as a personality, and will allow nothing to confuse the picture of him until then. Plutarch tells us (*Per.* 29.1) that he was instrumental in persuading the Athenians to make an alliance with Corcyra, but Thucydides has kept that debate completely anonymous.[4] Aristophanes' *Acharnians* (530–34) lays the Megarian Decree at Pericles' door, and makes it the paramount issue in the war (but perhaps only farcically?); but Thucydides really pays it minimal attention as an *aitia* (grievance), and has Pericles defend it illogically as possibly a small matter, which is not small, because to concede it would lead to larger demands (1.140.4.–5).

In Thucydides' account, Pericles is not actually involved in any of the grievances leading up to the war; however, the general point is made that he was opposed to the Spartans on all points and urged the Athenians into war (1.127.3). This appears to be an honest concession, but in the context of Spartan enmity, which we have just had rehearsed for us in detail through the Pentecontaetia, his response seems reasonable. It seems especially so at this particular point, after a rather contrived attempt by the Spartans to get rid of, or at least embarrass, him. He therefore does not appear the prime mover in the antipathy. And we cannot accuse him of warmongering, given the suspicion and belligerence of national sentiment with which he must work: long before his first appearance in the work, the Corcyreans have already spoken of the war as inevitable (1.36.1).

By the time Pericles comes forward to speak, the Spartans have left the particular grievances behind ("making none of their customary points"—1.139.3), but have raised their claims to one general demand—"to let the Greeks go free" (ibid.). Such a claim is, of course, intended to set the terms of the impending conflict straight for public consumption: it is another demand that does not expect to be met. But it does allow Pericles to cast his speech "once and for all" in the tone of a defender, in conformity with his character as it has so far been defined: "I cling as always to the same conviction, not to yield to the Peloponnesians, . . . and now they are here no longer expressing grievances, but giving us orders, refusing arbitration even when we offer it" (1.140.1–2). We do not have to accept this position as unassailable. We have seen plenty of evidence to accuse Athens of treading a deliberate line of brinkmanship before the war, which raised the tensions all around and brought pressure on Sparta from her allies for intervention, even if it fell short of a formal violation of the truce. But I do not believe Thucydides intends us to second-guess Pericles here—he has protected him so thoroughly to this point in the narrative, and will vindicate his policies so completely at the end.

There are three other points, besides the refusal to compromise, which call for special comment in Pericles' first speech.

1. The first is his review of the strategic advantages in the coming war, and his finding that Athens is better prepared for the kind of war it will be: "Surpluses sustain wars better than forced levies" (1.141.5), and Sparta, an agricultural country dependent on an annual harvest, without naval experience and without capital, will be hard put to survive a protracted struggle and retain the support of her allies. At several points he

alludes cautiously to the Athenian superiority: "Know that we shall not be the weaker of the two sides in resources for the war" (1.141.2; cf. 143.3; 144.1–2). In the last passage he refers to a full account "to be given on the brink of action," and Thucydides reports this to us at 2.13. It amounts to massive military and financial reserves and Pericles' optimism about final superiority seems understated. Thucydides himself says that the reserves accumulated by Pericles sustained the war through its long duration and frequent mistakes, and justified his foresight that the city would prove superior in war against the Peloponnesians alone (2.65.13); in terms of the Thucydidean categories of foresight (*pronoia*) and preparation (*paraskeuē*), Pericles cannot be bettered. In his first appearance before the reader, Pericles uses hardheaded calculations of the factors that will win the war for Athens, rather than rhetorical and emotional arguments, and in so doing he has the last word in the strategic debate, which has been conducted at long distance and intervals, beginning with cautions to the Spartans from Archidamus and carried on more optimistically by the Corinthians at the second Congress (1.120 ff.).

2. The qualification that Pericles predicted a win against the Peloponnesians *alone*, brings us to his stern injunction that Athens should not try to add to the empire while the war was in progress (144.1; see 2.65.7 for the importance which Thucydides himself attaches to the injunction). This, coupled with the admonition not to be concerned with the loss of their land and homes in Attica, completes a strategy for the war of nonconfrontation on Athens' part. Again, this seems quite in keeping with the defensive posture which Pericles has adopted, though the designs may well see further than simply coming through a war intact. Pericles seems to be putting the onus on Sparta of proving to the Greek world that she can put an end to the Athenian empire. Once Sparta, the traditional liberator of Greece, was humiliated by her inability to live up to her former image, a lot of hopes elsewhere would be extinguished, and the task of policing the empire and even extending it would be easier for Athens. Pericles, then, was intent on putting the polarity between the sea people with resources and the agricultural people with no aptitude for a protracted war to work in Athens' favor; one has only to think of the low standing of Sparta's reputation at the end of the Archidamian War, despite Athenian slippage after Pylos and deviations from the Periclean plan elsewhere, to see how sound his calculation was (see 5.28.2

and, for the nadir of Spartan morale after the losses at Pylos and Cythera, 4.55).

3. These particular points have their ground in a larger critique of the two countries' positions: the question of unity and identity of interest.

The Corinthians in their speech at the second Congress had stressed the need for a collective effort. The leader should earn the honor he receives by serving the general interest (*ta koina proskopein*—1.120.1); those inland allies, away from the shipping lanes and Athenian harassment, should not regard the war as irrelevant to them (1.120.2): "If we do not all join together to ward them off, nation by nation, and town by town in one common goal, they will easily get the better of us in our divisiveness (*dicha ge ontas*)" (1.122.2); and again in the peroration: "So since there is every good reason to go to war, and since we are unanimous in urging this, and since our security lies in having both cities and individuals share this interest, . . ." (1.124.1) and so on, conventionally, to specific injunctions.

The insistence on unity may belie some anxiety. Pericles, in his answering speech, finds the Peloponnesians' unity suspect. In his review of the strategic options open to them, he lays the ground of their weakness in the looseness of their federalism:

> The Peloponnesians and their allies are capable of standing up to the rest of the Greeks in a single land battle, but they are incapable of maintaining a war against a power unlike their own, especially when it comes to emergency action; for they do not have one center of deliberation, or the unanimity of shared race (*ouch homophuloi*), but they all carry equal weight in the voting, so each pursues his own interest, and as a result nothing gets done. One group is intent on punishing someone, and another resists just as strongly for fear of personal loss. When they come together after some length of time, only a small part of their attention goes on the common interest, and most on their private business. No one imagines that his own indifference is causing any damage, but everyone still expects everyone else to look out for his own concerns, so that in the universal pattern of private obsession, they fail to notice that the common good is being undone. (1.141.6–7)

Athens, on the other hand, is "free from the faults which I find in them" (1.143.3). If the Peloponnesians take loans, for example, from Olympia or Delphi, to entice foreigners (*xenous*) out of the Athenian navy into their own, it will not make much difference, because the key members of the crew (the steersmen) are all citizens (1.143.1).

But Pericles shares the preoccupation with unity. He begins his speech with the same sort of appeal the Corinthians have used: "I call on those of you who share my views, to come to the support of our *common* decision (*tois koinēi doxasin*), even if we fail in some respect, or else not to share the credit for its intelligence if we succeed" (1.140.1). This has a clear echo in his last speech: "It is right for you to come to the support of the city and the honor it receives from the empire, in which you all take pleasure; you should not shun the labor, if you do not shun the honor" (2.65.1). In fact, the whole of Pericles' thinking, as Thucydides shows it to us, is dominated by the primacy of national interest over individual concerns. The very organization of the Funeral Oration stresses this priority: the praise of the city (its constitution, its way of life, and the national character of its citizens, who developed and preserved it) precedes the praise of the dead, who have died for it: "For such a city they fought and died, in their nobility refusing to be deprived of her, and it is right that all of us who survive should be willing to toil for her. That is why I have elaborated the qualities of our city, trying to convey the lesson that the struggle is not conducted on the same terms for us, as for those who do not share our advantages, and setting the eulogy which I am speaking for the dead on sure grounds and evidence. Most of it has now been said: the praises I have sung of the city, the virtues of these men, and others like them, further embellished . . ." (2.41.5–42.2).

At the start of the last speech, the priority is again starkly stated: "I believe that when the whole city prospers, it benefits the individuals in it more than when they all thrive on their own, while the city as a whole fails. For when a man does well on his own, but his country fails, he is destroyed just the same along with it, but when he fares ill, and his country prospers, he still has a better chance of reversing his fortune. So that if it is true that the city can support individual misfortune, but no single person can support the city's, surely we should all rally to her defense" (2.60.2–4). This cardinal principle opens the way for a definition of his own talents as a statesman—his ability to know the right policy and explain it, his incorruptibility, and his patriotism (2.60.5), qualities which he first modestly claims to possess "less than no-one" (*ibid.*), and then a little more assertively, "moderately more than others" 2.60.7). In between these two claims, there is a swiftly inductive sentence, which we discussed in chapter I, connecting these qualities into a definition of statesmanship: knowing the right policy is useless if you cannot explain it; without patriotism the care to give good guidance is in question; and without incorruptibility, the whole man is put up for sale.

Just as in the speeches of the first Congress at Sparta the reader was given the delineations of national temperaments as a guide to likely behavior by the two sides in the war, so in the speeches of Pericles he is given a set of standards needed to move nations by political leadership, with which he can measure the performance of prominent politicians in the work. Foremost among them is the submission of private ambition to the national interest. This kind of political altruism strikes us as a commonplace of rhetoric and philosophy, especially Plato's, but I do not believe that it would be one for Thucydides, or for contemporary readers who came to him from Herodotus and expected their history to be set closer to epic. For Thucydides, Clio is not a goddess of personal fame, and the *aretē* of the statesman is not the *aretē* of the epic hero. The proper stuff of history is large movements of power, to be found in nations, not individuals, and the greatest statesmen are those who serve the collective purposes of their countries and not their own. This is a considerable reorientation of the genre.

Thucydides confirms Pericles' claims to the virtues of statesmanship, and in fact makes him the unique embodiment of the type, to the disparagement of his successors:

> The others reversed his policy on all these points, both for the war and for other matters which had nothing to do with it; instead, with an eye to personal ambition and private gain, they shaped policies for themselves and the allies, which, when they succeeded, brought honor and success to individuals, and when they failed, damaged the city's war effort. Whereas his power was based on the authority of his judgment and his obvious incorruptibility, so that he controlled the people without any constraint, and was not led by them but rather led them himself. Because his power was not held on improper grounds, he did not have to say anything to please them, but because of his standing could oppose them even angrily. Whenever he saw them growing dangerously arrogant and overconfident, he would dress them down to caution again, and when he found them unreasonably fearful he restored their confidence. It was in theory a democracy, but in fact rule by the First Man. However, those who came after him were more on a level with each other, and while each one grasped for primacy for himself, they were all corrupted into indulging the whims of the people and so lost control of affairs. (2.65. 7–10)

This whole chapter casts a long shadow in the work, and one can see its influence in many of the later assessments of leaders, even as far away as the eighth book, where the oligarchs are said to have stopped "thinking of themselves as equals, but all sought to be first" (8.89.3). This impulse, whether in oligarchy or democracy, is the germ of *stasis*.

But if Pericles is the archetype of the statesman in his pristine virtue, Cleon, his first successor, must embody the decline from his standards. The portrait of Cleon is developed ironically, and apparently with the edge of Thucydides' own animus against him. The reader is encouraged to compare the two figures by Cleon's plagiarism in his speech of some Periclean phrases, and then finds that in substance there is no resemblance between them.[5] There are serious criticisms in the speech of the operations of democracy, and the tendency of the Assembly to avoid any sense of responsibility in their deliberations, and to look for entertainment instead (3.38.4–7). This is not the way democracy has to work, as we have seen from the close argument and elevated tone of Pericles' speeches. But it is the unfortunate aspect of a democracy without a true leader, when politicians are "corrupted into indulging the whims of the people," and it is typical of Thucydides that he gives his reader this critique at a general level, in the voice of an archetypical demagogue who benefits from the trend.

The trend to irresponsibility, and the irony of his earlier remarks, become immediately apparent at Cleon's next appearance, where he is the center of attention in the Pylos debate, and makes everyone behave badly: Thucydides, with privileged access into his motivation, sees his challenge to the generals as proceeding from a loss of standing from his rejection of the Spartan peace terms (4.27.3; cf. 4.22.2) and his personal animus against Nicias (4.27.5). Nicias, the trained soldier, irresponsibly accepts the challenge and steps down from his command, to allow the demagogue to make a fool of himself (28.1–2). And the people, enjoying Cleon's embarrassment, "as the crowd loves to do," urges the completion of the arrangement (28.3). "The Athenians were amused at his lightheaded boasting, but even the more sensible were pleased, calculating that they would obtain one of two goals—either getting rid of Cleon, which they rather expected, or, if they missed on that, getting the better of the Spartans" (4.28.5). A good case of politics as entertainment, but a far cry from Pericles' controlling interest in national security.

The same absence of real leadership, the same loss of control, causing others to abrogate their own responsibilities, this time disastrously, is shown in the last episode of Cleon's career. Cleon is doing nothing at

Eion, but then is forced (*ēnagkasthē*) by his men's discontent and adverse comparisons of his incompetence with Brasidas' efficiency, to make the move that Brasidas expected (5.7.1–2). When he sees the Spartans about to attack, he orders a retreat, but there is no cohesion in the Athenian army—the left wing flees, the center is routed, and the commander takes to flight, leaving his right wing marooned. "He (Brasidas) made his attack on the Athenians who were in a panic because of their own disorganization" (5.10.6). So much for Cleon's leadership—leadership that produced a crisis of confidence, and then a kind of military *stasis*.

The decline in Athenian fortunes seems so programmatic after Pericles, and he himself seems so secure in his judgment and so fully endorsed by Thucydides, that it is worth asking whether the historian has shaped his work as a kind of polemic, to protect his hero's name.[6] Writing after the war, he would be conscious of fighting a rear-guard action; it did not take the public long in their search for scapegoats to work back from the incompetence of the generals at Aigospotamoi to the architect of the war itself. There is, in fact, considerable delicacy in Thucydides' portrait of Pericles. We saw in the Pentecontaetia that the impersonality of the account obscured the earlier, demagogic phase of his career, which we find in Plutarch's *Life;* in Thucydides' version, his role was mostly conservative, reclaiming parts of the empire after revolt. There is equal delicacy in the summary of his career at the end of his last speech (2.65). The attacks against Pericles proceeded against two opposite aspects of him—against the well-born, authoritarian, Olympian figure who monopolized the government (fifteen consecutive years as *stratēgos*) on the one hand, and on the other against the crowd-pleasing politician of Plato's writings, who bribed the people with jury-pay and other funds taken from the allies.[7] Thucydides will not use the term *prostatēs*, or "champion" of the people, for Pericles, no doubt because of its demagogic connotation; he uses it, perhaps ironically, in the passage already referred to, of the oligarchs' ambition to be first (8.89.4). By the end of his last speech, Thucydides has his hero rejected by both oligarchs and *dēmos*— "the *dēmos*, because having started with little, they had been deprived even of that [by the war], and the powerful, because they had lost their fine estates in the country, with their expensive buildings and furnishings—but most of all because they had war instead of peace: altogether they were not appeased in their anger until they had fined him"

(2.65.2–3). Pericles, therefore, cannot be classified by narrow party labels. He receives a title of his own; he is the First Man, which allows him to be unique, and his isolation is the measure of his transcendence of partisan interests: it is the isolation of the First Man who is always right.

All of this is a little hard to take. The paragon has been so precisely defined that possible rivals through history can be eliminated on one or other of his criteria in comparison with him. Alcibiades lived an extravagant life, and was certainly motivated by self-interest (6.15.2; cf. 6.16.2–3 for priorities, and also 16.6), and Themistocles was possibly venal (though Thucydides will not mention Herodotus' slur),[8] and both of them on rejection by Athens went over to the enemy and might be disqualified on the count of patriotism.

It is important to analyze the exclusiveness of the treatment of Pericles to see what Thucydides is doing. Though his status is unique, it is certainly not the status of the epic hero; there is no concern for *kleos* for himself, and his strategy of nonconfrontation for the war, for all its rationality, is the antithesis of epic initiative. Yet it is clear that Thucydides supports him, and protects him to a degree never afforded any other leader, and perhaps, as Wade-Gery says, noting the family connection with Cimon, "with a convert's zeal."[9]

And yet I do not believe that the purpose of the portrait and its dominance in the book are purely polemical. I see beyond this a kind of philosophical interest in delineating the ideal relationship between a state and its leaders, along with a depressing awareness that such a relationship rarely exists and must in fact be doomed, because of the imperfections inherent in any citizen-body (the state as a whole) and in the average type of individual who aspires to lead it. In this sense, then, Thucydides makes Pericles a perfect archetype of the statesman in the same way that he makes Cleon a kind of archetype of the inadequacy of his successors. A purely polemical account could not afford to juxtapose the Funeral Oration and the Plague so starkly, obscuring Pericles' message and raising all sorts of dark questions about human nature. But this is exactly the point Thucydides wants to make: there is a period in a nation's history when it rises to greatness, as Athens did from Marathon to Pericles. But it is hard to sustain. Pericles will always appeal to his listeners "not to be inferior" to the tradition they have inherited (1.144.4; cf. 2.36.1–3; 2.41.5; 2.43.1; 2.63.1); he sees a hard *agōn* for the children and the brothers of the dead (2.45.1), to live up to the example they have shown. History is a competitive struggle, and increasingly so in a long war, and ultimately, as far as a nation's greatness is concerned, it is a struggle that will be lost. Thucydides has Pericles recognize this, in a parenthesis in the last paragraph of his last unanswered speech: "For all things are born to be diminished" (2.64.3). But for a time, at least, "under him it was greatest." What the Plague does to the Funeral Oration is to reduce it to the private vision of its speaker, Pericles; but it is a vision that Thucydides has shaped for his First Man, and fully shares. And historically, in Thucydides' view, it is the kind of vision that brought Athens to her *akmē*.

6

MELOS

We saw in the Archaeology that Thucydides, tracing the development of his civilization, seemed to accept the operation of the law of nature that the strong exploit the weak. Small things to great by violence grow. In the earliest days, communities did not take root, but let themselves be easily (*rhadiōs*) uprooted by the regular arrival of greater force (1.2.1); piracy was an accepted way of life, and people would ask new arrivals whether they were pirates, without intending any insult by the question (1.5.1–2); and when power became more concentrated, weaker communities would willingly accept the position of subjects, because of the profit attached to it (1.8.3). The development of states into something "significant" (*axiologon*) is thus recorded matter-of-factly in the Archaeology; and in the speeches the status of the Athenian Empire is established with pride, particularly in the Funeral Oration. In fact, the claim that Athens is the School of Hellas (2.41.1) is based strikingly on the evidence of her *power:* "The very power of the city, which we have obtained through this national character of ours, bears witness that this is not merely boastful talk for the present occasion, but actual fact" (2.41.2).[1] This is hammered home uncompromisingly at the end of the paragraph: "Because of the power we have shown, we will be a source of wonder to posterity, . . . making every land and every sea accessible to our daring, and establishing everywhere monuments of good and evil done" (41.4). And shortly afterwards, Pericles urges his audience not to make a mere mental calculation about the advantages to be reaped from resisting the enemy, "but actively to contemplate the *power* of the city day by day and become her lovers (*erastai*)," like the dead who made the final perfect offering (*eranon*) to her (2.43.1). The language is striking and uncompromising, and there is more of it in the peroration of Pericles' last speech (2.64.3). As we have seen earlier, prominent figures, whom Thucydides clearly respects, seem to acknowledge the rights of aggression, even when it is directed against them, e.g., Hermocrates (4.61.5; see also Brasidas, 4.86.6).

For Thucydides as a historian it is the concentration of power that makes history—that performs works that are "great and significant." His acceptance of this fact exposes him to reproach for acceptance of the *excesses* of power, but his *History* shows that he is alive to the issue; the debates he gives on the episodes at Mytilene, Plataea, and especially Melos are *moral* debates, all bearing on the question of whether a particularly severe action should be taken towards the defeated. In this chapter, we will discuss what conclusions he reaches: where, in particular, does he stand on the Athenian argument and action at Melos?

This is a very difficult question. Andrewes, continuing Gomme's *Commentary* over the relevant passage, himself "believes that the view of the Dialogue as an indictment of Athens is mistaken," but is less sure of Gomme's own view: "He once told me, but briefly and without argument, that he regarded it as intended to show the moral decline of Athens."[2] The tentative note is appropriate. But it is still worth trying to examine Thucydides' intentions with the passage.

The first point to make is that Thucydides has clearly set up a progression towards the most ruthless application of the law that the strong exploit the weak. The law is announced by the Athenians at Sparta, with the stipulation that they deserve credit for the moderation with which they have applied it. This moderation is tested at Mytilene and narrowly prevails. At Melos there is no evidence of any Athenian moderation, and the punishment that was first voted for Mytilene is exacted without second thoughts. There are other incidents which relate to one phase or another, but these three stages are highlighted by the arguments which accompany them; we will attend to these arguments in some detail.

The first statement of the rights of the strong is made by the Athenian speakers at Sparta, who were there "on other business," and obtained permission from the Spartans to speak, "not to answer the charges which the cities had brought against Athens, but to show that the whole matter should not be decided in haste" (1.72.1). I have suggested that the anonymity of the speakers and the fact that they are there on other business indicate that we are not about to receive an official, diplomatic answer to specific complaints, but an unofficial, though presumably fairly prevalent, point of view of the Athenians at the time. I will quote the nub of their argument again:

> We have done nothing astonishing, committed no perversion of human nature, if we took an empire when it was offered, and now refuse to let it go, overwhelmed (*nikēthentes*) by the three great factors of honor, fear, and profit. We were not the first to do this. It has always been an established practice that the weaker should be constrained by the stronger. Moreover, we consider ourselves worthy of our role, and you seemed to think so too, until calculations of self-interest prompted you to use the argument of justice, which no one in history ever took seriously enough to deny themselves a profit, when there was a chance of acquiring something by force. The people who really deserve praise are those who, while following their natural instincts to rule others, have more respect for justice than the power at their disposal requires. And we are sure that anyone who inherited our empire would prove our moderation convincingly. (1.76.2–4)

Worthiness to rule, then, belongs to the strong, and praiseworthiness for the manner of ruling comes to the moderate. We may take this argument, with the small space allowed in it for moderation, as part of the prewar climate of opinion at Athens, perhaps under the civilizing influence of Pericles, who "led (*exēgeito*) them *moderately*" (2.65.5).[3]

In the Mytilenean situation, moderation appears in the final decision, though it is not argued for in the debate as though it had any merit of its own. But Thucydides makes it clear that it still had a place in the public conscience; after the first debate on the fate of the Mytileneans has reached the verdict to kill the men and enslave the women and children, he describes the overnight reaction at Athens: "But on the next day they had second thoughts, and on reconsideration found their decision, to destroy the whole city rather than merely the guilty, cruel and excessive (*ōmon kai mega*)" (3.36.4). When Mytilenean representatives approach the Athenian officials to have the matter reopened, they convince them fairly easily, "because it was clear to them that the majority of the citizens wanted a chance to deliberate on the matter again" (3.36.5). However, when the final vote is taken, the result is close, with leniency only a narrow victor; and the stay of sentence was also a very near thing: the original decree was on the point of being carried out by Paches, when the crew of the second ship, urged on by special food and promises, arrived after rowing all night. "So close did Mytilene come to disaster" (3.49.4 *fin.*). The involvement on the side of leniency of the majority of the citizens and of the rowers (the *first* crew had rowed slowly because of the uncongeniality of their mission) saves the day.

But the debate between Cleon and Diodotus on the issue does not acknowledge this sentiment. Cleon, after castigating the Assembly for its fickleness and frivolity, like the attitudes of spectators to the serious business of politics, argues predictably that leniency will only encourage other subject states to revolt: "And we shall have to risk resources and lives in every state, and if we are successful, we will recover a city that has been ruined, and thus be deprived of her revenue afterwards, which is the principal source of our strength. And if we fail, we will be adding enemies to those we already have, and the time we ought to be spending on an adversary already drawn up against us will go on beating down our allies" (3.39.8). Coming from Cleon, the violent and persuasive demagogue, this argument does not surprise us. But when Diodotus speaks, we are, I think, surprised, in view of the swing in public opinion, that the tone he adopts in certain passages seems so relentlessly, and even inhumanly, businesslike and calculating:

> I have not come to refute arguments about the Mytileneans, or to make accusations. If we are wise, the issue we are debating is not the question of their guilt, but what is the best policy for us. I might find them altogether guilty, but would not on that account urge you to kill them, unless it was to your advantage; nor if I found some excuse for them, [the text is corrupt here but the sense is clear] would I necessarily let them live, unless it seemed the right thing for the city. (3.44.1–2)

And he goes on to argue that there has never been a deterrent, not even the death penalty, to keep people from taking risks, if they have hope of success: "It is simply the height of folly to imagine that when human nature has set its heart on doing something, it can be deterred by force of law or some terrible sanction" (3.45.7). Again we have the skepticism about the ability of manmade convention (*nomos*) to control nature (*phusis*), which echoes the Athenians' sarcasm about the Spartan use of the argument from justice. In this case, the argument runs, fierce punishment for revolt would be counterproductive, because subsequently rebels would resist to the death, in the knowledge that there would be no hope of salvaging anything from surrender—this would protract the business of reduction and add to the cost (3.46.2).

Thus after the siege of Potidea, the cost of subduing a revolution figures strongly at Athens, and both Cleon and Diodotus attend to it, though they disagree on whether severity or leniency is ultimately more expensive. Both steel their audiences against pity and gentleness (3.40.2; 3.48.1), and ask them to judge the matter on a rational assessment of what serves the city best. But buried in the midst of severity, there is a small hint in Diodotus' speech that Athenian policy with the allies, whom he twice refers to as *free*, should not be one of vengeance, but of preventive caution, "so that they do not even form the intention of revolting," and when the inevitable revolution does occur, "to hold as few as possible responsible" (3.46.5–6). Diodotus' reason for this, it seems, is given in the next chapter: "The *dēmos* is well disposed to Athens in every city, and either refuses to join the oligarchs in their revolt, or, if it is forced to join, remains hostile to the instigators, so that when you tackle a city in revolt, you enter the conflict with the majority on your side" (3.47.2). This comment on the friendliness of the *dēmos* is as close as we come in Thucydides' work to a recognition that it may be possible for a democracy to maintain an empire without incurring the hatred of one's subjects. Moderation in this view does not merely earn praise for those with an empire, but is the correct tactic for keeping it. At Mytilene, after a close call, this turns out to be the majority view.

But when we come to Melos, we find the law of nature that the strong exploit the weak enforced with full rigor; there is no indication of any climate of restraint at Athens. The issue is debated simply between aggressor and victim, and in the end the sentence which Mytilene avoided is carried out. In the context of Mytilene that sentence was labeled *allokotos* ("monstrous" or "unprecedented"—3.49.4) and "cruel and excessive" (*ōmon . . . kai mega*—3.36.4): if it was so for a prominent subject that had revolted, should it not be at least the same for a gratuitous assault on an independent island? And must not Thucydides, having set off on a straight-line progression, beginning with moderation and departing from it in stages, have arrived at a point, by the time he has reached the end, that he is prepared to call *excess?* Unfortunately, I don't believe the matter is so schematically clear-cut, or that he is entirely sure by the end where he should draw the line. The difference between Mytilene and Melos is an interval of twelve years, which Thucydides sees as one of unremitting war, hardening attitudes, and the actions resulting from them. I do not believe that Thucydides remained entirely proof against the trend himself. But to establish his view more precisely, we must attend more closely to the argument of the Melian Dialogue.

The Athenians begin by setting the ground rules for the discussion: "As for us, we will not string out an unconvincing argument of fine-sounding words about how we are right to rule because we freed the world from the Persians, or are now invading you because of the wrongs we suffered from you, and you should not imagine you will persuade us with speeches about how you never joined the Spartans in their fight against us, though you are Lacedaemonian settlers, and how you never wronged us. We should both proceed from our knowledge of the way power really works, since we both realize that justice is a term that only has validity in human argument when the two sides can bring equal force to bear; otherwise the strong do what they can, and the weak must go along with them" (5.89).

Such a statement purports to bring us down to the bedrock facts of the situation, which both sides should acknowledge to be true. The shift to a dialogue from formal, balanced speeches (*dissoi logoi*) enhances the impression of matter-of-factness, cutting into the rhetoric at every point before it can hit its stride. The argument of Athenian services to Greece in the Persian War, which the Athenians at Sparta first elaborated, and the arguments of justice—of rights and wrongs—are pronounced specious or irrelevant.

After such restrictions, what is left? The first point to note is that the argument is by no means as factual as the Athenian rules suggest it would be, or in fact as an actual debate in the circumstances was bound to be—we are not told how much tribute Melos would have to pay, whether they would have to give hostages, or whether an Athenian garrison would be posted there. Secondly, the narrative is deliberately cleared of all contextual information, any record of grievance or politics attending the event, so that the Athenian action is made to appear a perfectly gratuitous act of aggression.

The Melians have been challenged by the Athenian opening statement to find advantage for themselves in obliging Athenian self-interest. They first attempt to alter the rules with some redefinition: "In our opinion, it is convenient (useful, *chrēsimon*) (if you must have it this way, with your insistence that we should speak about what is expedient at the expense of what is just), for you not to abandon the concept of a goodness that is common for all, but to allow that there is room for equity and justice even for those who are desperate, and that a man in this predicament should be given the benefit of making arguments even though they fall short of absolute precision. And this principle is particularly in your favor, because if you ever fall from power, you would be made an example for the rest of time for the scope of the vengeance exacted from you" (5.90). However, the Athenians do not accept this appeal to general principle, and are not daunted by the threat of future retribution: if they are brought down, it will be by an imperial power, and imperial powers understand one another.

The Melians, limited to the discussion of their present predicament, ask whether Athens would not accept them as friends, pledged to neutrality, instead of enemies (5.94). The answer is an uncompromising refusal but on sophistical grounds, which are hard for us to accept: "Your hostility would not hurt us as much as your friendship, which would be a sign of weakness to our subjects, just as hatred is a sign of power" (5.95). The Melians go on to ask whether the Athenian subjects cannot make a distinction between those who have no previous connection with Athens, and those who are colonists or else have been suppressed after a revolt (5.96). The answer is that there are no grounds for such a distinction: the allies, like their masters the Athenians, calculate on the basis of power: "They think that those who survive do so because of their power, and if we fail to attack them, it must be because of our fear: so that quite apart from the increasing numbers we control, your suppression would also increase our security, especially as it would be a case of islanders who are weaker than others falling to a sea power" (5.97).

This leaves the Melians with the odds against them, with no recourse against the law of nature except intangible factors—hope, the gods, and their alliance with Sparta. The Athenians deride their hopes and make intervention by the gods and Sparta seem equally remote:

As far as the good will of the gods is concerned we don't think we have forfeited it; none of our claims or actions runs counter to the normal human notions of divine law, or indeed to the gods' own way of pursuing their will.

For as far as we can tell, we believe it is the divine law, just as it clearly is the human one, that in every situation, by force of nature, to the extent of their power, the powerful rule. We were not the ones who made the law, or the first to avail ourselves of it; we found it in existence, and will leave it to posterity, but in the meantime make use of it in the knowledge that you or anyone else, if you ever established yourselves with the same power, would do the same. So where the gods are concerned, we have no reason to fear that we will be at a disadvantage. And as for your views of the Spartans, who you trust will be shamed into coming to your assistance, we congratulate you on your naïve innocence, but cannot envy your folly. (5.105.1–3)

Thus the last ground of the Melian appeal is swept from under them, and having no words left, they prepare to withdraw to consider their predicament. As a parting shot, the Athenians define proper attitudes for people facing the realities of the world: not to yield to equals, to adapt oneself graciously to those who are stronger, and to treat the weaker with moderation (5.111.4). The last precept takes us back to the Athenians at Sparta, claiming praise for pursuing their natural advantage more moderately than their power requires them to, but it seems cruelly ironic in view of the punishment they design, and in fact will execute.

This last admonition might be a good place to begin in our search for clues to Thucydides' own attitude to the arguments he gives us. Does he expect us to condemn the Athenians out of their own mouths by their prescription that the correct attitude to ensure success includes "moderation to one's inferiors"? I do not believe Thucydides intends us to see this as a case of ironic blindness. The word for "moderate" (*metrioi*) in this phrase picks up the *metria* earlier in the same sentence, and seems to indicate the treatment to be awarded to those who *acknowledge* their superiors—that is the correlative stance specified along with moderation to the weak: one should also show respect for those who are stronger. The Melians by resisting are casting themselves as *equal*, and the prescription for dealing with *them* is refusal to give way.

There are two more substantial points, which seem to underline the negative aspects of the Athenian position.

The first is its contextual position in the work. Though it is true that the Athenian arguments are confirmed in the short run—nothing arrives to alter the inevitable consequences of resistance—in the slightly longer term, only three years later, the aggressor comes heavily to grief in Sicily. The Melian episode is the last event before the narrative of the

Sicilian expedition begins. Is it correct to see this episode, as Cornford does, as a case of *hubris*, emphasized by Thucydides with a forward look to the nemesis of 413?[4] The similar action at Scione a few years earlier received no particular comment (5.32); the chronological juxtaposition of small Melos to the much larger invasion of another uninvolved island may give us the reason for the emphasis here, despite its comparative strategic unimportance.

The irony of the Sicilian disaster is certainly not wasted on Thucydides. He stresses not only the glory of the panoply which sailed out of the Peiraeus (6.30–32), but also the fact that the sight of it reassured the spectators in their apprehensions of the dangers that lay ahead (6.31.1); there is a similar piece of false reassurance earlier, at the end of the debate on the expedition, when Nicias has been driven to specify the numbers needed: the younger citizens were full of anticipation, "and confident that they would be safe," but even the older ones were enthusiastic, sure that they would either complete the mission for which they left, or that at least such a great power could not come to grief (6.24.3).

On the other hand, the Melians, in their warnings to the Athenians that they may in the future find themselves in the position of underdog, seem to direct their prediction beyond Sicily to the end of the war and the Athenian empire (5.90). At least, that is the way the Athenians interpret it, thinking of their empire being brought to an end by the Spartans, "who themselves rule others" (5.91). The prospect does not worry them at this distance (though Xenophon says that there was some fear at the end that the fate of Melos would be visited on Athens—*Hell.* 2.2.3). And again, we have to say that the Athenian assurance on this point is, in the longest term, by a narrow margin justified: they were defeated by Sparta, and they were not annihilated.

Furthermore, Thucydides does not seem to choose to make further use of his juxtaposition of Melos and Syracuse: in the final throes of Athenian defeat in Sicily, he never draws the conclusions of nemesis, but seems rather to see the aggressor-come-to-grief as victim; and in the aftermath of defeat, having underlined the desperation to which the Athenians were brought, he emphasizes their resilience despite everything (8.2.1). At least for Thucydides, the Sicilian disaster is not the end of Athens, in the sense that the Athenian action at Melos was the end of the Melians.

The second point is harder to deal with, but equally important. Perhaps the most influential factor in the reader's acceptance of the Melian Dialogue as a cynical exposition by totally unprincipled aggressors is the fact that the tone of hardness is adopted prospectively, to match the final outcome of the confrontation. Instead of using the carrot before the stick, the stick is obviously in evidence before the start, and clearly impatient with the talk that is delaying its descent. The very structure of the Dialogue, chosen over set speeches in the preliminaries to the debate (5.85), emphasizes the impatience. There are to be no "fine words" on either side. This is an effective device for carrying the sense of desperation one stage beyond that of the Plataeans, who, though faced with a single question, were finally allowed to widen their appeal beyond it (3.52.4–5).

It is clear that the tone of the argument is fitted by Thucydides to the pending Athenian action: tough action calls for tough argument. Just as Athenian action proceeds from moderation (the Athenians at Sparta allow their subjects access to law courts, and justice—1.77), to second thoughts at Mytilene, and on to the massacre of the Melians, so the argument that accompanies the action becomes more severe. There is common ground between the various stages (all acknowledge the role of self-interest, all see the inefficacy of manmade law or sanctions in the face of nature—1.76.2; 3.45.7), but in the case of Melos, the antinomian argument is pursued far more extensively and made apparently absolute and watertight. Justice is a matter of human convention, dependent on the power of enforcement, and the law of nature has supremacy over it and carries the endorsement of the gods. It is therefore completely untrammeled and need acknowledge no restraints, even of the highest authority. The gods are on the side of the big battalions.

This progression towards extreme violence is followed most noticeably in the Athenian development, but, as I have indicated, I do not believe Thucydides intends to make his point onesidedly. The episodes at Melos or Plataea show the same tendencies in the war at large which he has described in detail in his account of the Corcyrean Revolution, extracting from it a general theory developed on "neutral" ground. Violence escalates from past experience: "And later attempts, in the knowledge of what had gone before, brought excess (*huperbolēn*) to the revolutionary spirit, both in the design of their tactics, and the outlandishness (*atopiāi*) of their vengeance. To fit their actions, they changed the established meanings of words . . . moderation was just the pretext of cowardice" (3.82.3–4). Revolution is a particularly intense microcosm of the processes of war in general; the passage just quoted follows immediately on the description of war as a "harsh (or violent) teacher" (*biaios didaskalos*), which scholars have often been tempted to translate as a "teacher of violence":[5] a good teacher is supposed to make his students *better* at his particular discipline.

The fact of escalating violence under pressure of war or revolution is, Thucydides believes, universal and inescapable. The universality may account for the fatalism of so much of the tone of Thucydides' narrative. It is no good decrying the inevitable. The hardness of tone which on one view of the Melian Dialogue and other debates invites condemnation, on another serves simply to underline a persistent and perhaps cynical display of the fragility of the moral code, constantly rubbing the scrupulous reader's nose in the inefficacy of principle or virtue. I do not believe that this is Thucydides' intention; however, neither do I think his attitude towards the Athenian action at Melos is one of unqualified moral condemnation.

Having given the "negative" aspects of the Athenian argument, it is worth accumulating whatever "palliatives" we can find for their position from the Dialogue itself or from other contexts in the *History:*

a) The Melian leaders restrict the negotiations to a closed session; the Athenians seem to expect that they would have a better chance of acceptance if they spoke to the people at large (5.85). Are we expected to look on the Melian intransigence as a selfishly partisan decision, as well as an unrealistic one?

b) The Athenians are candid about their intentions and their advantage. There are no euphemisms which might delude the Melians; the chances of their *surviving* by resistance are ridiculed at 5.111.2.

c) The Athenians are correct in their judgment of the realities of the situation: Melos cannot hold out, the Spartans do not intervene, and the gods do not appear to be interfering with the common law of gods and men, that whoever is stronger rules (5.105.2). Is the accuracy of the argument a sign of Thucydides' sympathy with it?

d) Extreme as their action strikes us, the Athenians do not in their final reduction go as far as they might: they do not kill the women and children, as the Thracian slingers, returning north after missing the boat for Sicily, do to the people of Mykalessus (7.29.4). This latter is looked on with as close to obvious outrage as Thucydides allows himself to come (7.30.3), and the barbarism of the Thracians in such situations is alluded to (7.29.4). The Athenian action at Melos may remain within the bounds of what is acceptable in the Hellenic world. It is, after all, virtually the same as what Priam predicts will be the result of a Greek victory over Troy (*Il.* 22.62–65).[6] Within the Peloponnesian War, the same treatment has been meted out without particular comment to Scione (5.32), and also in essence, in a highly charged episode, to Plataea, though there were no children there (3.68.2).

e) A sortie by the Melians during the siege killed some Athenians: the final action may have the harshness of a reprisal (5.115.4).

f) There had been Athenian intervention at Melos in 426, when Nicias had led an expedition there; Melos had also appeared in the tribute assessment of 424, though it had never paid. In the present expedition there are subject islanders present in the Athenian force, helping to bring the recalcitrant island to heel. Some have inferred from this that Athens has a grievance, possibly a legitimate one, for this apparently wanton aggression.[7] (Logically, we should not use this: we cannot argue that Thucydides intends to excuse the Athenians on these grounds, because he has not told us what the grievance was.)

g) The Athenian skepticism about the gods' intervention seems at root akin to Thucydides' own in the narrative of the Plague (2.53.4; 2.54.2–5). There are two other passages in the work that appeal to the same sort of divine understanding of, and leniency with, human aggression as the Athenians claim at Melos. Both occur after Athenian defeats, when the opportunity was certainly open to the historian to belabor the penalties of *hubris*, and to show that assertive power contains the seed of its own destruction, because it is always likely to assert too much. But in neither case does this seem to be the lesson Thucydides wants us to draw: in fact, I can think of no passage that unequivocally has that intent.

The first passage to consider is the exchange between heralds after the Athenian defeat at Delium (4.97–98).[8] The Athenians still occupy the temple there, and the Boeotians make the return of Athenian dead conditional upon their withdrawal from it. They argue that the Athenians are violating the Hellenic custom of respect for temples in territory that is overrun, by fortifying them, and by drawing water for ordinary purposes and treating it as unconsecrated (4.97.2–3). The Athenians answer that it is customary (*nomon*) among the Greeks for an occupying power to occupy the temples as well, maintaining as much as possible the customary devotions (4.98.2). And they bring a countercharge of "much greater irreverence" on the part of the Boeotians, for making the retrieval of the dead, to which by ancient Greek custom (*kata ta patria*) the Athenians had an absolute right, conditional upon recovery of their temple. As for their own minor violations, they were committed involuntarily, and under necessity (98.6): "And it is altogether reasonable for actions done under the coercion of war or danger to be pardoned, even by the god."

When it comes to breaking the impasse, the Boeotians and their allies attack the Athenians' fortifications with a complicated flamethrower, and without any apparent scruples about sanctuary, and the garrison is routed (4.100). They then allow the Athenians to recover their dead without further comment. At least by taking the law into their own hands they have shown their acceptance in practice of the Athenian logic. It is hard to avoid the conclusion that Thucydides gives us this rather desultory exchange in the aftermath of an important battle for precisely this reason—to show that both sides in war follow their own interests; religious proscriptions are useful for taunting the enemy and putting an honorable front on one's own activity, but are not allowed to inhibit one's purposes.

The other passage where divine leniency is invoked optimistically is Nicias' final exhortation to his army as it retreats from Syracuse (7.77). He speaks as one who has "spent my life in many regular devotions to the gods, and many just and ungrudging (*anepiphthona*) works to men" (77.2). Thucydides confirms after his death that he least deserved to meet such an end, "because his whole life was regulated according to virtue" (7.86.5). His credentials, therefore, on moral and religious grounds are high. He is prepared for a moment to entertain the hypothesis that the expedition may have incurred the grudge of some of the gods (*epiphthonōs estrateusamen*), but argues that they have already been punished enough. And he goes further: "Other men at one time or another have gone against other states, and having done what is only human (*anthrōpeia*) have suffered only what can be endured. So it is reasonable for us now to hope for a gentler treatment from the gods, because we now deserve pity rather than envy (*phthonou*)" (77.4). The religious cast of the language overall is designed to convey Nicias' respect for the gods, which Thucydides may not share; but the assertion that those who do "human things" do not call down on themselves any outlandish punishment, which he puts into the mouth of a man he respects, is not far from the Athenians' claim at Melos that they have done nothing to forfeit divine favor (5.105.1).

h) Thucydides apparently accepts the argument of fear. We return to the Dialogue and the Melian question of whether Athens cannot accept them as friends pledged to neutrality instead of enemies (5.94). The Athenians say that Melian enmity does not hurt them as much as friendship would, since the latter would be a sign to their subjects of weakness, whereas their (Melian) hatred is a sign of Athens' power (95). The underlying assumption is that those who survive do so because of their power, and that the only reason that the Athenians do not attack them is because of fear (97). On this argument both oppressor and subject seem to operate on the same calculus of power, the subject always testing the oppressor, and the oppressor always ready to prove his power, and, despite the constant profession of self-interest, fear is the dominant motivation on both sides. Athens, then, invades Melos to prove to the rest of the empire that she can still do it.

This seems preposterous. The Melian Dialogue is presented as a candid exchange, without the embellishment of rhetorical set pieces, without the distraction of strategic considerations, and above all without pretense. The "fair words" (*onomata kala*) are supposed to have been discarded, and Athens, along with the advantage of overwhelming superiority, could afford to be blunt; but is not her argument that Melos must be suppressed because it is there, because it is necessary to prove to a watchful and resentful empire, consisting largely of subject islands, that another island is too weak to stay independent—isn't this just another false justification, another *onoma kalon* in its way, without being particularly elevated? At the very least, it seems, the argument has been generalized and distorted. We would believe them if the Athenians had said that they attacked Melos to prove to the rest of the empire that, despite the convincing Spartan victory at Mantinea in the previous year, the subjects should not imagine that the Spartans would assist any revolt, seeing that they would not come to help their fellow Lacedaemonians when wantonly attacked but too far off shore. The notion that one must constantly expand to maintain national security seems patently false, yet Thucydides seems partly inclined to believe it.

Fear is not the only factor involved. Thucydides is aware, of course, that *profit* is a strong motive force behind imperialism. In the Archaeology, the reason why pirates plunder, apart from making a living, is profit (1.5.1), and the reason Minos purges the seas of piracy is that the income would come to him (1.4); profit is also the reason why weaker states endure subjection to the stronger (1.8.3). There is no question that self-interest is the dominant motive behind most aggressive acts in Thucydides' account, and self-interest may be self-confident and not fearful.

This is clearly the case when we look at the motivation of the Sicilian expedition. Thucydides says of the exploratory force which sailed out in 426 that it was there on the pretext of kinship with Leontini, but really from the desire to stop food being exported to the Peloponnese and "to take a sounding to see if it would be possible to bring Sicilian affairs under their control" (3.86.4). When it comes to the great expedition, Thucydides leaves no doubt about the motivation: the Athenians were intent on conquering the whole of Sicily, as Nicias saw, on a slender pretext (6.8.4), and they saw this venture as profitable; Alcibiades hopes to take Sicily and Carthage, "and by success to increase his personal fortune and fame" (6.15.2); and the rank and file look forward to the work of conquest and the possibilities of perpetual pay once it is complete (6.24.3). There is hardly a hint of fear in the motives that influence the decision, or in the exuberance with which the glamorous expedition sails. Alcibiades' rationalization about the need for an imperialist power constantly to build its power bigger (6.18) seems disingenuous: "It is impossible to make any accountant's calculations about how much we want to rule; it is, in fact essential, since we are in this situation, to form designs on other people, and not to let go what we have, because there is the danger that if we do not rule others ourselves, we will be ruled by them" (6.18.3). When the Athenians and Syracusans converge on Camarina in the winter of 415/4, each bent on winning the town for their alliance, Hermocrates, who has just been praised by Thucydides for his intelligence (6.72.2), strips the Athenian propaganda bare: "You have heard the pretext on which they came to Sicily, but we all suspect what their real intention is. I don't believe they are interested in establishing Leontini, so much as in displacing us. For what sense does it make for them to be setting up cities here, and overturning them there, to be caring for their Chalcidian kinsmen in Leontini, while holding the mother city, Chalcis, in subjection in Euboea?" (6.76.2). When Euphemus, the Athenian representative, comes to rebut these criticisms, he must move cautiously. His argument is full of echoes of the Athenian speech at Sparta, but some of the ground has changed. The Athenians are still worthy of their empire "because we contributed the biggest fleet and the most uncompromising courage to the Greek cause" (6.83.1; cf. 1.75.1), but in the climate of candor of the Melian Dialogue, "we will not spin fine words (*kalliepoumetha*) that we are right to rule because we destroyed the barbarian single-handed" (6.83.2; cf. 5.89).

Instead, the argument returns to the motive of fear: the Athenians hold their empire because of fear (6.83.4)—not, this time, fear of the allies and their revolts (which would be tactless to a prospective ally), but fear of Sparta and the Peloponnesian bloc. Euphemus picks up Hermocrates' point of the "eternal enmity" between Ionians and Dorians (6.82.2; cf. 6.80.3). There is indeed such enmity, and that is why Athens needed her empire—to claim and to hold her independence from the Spartan empire (*archē*) and hegemony (6.82.3). The reason the Athenians are in Sicily is to cement their security at home: "Let none of you imagine that our concern for you has no ingredient of self-interest. You should realize that as long as you are safe and strong in your resistance against the Syracusans, *we* are less likely to be damaged by their sending a force to help the Peloponnese" (6.84.1). It is in Athens' interest to have different kinds of relationships with her allies; some are subject and pay mandatory tribute, some are independent and provide naval assistance, and some in strategic positions around the Peloponnese are entirely free (6.85.2). It would clearly be impossible for Athens to police places as far away as Sicily as rigorously as they police the empire at home, nor would it be in her interest to do so. The premise behind the Athenians' position, and the picture they try to get Camarina to see, is that in the completely polarized world in which they live, Athens must protect herself or be swallowed up, and so must Camarina, and if she rejects the Athenian alliance, then in all likelihood she will be swallowed up by Syracuse. Again, this does not seem completely plausible to us, but it

clearly makes at least *some* sense to the people of Camarina. In their deliberations after the debate, Thucydides says that they were well-
disposed to the Athenians, "except insofar as they thought they would
enslave Sicily," but they have substantial fears about their neighbors the
Syracusans. They end up deciding to help neither side. Thus even in the
motivation of the Sicilian expedition, which Thucydides seems to have
drawn so tellingly at its outset in the colors of self-interest, he leaves
some room for arguments drawn from fear, and the desperate or farfetched measures of national security.

These arguments run persistently through the work, beginning, like
many other refrains, with the Athenian speech at Sparta. The argument
there allowed other possibilities than those of fear, including honor and
self-interest; we also heard of "worthiness" to rule, based on the Athenian contribution against the Persians, a "benefit" (*ōphelia*) to the Greeks
which earned the benefits of rule. The Melian Dialogue dismissed the
Persian argument and reduced matters to self-interest and fear. Alcibiades adopted the basic point: one rules so as not to be ruled by others
(6.19.3), and this is the brunt of Euphemus' defense of Athenian imperialism (6.87.2). Fear is at this stage virtually the first impulse to imperialism, whereas for the Athenians at Sparta it is the reason not to surrender
an empire once gained. They put it like this: "It no longer seemed safe to
run the risk of letting it all go, when we were almost universally hated
and some of our subjects had already revolted and had to be subdued,
and you yourselves were no longer friendly, but were now at odds with
us, and so were viewed with suspicion" (1.75.4).

The Athenian speech at Sparta is the first step in a rhetorical debate
on the issue of imperialism in Thucydides' work, and Euphemus' speech
is the last. There are other shadings of the argument by other speakers in
between, as we shall see; but taken together they form an interconnected
web of rationalization, which the emphases of Thucydides' narrative
seem to support at several points. We noticed in the Archaeology that
fear and the need for security seemed to walk hand in hand with the
quest for profit in the accumulation of power: in the case of the *tyrant*, it
became an overriding obsession (1.17). And we saw that the second long
excursus in the book, the Pentecontaetia, was structured to emphasize
revolts, and Athens' problems with keeping the empire which had been
given to her.

If we were to trace the vicious circle which seems to circumscribe the operations of power in Thucydides' thinking, it might run as follows:

To be defenseless is to be a constant victim of aggression. One of the first steps after accumulating power and resources is to build walls. But having power means ruling others, which entails earning the hatred of the ruled. No level of power is absolute, and therefore no level is adequate because there is always a rival, with whom the nonaligned can take refuge against *you*, and to whom your own subjects can appeal for help in escaping your rule in revolt. Those whom you lose in this way, therefore, go over to the enemy (1.75.4), and thereby increase his power and the odds against you in any future confrontation. This becomes increasingly alarming as the world shrinks to one of exclusive bipolarity, which Thucydides seems to see as the situation of his day—"seeing the rest of the Greek world either actually joining one of the two sides, or planning to" (1.1.1; cf. 1.18.3; 2.8.1; 8.2.1). In this highly charged situation, the revolt of allies becomes doubly critical. In all the talk about its being "dangerous to let the allies go," the speakers envisage, not a solitary or even united sailing by emancipated Chians or Melians against the Peiraeus, but secession to the other side, and the consequent weighting of the balance of power against them.

The most striking case of the danger involved in "letting it go" occurs in Pericles' last speech, in a passage where he has been driven by opposition from the idealistic rhetoric of the Funeral Oration to a more pragmatic tone: "It is no longer possible to step down from [the empire], if anyone, intimidated by the present situation, wants to play the noninterfering philanthropist: you hold it like a tyranny, which it may have been wrong (*adikon*) to take, but which it is dangerous to let go" (2.63.2). This seems an important concession: the high moral tone of the Funeral Oration has not prepared us for a tentative admission that the Athenian empire may be founded on an injustice. It once seemed to me that the concession is not a real one—that 2.63 is an anomalous chapter in which Pericles is not so much expressing his own view, as making an *ad hominem* argument against his opponents and confronting them with the consequences of their policy of noninterference (*apragmosune*).[9] The argument, in this interpretation, would run as follows: "Let us concede that the empire is like a tyranny; in that case we must hold on to it, because tyrants, when they fall, are done away with." This would emphasize the ironic character of the passage, with the contemptuous overtones of the word *andragathizetai*—"playing the gentleman or philanthropist," the assumption that such moralizing proceeds from *fear*, and the final sting in the last clause of the chapter, "only in a subject city can one afford to be a slave in safety" (2.63.3).

It is worth noting that up to this point Pericles has used the word *archē* warily; he uses it once at 1.144.1, with the negative injunction not to add to it during the war, and once at 2.36.2 of the empire that the present generation inherited from its fathers. There is a small periphrasis at 1.143.5, where he talks of "the resources of our allies (*ta tōn xummachōn*), which are our strength," and then of the need to have adequate forces to keep them quiet. We might see in this a reluctance to call an empire an empire. But in 2.63.1, such delicacies are dropped and we have two uses of the noun *archē* and one of the verb *archein* hammered home in the space of a few lines. And whatever the ironies of the latter part of the chapter, I cannot now see anything but straightforward bluntness at the beginning. Furthermore, the talk of empire is made in the context of an explicit abandonment of the freedom motif (2.62.3), which has been well worked rhetorically in the Funeral Oration (2.36.1; 2.40.5; 2.43.4), in favor of the concrete aspects of Athenian power, and the dangers of losing it, and the benefits (or honors) that accrue from it. We conclude, then, that Pericles is not playing with his opponents' argument in this passage, but, beleaguered by his opposition, becomes more pragmatic.

The comparison of Athens to a tyranny is made at intervals in the work. The Corinthians at the Second Congress of the Peloponnesian League, setting the task for their allies in the traditional role as liberators of Hellas, twice refer to Athens as a *polis turannos* (1.124.3; cf. 1.122.3); Euphemus, without attaching the label to his own city, makes an explicit comparison between a tyrant and a city with an empire: "To an individual who is a tyrant or a city which has an empire, nothing is illogical provided it is convenient, nor is there any natural bond unless it is trustworthy" (6.85.1). Between the two, Cleon works some changes on the theme, while borrowing conspicuously from Pericles' phrasing. He first complains about Athenian complacency: "Because you have nothing to fear in your daily lives and don't conspire against each other, you attribute the same spirit to the allies, and whether your mistake is due to their powers of persuasion or your own surrender to pity, you fail to rec-

ognize that your softness is dangerous for you and does nothing to win
the allies' favor—that in fact you hold the empire as a tyranny in the
teeth of people who have no desire to be ruled and are constantly con-
spiring against you" (3.37.2). Towards the end of the speech, in a passage ironically loaded with ethical terminology, he explores the theme
further, again with echoes of Pericles: "For if they were right (*orthōs*) to
revolt, you would clearly be wrong to rule. But if you think it best (*axi-
oute*) to continue to do this, even if it is not right (*ou prosēkon*), then it
must be expedient (*xumphoròs dei*) for you to punish these people, even
against the claim of equity (*para to eikos*), or else to stop ruling and play
the philanthropist (*andragathizesthai*) without danger" (3.40.4).

Cleon is not a reputable source for many things, and in this case, as
we have seen, he is corrected by Diodotus, who argues that at least "the
dēmos is friendly to you in all the cities" (3.47.1). But the drift of the
argument through the work runs counter to Diodotus' isolated qualification. Furthermore he seems to be bypassed by the Mytileneans themselves, in the only speech Thucydides gives us about Athenian imperialism from the subjects' point of view (3.9–14). It is in many ways an
artificial construction. The Mytileneans go to Olympia to ask for Spartan
help and justify their revolt (3.9.1). Justification would seem in the context unnecessary: a vassal state does not have to explain its desire to
revolt from oppression to its oppressor's principal enemy, especially one
that is explicitly dedicated to liberating the oppressed. However, it does
allow the speakers to describe in the course of this justification the attitude among the allies at the time towards Athens, and the Athenian attitude towards them. They do not tell us anything new, but they endorse
the imperialist argument: "Our fleet frightened them (*phobon pareiche*) in
case it moved in a bloc and attached itself to you or someone else and
created a threat to them" (3.11.6). "What sort of friendship could there
be, or what confidence in freedom, when we made our promises to each
other against our better judgment? They paid attention to us in wartime
through fear (*dediotes*) and we reciprocated when it was peace. Where, for
other people, good will makes their sense of trust secure, for us it was
fear (*phobos*) which made the bond secure, and, united in fear (*deos*) rather
than friendship, we formed our alliance" (3.12.1). There is some special
pleading in the speech, to persuade the cautious Spartans that it is worth
their while to commit themselves so far from home, and in the event the

Mytileneans are found to have exaggerated Athenian weakness. But I do not think Thucydides means us to conclude that they have also exaggerated Athenian fear. As Andrewes comments, "his temperament somehow inclined him to believe that Athens' relations with her subjects were generally bad, probably worse than they were in fact" (Gomme, *Commentary*, IV:186).[10]

But the fact is that for Thucydides bad relations do not end with one's subjects. He sees fear of one's neighbor as one of the strongest determinants of human behavior (it is put first of three influences on Athens at 1.75.3), not merely between master and subject, but comprehensively between man and man. Before any form of civilization, men did not associate with each other without fear (1.2.2); they carried arms because their towns were not fortified and communications with each other were not safe (1.6.1). Once they formed walled communities and gathered larger spheres of influence, propelled both by self-interest and the need for security, the power blocs that resulted were still in a constant state of embattlement against each other (1.18.2–3). Spartan fear of growing Athenian power was, in Thucydides' judgment, the true cause of the war, and fear of Spartan hostility, and of secession of her allies to the Spartan camp, was Athens' reason for retaining the empire (1.75.3–4). We saw Thucydides confirm both these points by the structure and emphasis of the Pentecontaetia.

The Corinthians at the first Spartan Congress see the Athenian policy of intervention as mere meddlesomeness: "In short, if anyone were to say that their whole nature was directed to the avoidance of peace for themselves, and the refusal of it to anyone else, he would be correct" (1.70.9). Thucydides will entertain this as a possible interpretation of Athenian policy, but all the signs are that he himself believes that principles of nonintervention would be dangerous for Athens. As we have seen, he puts the language of fear into the mouth of such a moderate speaker as Pericles (2.63); the final ironic sentence of that paragraph states firmly that "principles of nonintervention can only survive when they take their place alongside activist ones" (63.3). And even outsiders will make the same point; the Corcyreans speaking before the war, admittedly to an Athenian audience, acknowledge that their policy of nonintervention has been a mistake and left them exposed (1.32.3–5, especially the last section).

What one has, then, in the Melian episode is the convergence of two kinds of expectation about human behavior. One looks for the maintenance of decency and restraint even in wartime, as certain people managed to maintain them in the Plague, perhaps especially those, including Thucydides, who had had the disease themselves and seemed to live charmed lives (2.51.5–6). The other expectation is that war, the harsh teacher, by removing the comfort of their daily lives, reduces the passions of most people to the level of their circumstances and imposes its necessities on them (see 3.82.2). It is clearly absurd to say that the Athenians had valid reasons for fearing the Melians. But the truth is they are looking beyond the specific situation to a wider context of fear; and I believe that at least part of Thucydides does the same.

Such ambivalence explains the confusion of intent that is so puzzling about the episode—does it express outrage or fatalism? The answer is that part of Thucydides sees the Athenian action at Melos as a clear excess (an extreme departure from that moderate use of power, which the Athenians at Sparta claimed entitled them to praise—1.76.3); the other part, which has learned the lessons of war, finds what happened natural.

7

ALCIBIADES:
A PATRIOT FOR HIMSELF

In the last chapter we followed the course of Athenian moderation through the war to its brutal demise at Melos. The thematic progression and the lessons to be drawn from it seemed clear enough until the final phase, when certain ambivalences in Thucydides' mind seemed to hold him back from enforcing a moral conclusion with any clarity. In this chapter we will find the same kind of indecision in the depiction and judgment of the flamboyant character of Alcibiades—a personality who, according to categories set up early in the work, seems to invite condemnation for his selfish use of the war for his own ends, but who, from some shading of the picture, emerges as unexpectedly sympathetic.

Thucydides' overall judgment on Alcibiades reads as follows:

> Being much in the public eye, he indulged his appetite for horse-racing and other luxuries more lavishly than his wealth could support. And this subsequently played a significant part in ruining (*katheilen*) the city. For the people at large were afraid of the scale of physical excess in his private life, and also of his ambition in everything with which he was involved. They became his enemy because they thought he was aiming at tyranny; and though in fact his public management of wartime affairs was excellent (*kratista*), they were personally angered by his way of life; so, by entrusting the state to others, they soon brought it down (*esphēlan*—6.15.4).

This evaluation is given as an introduction to Alcibiades' speech before the Sicilian expedition, but I agree with Dover [1] that the ruin envisaged is the final defeat after Aegospotamoi rather than the more proximate failure of the expedition; the judgments therefore apply to the whole of Alcibiades' career, and not merely to an episode.

When we examine these few sentences, we can detect a trace of ambivalence on Thucydides' part. This is most apparent in the shift of the burden of responsibility for defeat. The subject of *katheilen* must be Alcibiades' indulgence of his appetites: but in the last sentence the *people* seemed to be blamed for failing to see their way past his personal extravagance to his excellent management of affairs; instead they give the state to less talented people and so ruin it. Thucydides' own disdain for personal anecdote shows here; just as he excludes personal foibles from his record of events, so in real life he expects them not to influence judgments on those who shape events. Alcibiades is among those who benefit from this purist reticence. Thucydides tells us that Alcibiades had his differences with the Spartan king Agis (8.12.2), but he does not tell us that one reason for the difference was that he seduced, and had a child by, Agis' wife (see Plut. *Alc.* 23.7, *Lys.* 22.3, and Xenophon *Hellenica* 3.3.2).

But the world at large does not maintain such orderly dichotomies between public and private, as Thucydides is aware. Whatever the actual motives behind the mutilation of the Herms and the desecration of the Mysteries, the Athenian people treated the actions as politically subversive, and Thucydides must attend to them. But he does so in a style, and a context, which reveal his contempt for popular alarmism and mishandling of evidence and some sympathy for Alcibiades as their most distinguished victim. His account of the investigation immediately follows the critique of the popular version of the Pisistratid tyranny and its removal—a version full of errors of fact and interpretation (6.53.3–59). When we return to the present and hear the wholesale accusations against notable people (*axiologoi*—6.60.2), the death sentence against all who had been accused (60.4), and the farfetched accusations leveled at Alcibiades himself (61.2), we do not blame him for escaping from his escort at Thurii, "in fear of the voyage home to face trial on a false charge" (*diabolēi*—6.61.6).

The passage as a whole shows Thucydides' antiplebeian bias: it is the alarmism of the *dēmos* that fears conspiracies of oligarchs or would-be tyrants (6.60.1), sends it in pursuit of the "notable" (60.2), and in fact makes it behave *tyrannically;* and of all the victims of its repression, Alcibiades, at least in Thucydides' regard, is clearly the *most* notable: his is the only name given. It is interesting that earlier, at his first appearance, he is introduced as an aristocrat, and thereby at once distinguished from a mere demagogue: he is "honored for the reputation of his forefathers" and he seeks to be honored in his own right (5.43.2). When Alcibiades makes his defense at Sparta he allows his aristocratic arrogance full rein:

> If anyone disparages me on the grounds that I am attached to democracy, he should realize that his dislike is not soundly based. It is true that our family has always been opposed to the tyrants, and that is the basis of our continued leadership of the people; and one might give the name of democracy to anything that opposes absolute power. Besides, given the fact that the city was governed by an actual democratic constitution, it was on the whole necessary for us to go along with the situation. But we always tried to be more moderate (*metriōteroi*) politically than the prevailing extremism (*akolasia*). There have always been others, both in earlier times and now, who have led the mob in shameful directions—and these were the ones who contrived my exile. As for us, we presided over the whole, and thought it best to preserve those structures of the city which we inherited, and under which it had become so great and free. Anyone of any sense could see how to disparage the democracy—myself not least. It is an acknowledged idiocy and nothing new can be said about it. But as for *changing* it, that did not seem safe as long as you were our enemies and had us under siege. (6.89.4–6)

We recognize the contrivance of the argument, designed to appeal to his conservative audience: Alcibiades claims a lofty superiority to the plebeian government that has rejected him (and also steered Athens into this war against Sparta). But at least one strand of Thucydides' account endorses this claim—Alcibiades was seen at home as "beyond the norm" and that was the source of his trouble. As we have said, there is a note of sympathy for his predicament; Thucydides, of course, was another aristocrat rejected by the democracy.

We turn from domestic problems to Alcibiades' public activity during the war, which is Thucydides' principal interest. Alcibiades is the instigator of the alliance that forces Sparta to the full-scale battle at Mantinea, even though there is technically a peace in effect; he is the promoter of the Sicilian expedition, and sees beyond it to future ventures against Carthage (6.15.2; cf. 6.90.2); and he is influential in having the Spartans expand the war to Ionia (8.12.1–2). Behind all these important developments it is made clear that Alcibiades' prime motive is self-interest. He is converted from being the Spartan representative at Athens to his anti-Spartan policy by pique, because his youth is slighted and especially because the Spartans have negotiated the treaty with Nicias and Laches instead of himself (5.43.2). (He therefore seems to move perversely against the current at this point: when he is the representative (*proxenos*) for the Spartans at Athens, the war is still on and he is presumably for conciliation; once the Peace of Nicias is in effect, he is for renewing the war.) He espouses the expedition to Sicily because he hopes for personal profit from the campaign (6.15.2, confirming Nicias' charge at 6.12.2). And he urges the extension of the war to the Ionian theater, in hopes of scoring a personal coup against the Spartan king Agis (8.12.2). In all of this, Alcibiades seems a large-scale embodiment of the basic state of nature we described at the end of chapter 2: he is a sign of contradiction at home, and a disturber of everyone's peace abroad. With this much to go on, we would not have much difficulty in including him among those of Pericles' successors "who, for private ambition and private gain, embarked on policies which seemed to have nothing to do with the war, which were bad for Athens and her empire, and which, when they succeeded, brought honor and profit to individuals, and when they failed inflicted grave damage on the city in the war" (2.65.7).

But Thucydides calls Alcibiades' management of wartime affairs "excellent," as we have seen, and at no point does he unequivocally blame him. He does not blame him for disturbing Nicias' fragile peace after 421—in Thucydides' view, it was no peace at all, but rather a continuation of war, so one cannot criticize Alcibiades for acting accordingly. Besides, his maneuvers brought the enemy into the greatest danger, without committing any great expense of money or manpower from Athens (6.16.6). The Sicilian expedition takes some explaining, as it is the most signal violation of Pericles' injunction not to add to the empire while the war was in progress. Thucydides cannot ignore it, and in fact explicitly acknowledges that it was a mistake, but immediately qualifies his judgment—"a mistake (*hamartēma*) not so much in the choice of goal, as in the failure of those who sent the expedition to provide adequate support once it had gone. Instead, by personal attacks in the struggle for leadership of the democracy at home, they weakened the situation with the army, and by their internal conflicts threw all the city's affairs into confusion" (2.65.11). Such a qualification clearly protects Alcibiades. The

personal attacks send him to Sparta; his good judgment in public affairs
in wartime is now in the service of Sparta, and immediately shown by
his insistence that the Spartans send support to Syracuse (6.91.4) and
fortify Decelea as a base in Attica (91.6)—two points that were acted on
and damaged Athens greatly.

We turn to the Ionian narrative. Once again, Alcibiades shows himself
totally self-interested and totally in control of a very complex situation.[2]
His manipulation of Tissaphernes, "becoming his teacher in everything"
(8.45.2), and the policy he has him adopt of playing Athens and Sparta
off against each other and so wearing them out (8.46.2), in effect makes
him the manager of the war in the area. Tissaphernes' great dependence
on him, of course, is the principal card he has to play in winning his way
back to Athens (8.47.1), and it is ultimately successful.

In the meanwhile the mere prospect of his recall is one of the factors
agitating the political situation there: both democrats and oligarchs pro-
claim the desirability of his return, and in fact the oligarchs succeed in
persuading the *dēmos* that it must accept the oligarchy if it hopes to bring
Alcibiades home, and obtain the Persian support which he will bring
with him (8.53.1 and 3). Thucydides has already reported, and
approved, Phrynichus' argument that it is all one to Alcibiades whether
democrats or oligarchs are in power, and that his sole preoccupation was
to be recalled (8.48.4). Phrynichus himself acts on the assumption that
oligarchs would be unlikely to recall Alcibiades (8.68.3); and Thucydides
confirms *this* argument too at 8.70.1: "They did not recall the exiles
because of Alcibiades"—i.e. they did not want Alcibiades back so they
did not recall anyone else.

Thus Alcibiades, even when he is indifferent, becomes a catalyst of
personal and national upheavals. The statesmanlike Phrynichus becomes
a traitor and an oligarch for fear of Alcibiades; the democracy itself
reluctantly allows an oligarchy to be imposed for his sake; and Alcibiades, scornful of democracy, accused of conspiracy for oligarchy and
tyranny, and a traitor to first Athens and then Sparta, comes back to the
army at Samos, and commits himself at last to saving the state: when the
fleet, outraged by reports from Athens that their families are being
abused by the oligarchs, intends to sail on the Peiraeus, Alcibiades stops
them. "Then for the first time,[3] it seems, Alcibiades performed an outstanding service for his country; for when the Athenians at Samos were

bent on sailing against their own people, at a time when the enemy clearly controlled Ionia and the Hellespont, he stopped them. There was no one else at that moment who would have been capable of restraining the mob, but he managed to stop them sailing, and also by his rebukes to deflect their rage at the (oligarchic) ambassadors" (8.86.4–5). We do not have to be impressed by the altruism of these actions: Alcibiades has not yet completed his circuit home, and he wants there to be something left when he reaches Athens (cf. 8.47.1).

There are several puzzles in this full but variously accented account. Alcibiades' name occurs more frequently than that of any other character in the work. Almost all his other associates, as we shall see, are caught up in the vortex of the war, and ground very small by it. Their personal fears and ambitions are shaped by the war, which they are powerless to change. Whereas for Alcibiades, the war is *his* natural element, and at every point he seems able to make it serve his own interests. He therefore dominates the second half of the work, the way Pericles and his plans dominate the first. Thucydides says of Pericles that "those who came after him were more on a level (*isoi*) with each other" (2.65.10): Alcibiades is the most conspicuous exception to this; he enjoys the same kind of preeminence over his contemporaries that Pericles did over his, and this shared elevation, even though Thucydides does not explicitly couple the two personalities or allow any overlap between their careers, invites comparisons.

To pull together the various strands of the narrative into a coherent estimate of Alcibiades' career, we should test three possible hypotheses:

1. Alcibiades is intended to be the archetype of the selfish politician whose personal ambition ruined Athens.

2. Alcibiades is above and apart from inferior, selfish politicians and is hounded by their persecution to protect his own interests.

3. Thucydides sets out to offer the reader explanation 1, but is constantly prompted by his sympathy for Alcibiades to shade it toward explanation 2.

We will examine the three hypotheses in turn, but I will say at the outset that I believe the third answers best to the various nuances of the text.

1. The key evidence for the first hypothesis is what we learn by comparison of Pericles and Alcibiades. Such comparisons are invited, as sug-

gested above, both by the unrivaled stature the two Athenians enjoy in their respective halves of the work, and by Alcibiades' explicit deviation from certain cardinal Periclean principles which the reader carries with him from one half to the other.

a) His inversion of Pericles' priorities governing the relationship of the individual and the state. Pericles had insisted that a citizen should put his country's welfare before his own—because even if his personal fortune declined, it had a better chance of recovery while his country thrived; whereas if his country collapsed, it pulled individuals down with it, however prosperous they might be (2.60.2–3). We saw the acceptance of this priority as the essential mark of the patriot (*philopolis*), as Pericles defined the term and embodied it. In his case, this went beyond a calculus of self-interest: the Funeral Oration was organized and driven to its emotional climax along the lines of this priority, ending with the injunction to the audience to "contemplate daily the city's power in action, and become her lovers" (*erastai*—2.43.1), like the dead who were prepared to make the "fairest offering" (*eranon*—43.1) to her. In Pericles' case, such devotion, even when he falls from favor and is fined, keeps him at his country's service.

Alcibiades inverts these priorities. In the first paragraph of his first speech, in reply to Nicias and other critics of his horse-racing extravagances, he makes it clear that he looks for his own glory first, but argues that the city benefits derivatively from his success: "As for the loud denunciation of me, my actions bring glory to my ancestors and myself, and advantage to my country"—in that order (6.16.1). The whole passage resounds with the kind of egotism, which, even allowing for differences of cultural emphasis, seems frivolous and, despite Alcibiades' protestations, immature. We are not surprised, when he goes over to Sparta, to find that his view of patriotism is quite different from Pericles', and allows room for his large ego:

And I should not seem contemptible to anyone, if I, who was thought to be patriotic (*philopolis*), now join my country's greatest enemies in a strong attack on her, nor should I be suspected of arguing simply from the longings of an exile (*phugadikēn prothumian*). For I am a fugitive from the malice of those who expelled me, and not from the possibility of helping you, if you will listen to me. Real enemies should be defined not as those like you, who do harm to those who are obviously your enemies, but as those who, when they have friends, force them to become their enemies. Patriotism in my view does not extend to suffering injury, but only so far as one is left secure in one's citizenship. So I do not consider that I am proceeding against what is still my country, but rather trying to recover her, now that she has ceased to be mine. The true patriot is not the one who refrains from attacking his city once he has been deprived of her, but the one who, because of his desire, does everything in his power to get her back. (6.92.2–4)

The sentences are crowded with sophistic redefinition, and what Dover says of 92.3, that its sophistry is "obscure and lame," may well be true of the whole.[4] At least the inversion of Pericles' priorities is clear.

b) Alcibiades' instability. Pericles' consistency had been a hallmark of his character: "I am the same and do not change" (2.61.2). We acknowledged the justice of this claim in Pericles' case, and rejected it as pretension on the part of Cleon. Nor could Alibiades validly make the claim for himself; in fact, the matter of stability makes us question again his ability to control his situation.[5] Comparisons with Pericles are helpful: Pericles, throughout the portion of his career that Thucydides gives us, is *master* of Athens. He does not have to become a fugitive, or work elaborate schemes to get home, because he is always there, retaining a degree of power that transforms what is "in theory a democracy" into "rule by the First Man" (2.65.9). Even when the Athenians, at their worst demoralization under the plague, remove him from office and fine him, they quickly discover that he is indispensable and reelect him: "Soon afterwards, as is typical of the crowd, they chose him general again, and entrusted everything to his care, being less distressed at the time by domestic ills, and considering him indispensable for all the city's needs" (2.65.4). Alcibiades, on the other hand, so far from commanding the same consensus, incurs enough suspicion to be made an outcast. For all the brilliance with which he plays his role, it is a lesser status.

c) Venality. Pericles' authority in the city was based in part on the fact that he was "conspicuously incorruptible" (*chrēmatōn . . . diaphanōs adōrotatos*—2.65.8). Shortly before this, in his last speech, Pericles has included incorruptibility as an essential quality in a statesman—without it "he puts everything up for sale" (2.60.6). We do not hear of Alcibiades accepting bribes, but we do hear, in the initial character sketch of him, that the extravagance of his personal life had a lot to do with his advocacy of the Sicilian expedition: "He was especially eager for the command, and hoped that both Sicily and Carthage would fall to his efforts, and that personal success would bring him benefits in terms of money and reputation. For being much in the public eye, he indulged his appetites . . . on a greater scale than his resources allowed" (6.15.2–3). Again, personal motivation has clearly obtruded on public policy, and we may ask whether in this instance Alcibiades has not "sold" his country's interests to meet his own financial needs.

2. Alcibiades as victim. For the defense we can submit that all the above argument misses the essential point of Alcibiades and the role Thucydides intends him to play in his work. Instead, we argue that Thucydides does not expect his reader to *identify* Alcibiades with the political structure at Athens, which in fact rejected him, but to see the very rejection of him as a sign of Athenian decline, showing the disintegration of a coherent and successful imperial policy at the hands of incompetent and divisive politicians, who pursued their own self-interest without seeing any larger designs behind it. Petty jealousies eliminate the one man of genius they have. What evidence does the text give us for such a reading?

There are, I think, two points one could use to show that Alcibiades is intended to lie outside the dominant patterns of Athenian decline and the strictures leveled at it—the fact of his *success* and the fact that he seems above *stasis* and party strife. The first point is very obvious. Where the curtain is going down for everyone else, Alcibiades steps from stage to stage as a star in every action, and somehow brings each one to a happy ending for himself. At every point the odds are heavily stacked against him. At the outset of his career, with Athens formally committed to peace and himself still a neglected quantity because of his youth, he yet contrives to bring Sparta to the greatest, most direct test of its strength in the war. The peace prohibited any large-scale use of Athenian troops for his ventures, but he makes do by converting Sparta's former allies into an alliance against her. In the case of the Sicilian expedition, Thucydides leaves us free to conclude that it might have been successful if Alcibiades had been left in charge. A bold venture should not be entrusted to the man least convinced of its possibilities, as happened in Sicily with Nicias. Before then Thucydides seems to suggest that Lamachus' forthright plan—to attack Syracuse as soon as they arrived—would have been successful (6.49; cf. 7.42.3), which implies condemnation of

Alcibiades' more conservative view, which was actually adopted. But Alcibiades had perhaps more to lose, and to win, than Lamachus, and had he stayed, we cannot conceive that he would have allowed the situation to stagnate as Nicias did. After Sicily, with both the Spartans and with Tissaphernes, he pulls off the impossible feat of winning control of the situation, though his only bargaining card is himself.

It is true that he finally runs out of entrepreneurial possibilities in the war, with the defeat at Notium—in his absence, and outside the pages of Thucydides (Xen. *Hell.* 1.5.11–18; Plut. *Alc.* 35–36). Plutarch implies that the degree of irresponsibility involved on his part may have been maliciously embroidered by his enemies, especially Thrasybulus. At all events, Aristophanes' *Frogs* more than a year later (February 405) still raises the key question of what should be done about Alcibiades (1422–23). The question is thrown out of the blue at the climax of the literary contest (*agōn*) between Aeschylus and Euripides, and the implication is that it is one that was on many people's minds, and also presumably that there was a sizable faction that wanted him home.[6] They never, of course, brought him home, and in the following year the Athenian generals effectively finished the war by allowing virtually the whole fleet to be caught having breakfast at Aegospotamoi; Alcibiades had ridden over from his castle to tell them that they were badly situated, but they scorned his advice and told him that they were in command, not he (Xen. *Hell.* 2.1.26; Plut. *Alc.* 37.1).

The other point to make in a possible defense of Alcibiades is the fact that he does not seem to be the *promoter* but the victim of *stasis:* one does not want to push this too hard. After all, as we have seen, the oligarchic revolution at Athens used his name to win acceptance (although the oligarchs never had any intention of recalling him). But we do not see Alcibiades himself stooping to any narrowly political intrigues inside Athens. Phrynichus said that oligarchy and democracy were all one to Alcibiades, and Thucydides confirms this (8.48.4): his self-absorption seem to have put him above party politics. In his speech before the Sicilian expedition, he warns his audience against Nicias' tactics of setting the old against the young (6.18.6) and appeals for unanimity: the divisiveness does not begin with him. Even in his most arrogant vein at Sparta, we saw him assert that for all the absurdities of democracy, his family had always made it a point to work with the established constitution (except when it was a tyranny) (6.89.4): "As for us we presided over the whole (*xumpantos*), and thought it best to preserve those structures of the city which we inherited, and under which it became so great and free" (89.6). Finally, we saw him succeed, where Thucydides says no one else could have, in stopping the fleet at Samos from sailing on the Peiraeus in anger at oligarchic excesses (8.86.4–5). It seems that one of the secrets of his selfish genius was his awareness that success on the scale he wanted for himself could only be won by enlisting the concerted support of large national groups to do his bidding; to this extent his actions may be Periclean, even where his motives fall short of the truly patriotic.

3. There is, then, a confusing ambivalence in Thucydides' account of Alcibiades. On the one hand, he seems to take his natural place in the system of explanation as the archetype of selfish ambition, who leads Athen to ruin in the second half of the *History*—the very antithesis of the selfless Pericles; on the other, this portrait is at intervals glossed or shaded with sympathy for the man, until at points he seems to stand as a victim forced to excess to protect himself against the excesses of democracy; the anomie of the state imposes its inconsistencies upon him, as we shall see it does upon Phrynichus. It is this note of sympathy, of course, that requires explanation.

It would be a distortion of Thucydides' picture to attempt to draw strong lines and distinctions across it to explain the confusion, but two possibilities are worth consideration. One is that the progress of his pessimism through the war, and possibly also his personal disappointments, have brought the historian to a point of skepticism about the prospects of holding a *polis* together under the pressures of a long war, where Alcibiades' sort of individualism and his sophistic definition of patriotism seem the only correct response. When everything is cracking around you, you are entitled to think of your own skin. At this point, then, Pericles' idealism appears irrelevant, just as it did during the plague, and Alcibiades' personal pragmatism is endorsed. This line can be argued, but I do not believe the balance of the text, as we have it, favors it: the endorsement of *Pericles'* career against the full context of the war seems too firm and decisive.

A more personal explanation seems to fit the case better—that Thucydides, like so many of his contemporaries, was caught up against his better judgment by the fascination of the maverick genius, who directed the currents of the war and made his way through its apparent chaos and through the resentment he created with such ease and unscrupulousness. In Thucydides' case, the fascination may have been developed by direct acquaintance. Alcibiades, after the debacle at Notium, retired to his castle in the Thracian Chersonese (Xen. *Hell.* 1.5.17; Plut. *Alc.* 36.2), and it seems a plausible assumption that Thucydides himself, as we are told, spending his exile in Thrace (Marcellin. *Vita Thuc.* 25 and 46), availed himself of the opportunity to gather information from such an important source. There are sequences of narrative in the work for which Alcibiades remained the only firsthand authority open to him— the strategic debate between the three generals prior to the attack on Sicily (6.46.5–49: the other two never returned) or the record of his private counsels to Tissaphernes (8.45–46). Alcibiades could be a persuasive apologist for himself, even among the initially unsympathetic, as we saw at Sparta; and with Thucydides there would be several points of personal affinity for him to work on—high pedigree and a shared disdain for the *demos* would be two of them. And beyond these would be the shared bond of exile: the phrase "the exile's eagerness" (*phugadikēn prothumian*—6.92.2) is given to Alcibiades, and they would both understand what it means.

But perhaps the most attractive aspect of Alcibiades for the historian would be his activism. We shall see in the next chapter that in the debate on the Sicilian expedition both Nicias and Alcibiades represented, quite apart from their personal differences, authentic veins of Periclean policy carried to excess. Nicias stood for conservative caution carried to the point of paralysis, and Alcibiades for imperial activism without any check on its goals. Of the two positions, as we saw in chapter 6 in a variety of contexts, Thucydides seemed closer to endorsing the latter, as more true to Athenian destiny. The Corinthians at the first Spartan Congress say of the Athenians in general that "they are by nature disposed not to have peace themselves and not to allow it to anyone else" (1.70.9). Alcibiades, then, is a true Athenian, and even when the sentence of death hangs over him (6.61.7), he still contrives not only to remain at the center of action, but to direct the course of the whole war in his favor. At least a part of Thucydides, an active man reduced to the role of sedentary historian, who must report on the action from the sidelines "at leisure" (*kath' hēsuchian*—5.26.5), could only admire such continual, if unprincipled, involvement.

8

INDIVIDUALS IN THE
TOILS OF WAR:
NICIAS AND PHRYNICHUS

In chapter 5, we examined Thucydides' portrait of Pericles, the patriotic First Man, who led the people rather than being led by it (2.65.8–9). After Pericles there is no other Athenian to whom Thucydides is prepared to give the title of First Man, though others are seen to "grasp" (*oregomai*) for it (2.65.10; cf. 8.89.3). In chapter 7 we followed the career of Alcibiades, whose genius qualified him to be compared with Pericles, and to dominate his period of the war as no one else can, but whose excesses, and the suspicion they aroused, constantly force him to maneuver from an outsider's position. In this chapter we will examine the careers of two other Athenians who were brought into prominence by the war, were tested by it, and at particular moments of crisis were found wanting, though Thucydides awards both of them high qualifications—Nicias for his virtue and Phrynichus for his intelligence.

Nicias.[1] Nicias and Demosthenes are the two most notable Athenians in Thucydides' account who are active both in the Archidamian War and in the resumption of hostilities after the Peace. They meet their end together after their surrender in Sicily (7.86.2). In Plutarch's *Life*, Nicias is said upon the death of Pericles to have assumed his *political* mantle against the demagogic Cleon (Plut. *Nic.* 2.2), but Thucydides does not assert any such succession. Instead, he introduces Nicias purely as a soldier, and follows him in that role down to the negotiations of the Peace which bears his name, and to the explicit comparison with the great Spartan soldier Brasidas (5.16.1). We will not cover this early phase in any detail but simply list the record of his activity.

1. Nicias first appears in the fortification of the twin forts on the island of Minoa off the coast of Megara (3.51.1–4). The plan is introduced as his own, and it provided a useful early warning station against Peloponnesian movement into the Saronic Gulf, and a springboard for activity against Megara itself (cf. 4.67.3–4).

2. Nicias commands the larger of two expeditions in the summer of 426, which proceeds first against Melos (3.91), then supports Athenian activity in Boeotia, and finally ravages the coast of Locris, before returning home. There is no success against Melos, and the force never seems to be heavily engaged.

3. Nicias steps down from his command in the Pylos episode (425) as a challenge to his demagogic critic, Cleon (4.28.1). We may take this as a first premonitory instance of his reluctance for difficult assignments.[2]

4. In the same summer, Nicias commands a large expedition against Solygeia in Corinthian territory (4.42). A beachhead is secured but the Corinthians have been forewarned, and the Athenians, after having had the better of an engagement, are forced to withdraw. The reembarkation is tidily managed.

5. In the next summer (424), Nicias with two others leads a large force against Cythera (4.53). This episode is the greatest coup of his career, and it is easily won: the town of Cythera itself comes quickly to terms as the result of previous negotiations (4.54.3). Athenian success here brought Spartan morale to its nadir (4.54.4).

6. In 423, Nicias is one of the signatories of a one year's armistice with Sparta (4.119).

7. Nicias is sent north to bring Scione and Mende back to the Athenian alliance (4.29.2 ff.). He fails with Scione and puts it under siege (4.32.1), and fails first in action against Mende, but the next day the town, after a piece of Spartan boorishness, opens its gates to him (4.130.3–4).

If we assess the career to this point, we find that Nicias has been entrusted with large numbers of troops and ships, that, unlike Demosthenes in Aetolia (3.98), he has suffered no major losses, but also that on the whole he has not been very heavily engaged. There are no outstanding military actions to put him in the class of Phormio or Brasidas. Mende and Cythera fall into his lap, though in the latter case he deserves credit for the earlier negotiations which softened the defense into capitulation. Nicias' known virtue and sense of honor would make him a sympathetic and trustworthy negotiator and receiver of surrenders. And a general does not have to do things the hard way. But taking this phase of his career as a whole we are probably not prepared for Thucydides' judgment that he was "the most successful (*pleista . . . eu pheromenos*) of his peers in his commands" (5.16.1).

Such a judgment invites comparison with Brasidas, who is unquestionably the most successful *Spartan* general of the Archidamian War, and we are given one. Nicias, we are told, has largely personal reasons for wanting peace:

> He wanted to preserve his good fortune (*eutuchian*) while he was still untouched (*apathēs*) by the war and esteemed, and so wanted for the present an end of labor for himself and for his fellow-citizens, and for the future to leave behind a reputation for having spent his life without having failed the city in anything. And he thought that this was best achieved in tranquil circumstances, by the man who entrusts himself as little as possible to the strokes of fortune; for peace offers tranquillity. (5.16.1)

In the Greek text, as we have it, this psychological assessment forms one of a series of contrasts in an inordinately protracted period. Brasidas and Cleon, who were opposed to peace for their own reasons, are contrasted with Pleistoanax and Nicias, who want it, also for personal reasons. The contrast between Brasidas and Nicias is clearly made, the one enjoying war "because of the good fortune (*dia to eutuchein*) and honor" he gets from it, and the other seeking to preserve his good fortune by staying out of it. (There is also a linguistic parallel between Cleon, who is afraid that peacetime will lay bare his "incredible slanders" (*apistoterōs diaballōn*) and Pleistoanax, who seeks peace so he can deal with the "slanders" (*diaballomenos*) facing him at home.)

The comparison that is contrived between Nicias and Brasidas prompts the question of whether or not Thucydides intends Nicias to be disparaged by it. He is not obviously so—his motives do not seem to be *entirely* selfish; he wants peace for himself, but he wants it for the rest of the citizens as well; and he wants a reputation of never having failed the city. It is, of course, honorable to look to one's reputation, and one might almost say that his final fate confirms his worst fears, and his philosophy with them. We have heard plenty about the uncertainties of war from Thucydides himself and from his most privileged speakers: isn't Nicias, an experienced and successful general, in a perfect position to make the same conclusion, which Archidamus and Pericles have made before: the good soldier does not go to war unless he has to? In fact, Nicias, as a notoriously *lucky* general, might deserve special credit for realizing that luck is a very fickle and unreliable aide.

But having said all this, one cannot avoid the conclusion that Thucydides in this small psychological sketch, one of a few where he seems to claim a kind of privileged access to private motivations, is laying bare an almost shameful passivity which is somehow un-Athenian. In fact, in the comparison of Brasidas with Nicias, we seem to have an inversion of national types. And there can be no doubt at all that Brasidas, who was too quick for Thucydides himself, is one of the characters in the work who cannot put a foot wrong. His always seems to be the innovative, determined voice, even in the early passages where his efforts are not successful (notably in his determined effort to force a landing at Pylos—4.114; see also his voice in the sailing on the Peiraeus—2.93.1). Brasidas' career, and the careers of other "totally" successful figures in the work, like Pericles and Hermocrates, seem to speak a judgment on Nicias' view of fate. Brasidas gains "good fortune" from the war, because by his initiative he is able to make fate serve him well; he forestalls *paraloga;* when he is deserted by Perdiccas, and surrounded by enemy tribes in the heart of Thrace, he still manages to turn crucial danger into triumph (4.124–128). In Nicias' case, it is not so much the devotion to peace as the avoidance of danger that strikes the wrong note; military men do not sustain their wartime reputations for long by refusing to fight, or by making a creed of pacifism. It seems likely that Thucydides is spelling out Nicias' personal reluctance at this point with hindsight of his conduct over the Sicilian expedition; on the evidence we have been given so far, the judgment may be a little unfair, with only the Pylos incident to support it. Yet the pattern seems a plausible one. The quiescence to which Nicias is prone resembles that of the tyrants, who were preoccupied with their personal safety, "and nothing significant was done by them" (1.17). The alternative philosophy to Nicias' hazard-free life (*akindunon*) is expressed by Pericles at the end of his first speech: "We should know that it is from the greatest dangers that the greatest honors come, both to the city and to the individual" (1.140.3). This is the authentic Athenian attitude, but it is typical of Thucydides that he does not have to draw out these contrasts in any moralistic way, when mere juxtaposition with an antithetic example will make his point for him; it is ironic that the example in this case should be a Spartan, Brasidas, whose career has just been concluded in such a heroic aura. At all events, by such comparisons, Nicias is diminished, enclosed in a world of private aspirations. But for the moment the tide of war has abated and left him free to negotiate first peace (5.18–19), and then a full-fledged alliance with Sparta for fifty years (5.23–24).

Thucydides does not think much of Nicias' peace, and refuses to accept it as a genuine remission in the war (5.26.2). He notes the fact that neither side fulfilled the terms of their agreement (it turned out to be difficult, as one would expect, for the principals to persuade their allies to restore the territorial status quo), and spends nearly forty chapters describing the climate of international suspicion and intrigue that prevailed between the truce and the Battle of Mantinea (5.27–65). Corinth, Mantinea, Elis, and Boeotia all have dissatisfactions with Sparta, and Argos, which had benefited considerably from her neutrality in the Archidamian War (5.28.2), rises as a rallying point against her. An anxious game of musical chairs for new alliances is played out between this group and Athens, with the new Athenian personality of Alcibiades aiding and abetting the confusion, and eventually succeeding in forcing Sparta to a full-scale battle for survival on her doorstep at Mantinea: "I pulled together the powers of the Peloponnese and forced Sparta to stake all on a single day at Mantinea" (6.16.2). Clearly with such an activist on the scene, and, still more dangerously, in his own camp, Nicias will not be left in peace for long. We have a glimpse of him in this period, trying to keep the glue stuck on his precarious alliance, after Alcibiades has persuaded the Spartan ambassadors to contradict themselves before the Assembly (5.45–46).

Apart from this incident, there is only one other commission for Nicias alluded to over this period, to win back Amphipolis, and he is reprieved from that by some more backsliding by Perdiccas (5.83.4). Otherwise Thucydides keeps him in the shadows while Alcibiades' star rises. But he cannot stay there. The restless energies of Alcibiades combine with activist groups to bring the Sicilian expedition at last to a head, and Nicias as the most successful general of the Archidamian War is indispensable for the command. It must be unusual in Athenian practice for a command to go to someone who is known to be opposed to the venture as a whole—for obvious reasons. But in this case, it is easy to see how Nicias' caution, if not his reluctance, would seem an added advantage for such a far-flung expedition—with so much invested at such a distance, he would provide a reassuring counterweight to Alcibiades' volatility (he had never had a serious loss). Nicias' own supporters among the conservative faction would expect him to go, to keep the venture from getting out of hand, given that they could not stop it once and for all; and on his side, with his constant eye on honor and reputation, it must have been clear that it was a command which he could not sidestep and still retain his political and military eminence.

Nicias accepts the command, but, true to the character we have had sketched for us at 5.16, immediately tries to talk the Athenians out of the whole venture. The debate that is given between Nicias and Alcibiades is another extremely skillful composition, in which personal characteristics—Nicias' reluctance and Alcibiades' youthful excesses and arrogance—are blended with political arguments on both sides. Nicias scores in his estimation of the false promises made by Egesta (6.12.1, confirmed by Thucydides at 6.46.1–2), and in his warnings to the Athenians not to write off the enemy at home simply because they find that they have survived the first phase of the war against them (6.11.5), but is judged wrong by Thucydides when he says that people like Alcibiades "commit public wrongs" (6.12.2; as we have seen, Thucydides says that Alcibiades' public management of the war was excellent—6.15.4). On the other hand, Alcibiades seems right in his assessment of the disunity and lack of strong civic feeling in Sicily, right in his small taunt at Nicias' "luck" (6.17.1), but wrong, as we have learned from Pericles, in his inversion of the priorities between his own honor and his country's: for Alcibiades, the city can only bask in his own reflected glory (6.16.3).

But behind these personal foibles there are more serious arguments on each side, and ones which reveal once more Thucydides' own ambivalence. Nicias stands for the first time clearly in the mantle of Pericles, and urges the Athenians "not to grasp (*oregesthai*, again) for another empire, until they have secured what they already have" (6.10.5). Pericles in his first speech had insisted that Athenian survival depended on their "not adding (*epiktasthai*) to the empire while they are engaged in the war" (1.144.1), and this is confirmed as a crucial point of his policy in the summary of his career (2.65.7). But Alcibiades can also avail himself of Periclean doctrine; he takes the argument about the dangers of nonintervention (*apragmosunē*) from Pericles' last speech (2.63.2–3), and applies it logically to the need for further conquest. And as we saw in chapter 6, this is an argument with which Thucydides has some sympathy.

What we have at root, then, in this highly charged and skillfully wrought debate is an encounter between a policy for the war and a philosophy of imperialism (the caution of the one embodied by Nicias, and the initiative of the other by Alcibiades), and Thucydides seems to find merit in both of them. That may explain why his own assessment of the Sicilian expedition remains in the end tantalizingly ambiguous. It is delivered first in the context of a deviation from Pericles' sound policies, and at the outset the expedition is called a mistake (*hēmartēthē*—2.65.11); but Thucydides immediately glosses this as "not so much an error (*hamartēma*) of judgment in their choice of adversary, as in the failure of those who sent them to keep them adequately supplied once they had gone" (*ibid.*). Such a judgment seems to let both Alcibiades, who was the original motive force behind the expedition, and Nicias, who first resisted it and then mismanaged it to failure, off the hook, and chooses instead as scapegoat, the democracy's "out-of-sight, out-of-mind" irresponsibility.

It is possible that Thucydides himself protects at least the conception of the Sicilian expedition, because he is to some extent caught up in its daring. We should not make much use of the long and impressive account of the preparations and actual departure of the expedition (6.30–32), because such a buildup would serve to underline the irony and scope of the defeat. But it must be said that he seems to have caught the spirit of the occasion; he mentions not only the glitter of the spectacle, but the *daring* (*tolma*) involved at 6.31.6. And later, after the Spartans have fortified Decelea, he stresses the incredulity caused by Athens' stubborn resolution to maintain two full-scale wars at once—"anyone who heard about it would not believe it. . . . They had given such an astonishing proof (*paralogon*) to the Greeks of their power and daring" (7.28.3). There is a tone of real admiration for such an enterprise.

But we should return to Nicias and his transformation of Athenian optimism into defeat. The first mistake, as judged by the Syracusans themselves (6.63.2) and by Demosthenes on his arrival (7.42.3), was in not pursuing the attack immediately upon arrival, as Lamachus had suggested (6.49), when the Athenians had the advantage of surprise and intimidation (*phobon*—6.63.2; *phoberos*—7.42.3). During the winter which elapses the Syracusans gain confidence and busy themselves with fortifications.

However, there are several successes in the early stages of the expedition, beginning with the Syracusan defeat at Catana (6.69–70). When the conflict closes on Syracuse itself, the Athenians are again successful and take the heights of Epipolae, amazing the Syracusans with their speed, even though they had been aware of its strategic importance and had resolved to deny it to them (6.96). In the engagements which follow, Nicias distinguishes himself by prompt action to save the Circle, the Athenian fort on the top of Epipolae (6.102.2), and by the end of the episode Syracusan morale is brought to its lowest point, and there seems to be a chance that the city will be betrayed to Nicias (103.4). In fact the news that reached Gylippus, on his way to support Syracuse, was so depressing that he was prepared to write off Sicily, and concentrate on saving Italy. But this Athenian success marks the high point of their fortunes, and contains an ominous note in the death of Lamachus (101.6). This, and the arrival of Gylippus which coincides with it, mark the point when all initiative swings to the Syracusans. The first two engagements with Gylippus are decisive in this change: the first occurs just when the Athenians are about to close the noose on Syracuse by completing their wall down to the harbor (7.2.4). By the end of the second, the Syracusan counterwall has intercepted them, so that there is no longer any possibility of putting the city under siege (7.6.4). From this point Nicias has run out of ideas, and writes his letter asking to be recalled. His strategic plans, while he waits for reprieve, are limited to defense (7.8.3—*phulakē*), and to talking to his contacts in the city, in the hope that it will be handed over to him (7.48.2): it had happened for him at Cythera and Mende, so why not here? But meanwhile the strategic position he has taken, especially with the fortification of Plemmyrion across the harbor, brings added hardship to his army, especially with the difficulty of bringing in supplies. This is stressed as one of their problems by Nicias in his letter to Athens (7.13.2), but at no point does he concede that there has been anything to blame in any of the decisions or actions: "You should now realize that for what we came to do in the first place, there is no blame to be attached to the soldiers or their leaders" (7.15.1)—again the care for his reputation, and again the desire to be relieved of his command, in this case because of illness.

With Demosthenes' arrival the tempo, as one would expect, quickens. He is aware of Nicias' first mistakes, and wants to exploit the advantage of his arrival with a fresh force, and the temporary demoralization it has caused at Syracuse (7.42.2). He chooses a night attack on the Syracusan positions at Epipolae. With the element of surprise, the first contacts favor the Athenians (7.43.6). But when the resistance stiffens, confusions in the night begin to tell against the attackers (Dorian battle cries from allied Argives are taken as the enemy's), and in the end they are comprehensively routed. Demosthenes has made his test, and it has failed. He now sees that their strategic position is hopeless and that the army is demoralized and ill, and he advises immediate withdrawal (7.47.2–3).

It is at this point that Nicias' resistance perversely asserts itself. He wants to be recalled, but he does not want to take the initiative in leaving. His state of mind in the conference which discusses the matter is described by Thucydides as vacillating (*eti ep' amphotera echōn*–48.3), but he comes out against making a retreat; they would not be well received at Athens, unless it had been voted there first (*ibid.*). He did not want to be put to death on a shameful charge unjustly, but preferred to meet it "if necessary" from the enemy (7.48.4).

There has been general denunciation of this predominant concern for his own reputation over his army's welfare, and it is indeed hard to condone it. But Thucydides himself clearly enters into this situation, again claiming a kind of privileged access to Nicias' uncertain state of mind, where it differs from his public decision. And he appears to offer a small endorsement of Nicias' view, that it is worth waiting for developments in Syracuse, by confirming the information he has from the city as accurate (49.1). As with many of the major engagements at this critical phase, so too with the judgments leading up to them; Thucydides, perhaps because he is anxious to give Nicias his due, finds them critically balanced. But this may be the last time where it is true.

Demosthenes now modifies his plan to advocate a withdrawal to Catana or Thapsus, where there would be room to deploy and supply themselves, and where the fleet would have the open sea to reap the full advantage of its technical superiority (49.2–3). Demosthenes is supported in this by Eurymedon, but Nicias again resists, allowing the suspicion that he has inside knowledge (49.4). As we have earlier seen the indecision in his mind, Thucydides lets us question his insistence, and see the emphasis he places (*ischurizesthai*—49.1 and 4), with its false notes of determination, as misplaced.

In all these exchanges, which correspond to the council of the three generals at the beginning of the expedition (6.47–49), we begin to take note of the ominous accumulation of words for delay. The soldiers are hard pressed by the delay (*monēi*) and sickness (7.47.1), and Demosthenes after the failure at Epipolae voted for withdrawal and not to delay (*mē diatribein*) (47.3). This is vetoed by Nicias who says that they should stay 'and wait (*tribein . . . proskathēmenon*) (48.6). At the end of the debate, Demosthenes, with his modified plan, insists again that "they should move out as quickly as possible and not delay" (*mē mellein*—49.3), but with Nicias' continued resistance an attitude of "hesitation and delay" (*oknos tis kai mellēsis*) developed and so the Athenians wasted time (*diemellēsan*) (49.4).

With the return of Gylippus from his successful recruiting drive through Sicily, the Athenian position is seen to be correspondingly weaker, and even Nicias is won over, until, while they are still waiting (*mellontōn*—50.4) the eclipse converts him again to his policy of delay, in response to his soldiers' nervousness and the soothsayers' injunction to wait thrice nine days. Since his loss to Gylippus, we have not seen a single strategic thought from the commander in chief, and there can be nothing said to mitigate his latest abdication of strategy for chance (*tuchē*). Nicias thought of himself as "lucky" and was, as Thucydides says, "unduly predisposed to divination and suchlike" (50.4).

Thucydides has carried us with careful detail over the passage where he considers the situation was redeemable. At the end of it, we know that the expedition is doomed. We now enter on the final phase. It is at this point that Nicias comes to life in the desperate circumstances which his neglect has allowed to develop. Nicias in defeat is no longer the detached and plaintive figure seeking release from his responsibilities, but is involved in every downward turn of events; in defeat he will dominate every phase to the end. It is interesting that the speech of encouragement (*parainesis*) before the battle in the harbor is given to him (7.61–64), though he is not actually going to be commanding the fleet to which it is delivered—Demosthenes will be the commander. Apart from conventional encouragement, Nicias mentions modifications to the ships, designed to counter the enemy's tactics (7.62); it is clear that their nautical superiority will be forfeited in the close confines of the harbor, and that now it is a matter of meeting the enemy's initiatives instead of dictating the form the battle will take—a bad sign.

But whatever his tactical deficiencies as a commander, and however banal his first *parainesis*, Thucydides immediately makes him humanly sympathetic by reporting a kind of desperate reprise, in which Nicias for the first time becomes involved with his men individually, making awkward but moving appeals to each commander by name (7.69.2–3). This kind of desperation and passionate involvement is unprecedented in the *History*, and is the keynote of the concluding chapters of book VII, manifest both in the range of emotions portrayed and the detail of the fighting.

Again we have an intense and close-fought battle, and again the final result swings to the Syracusans. Demosthenes is for trying again at dawn, as they retain a numerical superiority in ships (7.72.3), and on this occasion Nicias agrees with him, but their men by now cannot be persuaded to embark.

And so the stage is set for the final retreat by land. There is one more delay, as fatal as any of the others, overnight and through the following day, when Nicias, still attentive as ever to the voices from Syracuse, is persuaded by Hermocrates' false message not to move immediately (7.73.3–4). So the final march to freedom begins, already entrapped. Thucydides records its progress step by step in an extraordinary piece of writing, in which the labor and suffering involved in every action are fully conveyed, as the trap closes, so that the path seems always to lead uphill (see especially 7.78.4–79.6). It begins with the departure from the camp, and the abandonment of the unburied dead and of the sick and wounded, who in the final moments, with the desperation of their cries and appeals, seem stronger than those who are able to march, "plunging them into a sense of hopelessness" (*aporian* twice—7.75.4), so that "it was hard to take their leave, although it was from a hateful place, and they had already suffered past all grieving" (*ibid.*). It ends with the terrible scene of the defeated army fighting each other for water in the blood-stained river, while they are pelted with javelins from the banks (7.84.5).

In recording all of this, Thucydides makes inevitable comparisons with the luster of their first departure from Athens, their "sense of shame" and "humiliation" contrasted with the "brilliance and pride" of their setting out. "Though they had come to enslave others, it turned out they left in fear that they would suffer the same fate" (75.5-7). With such contrasts, it is easy to see how this passage could be taken as the final spelling out of a *nemesis* after the *hubris* (or *auchēma*) of their first undertaking.

But Thucydides seems to reach far beyond such systems of retribution, and involve himself so sympathetically in the sufferings of the former aggressors that it becomes irrelevant to talk of guilt. This is made clear in Nicias' last speech, the marvelous inversion of a *parainesis*, in which he gives a kind of absolution to his army, encouraging them with the argument that their misfortunes are *undeserved*. We have alluded to this briefly in Chapter 6, but will follow it in greater detail here. The argument proceeds by a kind of induction, from his own misfortune and his own virtue: "As for me, I have no advantage over any of you in strength (you may see how my disease has affected me). Though I never seemed to lag behind anyone in good fortune before, both in my private life and in other respects, I am now caught up in the same danger as the humblest of you. And yet my life has been spent in many regular devotions to the gods, and many just and ungrudging (*anepiphthona*) deeds to man. And because of this, I have a confident hope in the future, and my misfortunes do not terrify me, as though I deserved them (*kat' axian*). Perhaps now they will be taken from us, for the enemy has had its fair share of good fortune, and if we incurred the anger of any of the gods (*epiphthonoi*) in making this expedition, we have by now been adequately punished for it. Other men have gone against other peoples, and having done what is only human (*anthrōpeia*) have suffered only what can be endured. So it is reasonable for us to hope for gentler treatment from the gods, because we now deserve pity rather than envy (*phthonou*)" (77.2-4).

This argument, if anything, seems to me a refutation of the *nemesis* interpretation, and a most important pronouncement on the morality of imperialism, at perhaps an unlikely juncture. It is a skillful composition—to have the pious Nicias voice a small skepticism about the gods' inclination for full vengeance comes as close as a respect for character can allow to endorsing the harsh judgment of the Athenians at Melos (that the gods operate under the same laws as men—5.105.1–2), and perhaps close to Thucydides' own agnosticism. Nicias' virtues are not open to doubt, and are confirmed challengingly by Thucydides in the brief epitaph he awards him at his death (7.86.5). In fact, the language of the epitaph seems to echo the last speech, in the discussion of his virtue (*nomima dediōitēmai*—77.2; *nenomismenēn epitēdeusin*—86.5), in the discussion of worthiness, or deserts (*para tēn axian—kat' axian*—77.3, *axiōteroi*—77.4; cf. *bēkista axios*—86.5) and in the contrast of his *eutuchia* (77.2) with the *dustuchia* of his death (86.5).

But the key sentence in Nicias' own argument, it seems to me, is the very compressed comparison of other people's actions with the proportionate scale of the sufferings they endured. By the single word *anthrōpeia* (what men do) we are reminded of the universality of human aggression, and the law of nature governing it. This is the first time it has been invoked by the Athenians in the position of underdog, but the fact that it is invoked by Nicias, whose virtue is not in doubt, who is in the position of victim, who had opposed the particular venture from the start, and who had asked to be removed from it before the end, seems to give it a particular validity, and to make the absolution from guilt, which he speaks over his army, convincing.

In his final hours, Nicias is once more a soldier. He seems to manage his retreat better than Demosthenes,[3] and his surrender at the end for the first time really shows some concern for his army—though there is a shrewd calculation in his choice of Gylippus to receive the surrender (7.85.1).

What in the end are we to make of Thucydides' treatment of Nicias? The final judgment on his virtue cannot be the only verdict the reader is expected to give, if he assesses the record of his whole career. Although Thucydides enters into his thinking to a remarkable degree, and allows him considerable dignity in his final desperation (in short, finds him a sympathetic figure), the dominant impression is of someone who stands, with his persistent reluctance, somehow out of pace with the war, and as it progresses, is left further and further behind. Thucydides seems to endorse, and fosters in the full portrait, the irony of Alcibiades' taunt about his *luckiness*, showing us on balance a general smaller than his reputation, and one, as the situation worsens, increasingly bereft of strategic ideas, waiting for deliverance from his informers in Syracuse, as he had been delivered at Cythera and Mende, and finally losing control of the situation totally—his men determine the final stay after the eclipse (though his religious and superstitious views were inclined to it), and his men refuse to embark after the second defeat in the harbor. In fact, there is no generalship at all after the first defeat by Gylippus (7.6). But all the way through the Sicilian expedition, from the first arrival, when he refuses to launch an immediate attack, Nicias loses opportunities; the policy is to be cautious and to delay, and, as Pericles said in his first speech, in war opportunities wait for no man (1.142.1).

In the all-consuming demands of the war, which imposes its own harsh morality of pragmatism in the interests of survival, Thucydides allows Nicias' virtue, so evident as it encourages his army along the final steps to their catastrophe, to seem an irrelevant anachronism. Constantly resenting the fact that he was involved at all, he became half-involved, a would-be fence sitter at a time for rapid decisions, and so was consumed by his own delays. One seems to see in him an interesting tension between the public man looking for a reputation for public service and military heroism, which his conventional view of virtue may have driven him to acquire and sustain, and the man of peace, who always wanted to cry "enough" and rest on his laurels. The contrast between the genuinely heroic Brasidas, relishing the engagements which brought him glory, and dying at a moment of triumph, and Nicias' passive conception of honor seems, as we noted, to be almost explicitly made in their juxtaposition at 5.16. The comparison, I think, calculatedly diminishes Nicias.

Phrynichus. [4] After the death of Nicias, we follow the news of the Athenian defeat back to Athens; we hear the recriminations and laments, and see how low the city has been brought—no hoplites or cavalry, no youth to be conscripted, no ships in the dockyard, no crews for the ships, no money in the treasury (8.1.2). "But nevertheless, even in their present predicament, they thought they should not give in" (8.1.3). Thucydides records their decisions to put their house in order, and makes it clear that, like us, he is impressed with their resilience (8.4). "When they are defeated, they give ground as grudgingly as possible," the Corinthians had said at Sparta (1.70.5). The war must go on.

But it does not go on in quite the same way. The narrative changes its key as the book proceeds, and later, instead of a will to continue the war when all is desperate, we find that it cannot be brought to an end, though efforts are made to end it. (Compare the oligarchs' commitment to the war at 8.63.4, with their rejected overtures to Agis—8.70.2; cf. 8.71.3, and their final desperate attempt "to come to terms in any way at all" with Sparta, which was equally unsuccessful—8.90.2; 8.91.1.) We noted earlier that there are parallels between books v and viii. In book v, though a peace has been signed, the fear and uncertainty of war continue unabated, and the individual states grope for security by realigning themselves in new but usually ephemeral combinations. Corinth, disaffected like most of the Peloponnese with Sparta, forms an alliance with Argos (5.31.6), and then tries, and fails, to get the Boeotians to obtain a ten-day truce for her with Athens (5.32.6). Argos itself comes close to signing an agreement with Sparta (5.41.2–3), but finally finds one with Athens more compatible (5.44.1), and eventually clinches a one-hundred-year alliance there (5.47). Corinth now feels exposed and starts turning back to Sparta (5.48.3).

In book viii, there is the same climate of suspicion and agitation, but the focus is narrowed further; instead of international confrontations or international intrigues, or even anonymous party confrontations and party intrigues, as at Corcyra, we finally descend to the level of named individuals and their intrigues with and against each other. The principles of human nature, which had been projected until now on the activities of nations and parties, are finally seen properly grounded in frightened and self-seeking human beings. The largest set piece of this phase of war is the oligarchic revolution at Athens, and we shall follow the career of one of its prime movers, Phrynichus, as he gets enmeshed in it and comes to grief.

It is important to keep in mind the kind of climate in which all the activity over this period takes place, and for that purpose I shall quote again the passage which describes the demoralization of the democrats during the revolution at Athens:

No one else ever spoke in opposition because of fear, sensing the size of the conspiracy; and if anyone did speak out, he was immediately killed in some convenient way. There was never any search for the killers, nor if there were suspects, was there any trial. The people kept a kind of shocked silence, and considered they were well off if they avoided violence even when they were keeping quiet. Their estimates of the scope of the conspiracy were exaggerated, but served to intimidate them; and it was impossible to arrive at an accurate figure, because of the size of the city, and the fact that individuals were strangers to each other. For the same reason, it was impossible for anyone with a grievance to lodge a complaint with anyone else: he would either have to tell it to a total stranger, or to someone he knew but did not trust. All the leaders of the democratic party communicated with each other suspiciously, as any of them might be a party to what was going on. And it was true that the conspiracy included people whom one would never have suspected of turning to oligarchy; and this group magnified the suspicion of the rest, and contributed greatly to the oligarchs' security by cementing the democrats' mistrust of each other. (8.66.2–5)

Phrynichus himself begins as a convinced democrat, and one whom Thucydides seems intent on depicting at first as statesmanlike in his concern for his city's interests, and in his willingness to face apparently concerted opposition on its behalf. He appears for the first time, without patronymic or preamble, at 8.25.1, as one of the three generals sent to command the Athenian force at Samos. Two chapters later (8.27) he insists on the Athenian withdrawal from Leros, after the Battle of Miletus. His reasons for withdrawal are given, and strongly endorsed by Thucydides, with some insistence, against the unexpressed charge that to withdraw is disgraceful—it is a greater disgrace, he says, to involve the city in a defeat (8.27.3), and he will only give battle when the situation clearly favors Athens (*saphōs*). Thucydides commends his decision: "He won the reputation for intelligence (*ouk axunetos*), if not immediately at least afterwards, and not only for this but for everything in which he was involved" (8.27.5). This is one of the few passages where Thucydides approves of the *evasion* of a particular action, though he does endorse Pericles' conservative policy of nonconfrontation for the war as a whole. But Athenian caution was particularly necessary after Sicily. Phrynichus' larger thought for the safety of the *polis* beyond the particular engagement seems strongly patriotic.

His next appearance is in the same vein, at the debate at Samos on the recall of Alcibiades. Again, Phrynichus is the odd one out among his colleagues, arguing that the question of democracy or oligarchy is irrelevant to Alcibiades, except as an instrument of his own recall, and that the thing they should be most interested in is to see that they do not fall into internal dissension (*hopōs mē stasiasōsin*) (8.48.4). Again, Thucydides endorses this judgment on Alcibiades—"as was so"; and again we see the larger, statesmanlike view behind the particular question—interior harmony and peace with the allies, who, if they could not have freedom, preferred democracy to oligarchy, were better than dislocation with Alcibiades. The difference between the two situations is that Phrynichus in this case does not carry the day, and is left out of step with a major current of initiative; Alcibiades is bound to return, and Phrynichus will have incurred his hostility.

Phrynichus' solution to the problem of his exposure on this count is an act of betrayal. He writes to the enemy commander Astyochus, revealing Alcibiades' efforts to turn Tissaphernes in Athens' favor and against Sparta, "and that he should be excused for plotting the downfall of his personal enemy, even at the cost of damaging his city" (8.50.2). However, Alcibiades has now moved beyond the passive Astyochus' reach to sanctuary with Tissaphernes; "and he (Astyochus) had no intention of taking action against him (Alcibiades), but visited him personally to give him the news; his motive, it was said, was to attach himself to Tissaphernes for private gain, by making him privy to information on this and other matters" (8.50.3). Alcibiades then passes the information of Phrynichus' betrayal back to the authorities at Samos. We thus complete a quadrilateral of private self-seeking and intrigue, at the expense of national interests on both sides.

Phrynichus' answer to this further degree of exposure is to compound his treason by writing once more to Astyochus, and offering to hand over the Athenian force at Samos to him (8.50.5). Leaving aside the matter of his treachery, we are beginning by now to question Thucydides' judgment that he was "not unintelligent." Presumably he imagined that the military coup he was offering Astyochus would be too large a plum for even that inactive commander to decline. But although he was insistent on knowing enemy dispositions before taking action at 8.27, it is clear in this instance that he did not clearly understand the personality he was dealing with. In the climate of suspicion engendered by these intrigues, it would be easy for someone of Astyochus' caution or lethargic temperament to see this second initiative as a trap to entice him into committing large numbers to a dangerous action. Much simpler, therefore, to spurn the bait and pass it up the coast again to Alcibiades (8.50.5 *fin.*).

When Phrynichus realized that this letter, too, had misfired, and would presently be returned as still more explosive ammunition against him by Alcibiades, he forewarned the Athenian force of impending attack, and took the lead in fortifying Samos against it (51.1). Alcibiades' letter, when it comes, has already been refuted by his timely preventive measures (51.3). It is interesting that the letter is taken as a sign of Alcibiades' unreliability (*ibid.*), though it does nothing to slow the movement to his recall.

In fact, Pisander is already clinching the matter in Athens (8.53–54), while insisting on the need for an oligarchy, to win the confidence of the king (53.3). At the same time, he arranges for the removal of Phrynichus from his command, "considering him unsuitable" (*ou . . . epitēdeion*) for the negotiations over Alcibiades (54.3); he also implicates him in the loss of Iasus and the capture of Amorges (*ibid.;* cf. 8.28.2–3). We have no grounds for associating Phrynichus with these events, but the result is that he is out of favor, though not so far out as some of the recorded intrigues would warrant.

But he does not stay out for long. We hear of him next as a committed oligarch, flying in the face of his earlier convictions about *stasis* (though the oligarchy is now established), among the list of the intelligent leaders of the Four Hundred—Pisander, Antiphon, and Theramenes (8.68.3). The motive for this change of face since 8.48 is again personal security, and "fear of Alcibiades, and his knowledge of his dealings with Astyochus from Samos" (*ibid.*); in his judgment Alcibiades was not likely to return under an oligarchy. The context is one of such pervasive deception that we require no comment on the oligarchic intention of recalling Alcibiades, as stressed by Pisander to the Assembly shortly before (53.3). At all events, once Phrynichus had involved himself, "he was the most committed (*pherenguōtatos*) in the face of danger" (8.68.3).

But his security is short-lived. The fleet at Samos reacted against the oligarchy (8.73 ff.) and recalled Alcibiades (8.81.1–2). With all their military strength across the Aegean solidly opposed to the revolution, the

Four Hundred's days were clearly numbered. Alcibiades has to prevent the fleet sailing on the Peiraeus (in Thucydides' view nobody else could have done it—8.86.5), and insists to delegates from Athens that the Four Hundred should give way to actual government by the Five Thousand, and that the Council of Five Hundred should be restored (8.86.6).

The hostility of Alcibiades and the Athenians at Samos, and the harsh reception given to their delegates there, prey upon the internal unity of the oligarchy (8.89.4). The ambassadors on their return report Alcibiades' message, and thus "gave new incentive to most of those who, though they had been involved in the oligarchy, had grown discouraged with it before this and would gladly be rid of it, in any way that guaranteed their safety" (8.89.1). Theramenes, the moderate, whose changes of part earned him the nickname of Buskin (*kothornos*), took the lead with Aristocrates in advocating a broadening of the oligarchy to the full Five Thousand. Thucydides, though he approves the new constitution (8.97.2), does not rate its advocates' conviction very high: "This was the political stance of their program, but most adopted it out of private ambition, which is the principal reason why an oligarchy which develops out of a democracy comes to grief; for they all simultaneously stop thinking of themselves as equal, and each regards himself as first (*prōtos autos*). The situation at Samos, now vigorous under Alcibiades, gave them definite encouragement, as did the fact that the oligarchy did not seem to have any permanence. As a result each one strove to become the first champion of the people (*prōtos prostatēs tou dēmou*)" (8.89.3–4). Under the lash of ambition or fear for personal survival, the transition in ideology from oligarch to demagogue is easy.

Prominent among the inner core of oligarchs who resist the new move is Phrynichus; it probably became harder for him to see which way the wind was blowing, and certainly harder to let go, when he was so close to the hub of things in Athens: it would be easy to flatter oneself in such a position that the situation could be controlled. And there was always perhaps a maverick quality to Phrynichus' disagreements with the views around him. At all events, the response of the Four Hundred to the threat of the Five Thousand was to redouble their efforts to make peace with Sparta (8.90.1; cf. first approaches to Agis at 8.70.2 and to Agis again and Sparta at 71.3). Antiphon, Phrynichus, and ten others go to Sparta with a mandate to make any peace at all that could be lived with

(90.2); and at the same time they hurriedly fortify Eetionia at the Peiraeus. Theramenes argues that the fortification is not to keep "the army at Samos out (or anyone else), but to let the Peloponnesians in" (90.3). There was a Peloponnesian fleet supposedly destined for Euboea, which Theramenes insisted might be sidetracked to help the oligarchs at Eetionia. The exact whereabouts of this fleet and its intentions, the fortification of Eetionia, and the forced unloading of supplies into a warehouse there were important sources of agitation.

But what brought matters to a head for the oligarchs was the assassination of Phrynichus in the crowded Agora by a militiaman, upon his return from the embassy to Sparta (8.89.2). The assassin himself escaped, and though an accomplice was caught and revealed some vague information under torture, the Four Hundred did not pursue the matter. Thucydides seems to suggest that their hesitation was responsible for their downfall, as it further encouraged Theramenes and Aristocrates to take control.

Thus the death of Phrynichus is not merely the result of *stasis* but the spring to its next phase. What are we to make of his career as a whole? It is difficult not to see the two extended reports of his early, preoligarchic positions (not to endanger the city by premature commitment of the fleet—8.27; not to risk *stasis* to entice Alcibiades—8.48), which are as close to full speeches as book VIII allows, as a deliberate development to provide the strongest possible contrast to the intensity of his revolutionary commitment, which is also emphasized (*pheregguōtatos, diapherontōs prothumotaton*—8.68.3). What are we to make of it? There may be intended irony in the heavy laboring of what is "disgraceful" (*aischron*) in conduct regarding the city, in the report of Phrynichus' avoidance of battle at Leros. But Thucydides, as we saw, in the same passage calls him "not unintelligent" (litotes with positive connotation), and seems to make a point of projecting this judgment into the future—"if not immediately at least afterwards, not only for this but for everything in which he was involved" (8.27.5). Certainly Thucydides makes his way through this scene of treason and personal betrayal with almost disconcerting comfort; as usual, nothing surprises him. The mere fact of treachery does not disqualify a man from Thucydides' approval of his intelligence, as we noted in the case of Themistocles (1.138.3). It is rather a matter of practical intelligence to save oneself in a desperate situation by any means available. What is forfeited, however, in these extremes is Pericles' pure definition of patriotism (2.60.2); but Alcibiades, as we have seen, has already forged a new and more flexible definition of the concept for this confused and demoralized period (6.92.4).

What Phrynichus' career shows us once more is that even a remarkably intelligent individual (in fact all but the very greatest), who is alert to the developments around him, will still get caught up in the vortex of war, or in this case of *stasis*, a war within the war, and in trying simply to survive will be compelled by events to make all sorts of contrary decisions for himself. There is nothing particularly virtuous about Phrynichus, just as there did not seem to be great practical intelligence in Nicias, but both of them are victims of events they cannot control, in the same sense. In the oppressive context of the war, with its intimidating agents of violence, uncertainty, fear, and mistrust, Thucydides seems to find both Nicias' virtue and Phrynichus' treason historically irrelevant. Nicias failed to take any initiatives at all, though he was commander in chief, and the pace of war overwhelmed him. Phrynichus, after cool appraisal of events against the grain of opinion around him, found himself threatened, and tried to take a lead in shaping the course of things, only to be, at the time he is most committed, marooned by the drift of events away from him.

Thus the individuals caught up in the oligarchic revolution of 411 are no different from the political parties at Corcyra in 427, or indeed from the two national protagonists over the course of the whole war. They are all crushed by the same fears and necessities, the same vice of pressure which a long war exerts, forcing all alike to lose control of the situation and, with rare exceptions, their grip on peacetime conventions and restraints. Though Thucydides reduces the scale of his *History* in the eighth book, he maintains its direction consistently to the end.

9

HUMAN NATURE AT WAR
IN THUCYDIDES

In the last chapter, we followed the career of Phrynichus to its conclusion in the oligarchic revolution at Athens. Private enmity with Alcibiades, and fear of reprisals from him, changed him from principled democrat to committed oligarch, but the change, so far from protecting him, led to death by an anonymous soldier in the marketplace. The principal difference between the narratives of the Corcyrean and the Athenian revolutions is that the party strife of the latter is made specific with the names, actions, and motives of the participants, and this reduction enables us to see that the motives behind all the partisan involvements are self-centered—individual ambition or individual fear determines the decisions. This seems to make patriotism, at least in Pericles' sense, an anachronism—the larger claims of one's city are met just so long as they do not interfere with private fears or possibilities. Thus the scale of the war has shrunk, from the conflict of nations against nations, then of party against party at Corcyra, where they were "drawn up in two camps against each other" (3.83.1), and now finally to that of individuals against individuals.[1]

But we should examine the relationship between *stasis* and war more closely, and guard against the logical error of identifying one with the other against the author's intentions. *Stasis*, by definition, involves the fragmentation of society, and is more likely to occur when the society is under pressure, but why should we not see the various instances of it in the work as *episodes*, like battles, within the general context of the war, instead of reading comprehensive lessons from it about the nature of war itself? The first answer to this question is the stress placed on the phenomenon of *stasis* by Thucydides himself; we saw the importance attached to it in the Archaeology; it sparked the first incident before the war (Epidamnus), and the first unambiguous violation of the truce, which made war inevitable (Plataea); immediately after the destruction of Plataea (3.68.5), we embarked on the very impressive set piece of the Corcyrean Revolution (3.70), where Thucydides gave a detailed anatomy of the social effects of revolution, and put it under the influence of war, "the harsh teacher" (3.82.2). We noted that Corcyra was the mother city of Epidamnus, and had been involved on one side of the revolution there; now it is the turn of Athens, which had been peripherally involved in Corcyra's upheaval, to be herself immersed in *stasis*. Thucydides has thus brought it from the edge of the war, to engulf one of the protagonists.

But in the eighth book, he goes even further than that; he takes the climate of *stasis* and spreads it pervasively through the operations of the war itself, souring all relationships with mistrust between the various commanders and their allies and troops *on the same side*. The war is the common background of everyone's lives, but the immediate concern is not to win it for one's country by solid collegial action, but to protect oneself and win advantage against close associates.

Thus on the Spartan side, Astyochus falls out with his fellow Spartan commander, Pedaritus. Astyochus sends word to Pedaritus at Chios, asking him to send ships to support the revolt of Lesbos, and Pedaritus refuses (8.32.3). Astyochus sails off to Miletus, with many threats that he will never come to help the Chians, even if they need him (8.33.1). Sure enough, the Chians are soon under pressure, and Pedaritus asks Astyochus for help, and is in turn refused; Pedaritus denounces him to Sparta (8.38.4), and a commission under Lichas is sent out to review Astyochus' conduct (8.39.2). At 8.40.3, Astyochus is finally prompted by his own allies to come to the help of the floundering Chians, "though he had had no intention of doing so"; and in fact, he is immediately sidetracked by the news of the arrival of the Spartan commission at Caunus—his need to ingratiate himself there overrides all military priorities (8.41.1). No help to the Chians is recorded, and we finally have a last desperate appeal from Pedaritus to the Spartans at Rhodes, saying that Chios is now completely under siege, and that unless help is forth-coming "with the entire fleet," all will be lost (8.55.2). The Spartans again "intend" to respond, but in the meanwhile Pedaritus leads an attack on the Athenian positions; he is at first successful, but the Athenians counterattack, and in the fighting Pedaritus himself and a large number of Chians are killed (8.55.3). Chios is then put under an even stronger siege by land and sea, and suffers considerable starvation (8.56.1). So much for Spartan cooperation.

Even among the Persians, one finds the same spirit of jealousy and competition between Tissaphernes and Pharnabazus. Near the beginning of book VIII we find representatives of both of them at Sparta competing for Spartan resources to aid the revolt of Athenian subjects in their territories. "As both parties conducted their business quite separately, there was considerable competition" (8.6.2). The Spartans at first put all their weight behind Tissaphernes' offer, but his refusal, abetted by Alcibiades (8.45), to pay them what is contracted lures them north to Pharnabazus in the Hellespont (beginning 8.61.1). The *History* ends with Tissaphernes planning to go north to discuss the situation, "considering that he had been badly abused by the Peloponnesians, and fearful that he would suffer further damage from them; he was also concerned that Pharnabazus, accepting Peloponnesian support, should succeed better, more cheaply and more quickly, in his operations against the Athenians than he had" (8.109.1). Unfortunately the Athenians are in no position to benefit from all this dissension, because *stasis* has reached the army and fleet at Samos. When the Chians win a surprising naval engagement, and Astyochus, though he had no part in the victory, is finally encouraged to challenge the Athenian fleet off Samos, "they did not come out to meet him because of their suspicion of each other" (8.63.2).

Thus everyone is caught up in the same negative spirit. But Thucydides pursues it beyond the personalities into the very fabric of the Peloponnesian alliance, just as he shows it undermining the foundations of Athenian solidarity in the oligarchic revolution. The terms on which the Spartans buy Persian support cynically abrogate the principle of "liberating the Hellenes," with which they supposedly began the war. In the first alliance with Persia that is made by the Spartan admiral Chalcideus, the Spartans agree that "all lands and cities that belong to the Persian King or *had belonged to his fathers* should still be his" (8.18.1). This first agreement is superseded later by Therimenes (8.37), not on any grounds of principle, "but because its terms seemed inadequate and not in their favor" (8.36.2). Finally the question of principle is raised when Lichas arrives with his commission from Sparta; he says that according to the provisions of the first two treaties "all the islands, Thessaly, the Locrians, and all the territory up to Boeotia should return to subjection, and instead of liberty, the Spartans would be bringing the Persian empire back to the Greeks" (8.43.3; cf. 8.52). Such pristine principles are impressive at this stage of the war, but predictably Lichas is not able to maintain them for long. When the Milesians expel Tissaphernes' garrison, "the rest of the allies, and especially the Syracusans approve, but Lichas frowned on the move, and said that the Milesians and the rest of those *in the King's territory* should accept a modest subjection to Tissaphernes and do his bidding, until the war had been properly settled" (8.84.4–5). Understandably, the Milesians are angry with Lichas, and when he dies from disease refuse him burial in the ground the Spartans have asked for. The crusade of liberation has clearly faltered.

But so by this time has the discipline inside the Peloponnesian army. Alcibiades has gone over to Samos, and Tissaphernes, who at his suggestion has been keeping the Peloponnesians on short pay, is now regarded by them as totally unreliable. Their rage is directed against Astyochus, who was "responsible for everything, as he conformed for private gain to Tissaphernes' wishes" (8.83.3). An altercation rises to the level of mutiny (more Spartan arrogance), and Astyochus has to take refuge in a temple to avoid stoning by his own men (84.3). In the next paragraph he is relieved of his command (85.1).

This brief sketch of the actions and relationships of book VIII is sufficient to show how Thucydides has belittled the large business of war into small flurries of individual conflict and intrigue; the war is still there and will not go away, but rather provokes and intensifies the climate of *stasis* with its uncertainties. The focus narrows, as we watch individuals pursuing what they see as their own advantage, often disastrously, against the undifferentiated background of incessant war. Much play has been made of the lack of speeches in the eighth book, as a sign of its internal incompleteness, but perhaps wrongly: speeches serve to focus action, as we have seen, and Thucydides may well have decided to leave the actions in this book undiscussed in debate, precisely because they are never fully focused, or "collected," but rather fragmentary and often ill-considered.

It should be clear by now that I do not look on this last phase of the *History*, as Thucydides has given it to us, as any bathetic, ill-edited aberration from the rest of his account, but rather as the final stage of a planned recession to the ground of human nature in the human individual. The war is no longer the "greatest" war between Greek nations, but one of every man for himself against everyone else. We may say that war has become a "condition" of human nature. And looking back over the work, we can see how Thucydides' assumptions about human nature ever more closely inform his narrative. Already in the Archaeology, in a typically condensed sentence, he defended the *usefulness* of his work to posterity, by postulating the constancy of human nature. The careful student of the past, by attending to the context and sequence of events, will recognise recurrent patterns and be able, within limits, to predict the future (1.22.4). Such a statement, of course, says nothing about the *kind* of events that will recur. But we noticed in the course of the Archaeology that Thucydides himself had traced narrow repetitive patterns from prehistory to his own day in Greece, concentrating on acts of aggression of stronger against weaker, and the motives of profit and fear. In the Athenian speech at the first Spartan Congress, these assumptions about the essential drift of human nature are spelled out: the three great motives of action are honor, fear, and self-interest, and it is a law of nature that the strong exploit the weak (1.76.2; cf. 1.75.3). This is in the context of a defense of Athenian imperialism, but it maintains the same emphases that Thucydides places in his own narrative voice. So the notion of human nature has by now been given some content; it explains the typical movements of a complete society which bring it to the point of war.

But as we saw at the beginning of chapter 2, Thucydides is as much interested in what war does to people, as in how they wage it. As the war proceeds, it is transformed from a mere series of actions into an agent, with a set of characteristics and an identity of its own. It lays siege to human nature, imposes its necessities upon it, and lays bare its most fundamental character. By the time the war is four years old, Thucydides is prepared to personify it as "the harsh teacher" (3.82.2). This is metaphorical writing, of course, but it serves to convey the sum of hostile conditions and necessities with which both sides in a war must deal, and the author's preoccupation with the *effects* of these conditions. It is important to see what this change of emphasis does to Thucydides' narrative. We began with the notion of human nature as a kind of postulate, imposed to explain actions and events, including imperialism and the hostilities leading to war. But as the account proceeds, we find that the historian does not leave it as a postulate but defines it *by the events themselves*. War probes a society ever more searchingly and eventually severs the fragile bonds between its members; it therefore locates and defines human nature in its essential ground—the human individual isolated in his fear, self-interest, and aggression. War and human nature, then, are seen to be indissolubly connected: the brutality and general mistrust, which are part of the climate of war, are both expressions of human aggression and fear, and also drive it to further excesses along the same line. The vicious circle is now complete, and the iron has entered into the soul.

We can now see retrospectively that this view of the individual state of nature has been consciously projected, or in Plato's term "written large," in the accounts of the maneuvers between states and parties; and this gives us a new understanding of Thucydides' attitude to the war itself. The Peloponnesian War for Thucydides is not merely a circumscribed episode, which for its duration changes the accepted patterns of behavior and belief for those who happen to be engaged in it, but a cataclysm that occupies every corner of the world, and transforms all its relationships. At the very beginning of the war, we noticed Thucydides' insistence on its scope (its "greatness"), and his extension of it "to the Greeks, to some of the non-Greeks, and almost one might say the majority of mankind" (1.1.2).

This near-universality of the war is stressed at intervals in the text. Still in the Archaeology, the subjects of the Persians after their liberation are divided between the Spartans and the Athenians "for these were pre-eminent in power, one on the land and the other by their fleet. . . . For a little while their alliance lasted, but then they fell apart, and made war on each other with their allies; and if any of the Greeks disagreed on anything, they went over to these two sides" (1.18.2–3). The Spartan and Athenian spheres of influence, then, comprise the two hemispheres of Thucydides' constrained universe. The rest of the Greek world immediately joins one of the two sides, or intends to (1.1.1), and on the eve of the conflict, "the whole of the rest of Greece was in suspense as the two principal cities were about to converge on each other" (2.8.1). The war has the centripetal force of a whirlpool, sucking other states into it, because they are involved in their own internal disorders, and each group of partisans hopes to strengthen its own position (3.82.1); or, especially after the Sicilian expedition, because they want to be in on the kill, "assuming that Athens would have proceeded against them had she won in Sicily" (8.2.1; cf. 2.8.5). The climate of hostility is omnivorous and allows no respite. The Spartans, suing for peace at Athens after their loss of men on Sphacteria, warn the Athenians of the risk of "some unendurable incident intervening between us which would compel a *perpetual* personal and public hatred of you" (4.20.1); no single incident is recorded (they seem to be alluding to the Athenian killing of their Spartan prisoners), but the war between the two states still turns out to be irresolvable. When the Peace of Nicias is signed, Thucydides refuses to allow it to be considered an authentic break in the war: "As for the interval of the agreement, if anyone thinks it should not be counted as war, he is judging wrongly" (5.26.1). And a general warning that war may assume a life of its own in this way is made in the same Spartan speech just cited: "Wise men . . . should realize that one cannot deal with war on the limited terms one would like to put upon involvement in it" (4.18.4).

The demographic or spatial universality of the war and its temporal continuity are simple extensions of what Thucydides has come to see as an almost permanent condition of human nature, as it is found in the human individual. The climate of war and the spirit of suspicion and the fear it produces can be traced through the whole work from the beginning to the end. In the first of the incidents which Thucydides sees as "preliminary" causes of the war (*aitiai*), it is already assumed that war is inevitable (1.44.2; cf. 1.36.1; 1.42.2); the necessities of war are already asserting themselves, though no war is declared. At Sparta Thucydides projects into the atmosphere of seeming torpor before the war a fear of Athenian power, virulent enough to be the compelling and sustaining cause of the whole conflict (1.23.6; 1.88). And we have seen that the Athenians claim to be compelled to hold on to their empire by a reciprocal fear—Sparta is hostile, and those who secede from Athens go over to the other side (1.75.3-4).

What Thucydides seems to have done here is to take the personal terror of an individual in wartime, and project it, or write it large, on the international plane of the relationships between two states, *even before the war has begun*. We may be pardoned for finding this kind of induction from the personal not altogether convincing. We believe Thucydides when he describes Phrynichus' fear of Alcibiades, or the more general climate of mistrust between the democrats at Athens during the oligarchic revolution. It is certainly possible for a nation to be seized by a mass hysteria (one could make the case for Athens after the mutilation of the Herms and desecration of the Mysteries—6.27–29, and especially 6.53); and it is certainly possible in wartime for the international situation to be so uncertain and confused that a climate of suspicion is engendered for a time, as Thucydides shows in the period of diplomatic intrigue following the signing of the Peace of Nicias in book v. But human emotions are mercurial, ephemeral things, and seem to ring false when given permanence or made monolithic in the way Thucydides has done. The fact is that Thucydides shows too many other states of mind to allow this dominant emotion of fear to be sustained so overridingly for so long. We do not find the Spartans fearful when they are being goaded from their sluggishness by the Corinthians at the first debate at Sparta, and we do not find fear as the dominant emotion in either of the two speakers, Archidamus or Sthenelaidas, when they represent two sides of Spartan opinion at the same debate; we do not find fear, but rather a sense of opportunism and confidence in the rightness of their cause, as the ruling motives when they resume the war with new energy, under Alcibiades' guidance, at 7.18. On the Athenian side, we do not find fear, however much Thucydides insists on it, as the dominant motive behind Athenian meddlesomeness (*polupragmosune*), whether in the first involvement in the alliance with Corcyra, or in the large-scale venture to Sicily—as we saw, Alcibiades' personal self-interest was very much a factor there; on the more passive side, we do not altogether believe in Athenian fears that "it is dangerous to let the empire go." Thucydides, we would say, has overwritten this aspect of his causality.

But the essential point to note is that, whatever the historical validity of his explanations, they remain completely consistent with his view of human nature, as he sees it in operation in his own day, and as he projects it for the future; the same human nature that drives Phrynichus to make personal choices to avoid the malign intentions of Alcibiades drives the Spartans to prosecute a war of twenty-seven years to its conclusion against Athens. The consistency is won by inflating the individual's human nature, complete with emotions and appetites, to the national level. One step down, we see the same kind of inflation, or projection, at work in the analysis of the party strife at Corcyra. We are warned at the beginning of the analysis that we should expect such upheavals, "as long as human nature remains the same" (3.82.2); no individuals are named at this point, and in fact all differences between oligarchs and democrats are obliterated in their common violence and loss of restraint. All behavior has been reduced to uniformity, and in this kind of reduction it is possible to forget about party alignments, which are at first in evidence (3.82.5–6), and see the beleaguerment as one of every man for himself: where the text mentions their "being drawn up against each other" (3.83.1), the commentators supply from the context the notion of two ideological camps, but in the next sentence the climate of mistrust, which "no word or oath is strong enough to dissolve," is made universal and attributed to everyone (*hapantes*—3.83.2). The mistrust and hatred, in fact, penetrate the most intimate personal relationships, and fathers kill sons (3.81.5).

As we have seen, in the eighth book Thucydides systematically carries the disruptive spirit of *stasis* into the main action of the war itself, and extends it beyond any party influence to the irreducible level of individuals at war against each other. The book then takes its place as an authentic part of the work, and, in fact, the term of a progression that makes the whole more intelligible. When we arrive at this nadir of morale and look back over the rest of the work, we see that all the early emphasis, from the Archaeology onwards, on collective action, building empires, and setting up the confrontation of the two greatest powers in Greece at their peak of preparedness, is counterpoised against the long process of decline. The exact point where the balance tips downwards is in the long chapter 2.65, where Thucydides reviews the career of Pericles, the First Man, under whom "she (Athens) became greatest," and then distinguishes him quite simply from anonymous successors, "those who came after" (*hoi de husteron*—2.65.10), who shaped their policies "for private ambition and private gain" (65.12). But one could say, as we did in chapter 2, that the Plague had already forecast this process of decline by showing the fragmentation of society under pressure, and isolating Pericles with his priorities of the "city first." After Pericles' death, the signs of decay on both sides soon proliferate; immediately afterwards, Peloponnesian ambassadors to the Persian king are intercepted and killed without trial (2.67.4), the noose closes on Plataea, the last place where the Greeks fought a collective action, Athenian moderation is tested over Mytilene and only triumphs narrowly at the second attempt, *stasis* erupts at Corcyra and is followed in detail, and the disreputable character of Cleon emerges as a countertype to Pericles, pushing the war to serve his own interests. Cleon is disposed of by Brasidas, who is almost an anachronism at this point for his chivalric pursuit of honor, showing more positive aspects of war. Both Cleon and Brasidas go out in the same engagement, but it is found that the war, which was inevitable before it started, cannot now be stopped. It has assumed a life of its own, proceeding from fear on both sides and in turn intensifying fear, and Nicias' virtue and Phrynichus' intelligence are powerless against it. There are certain forces in human nature that compel it to war, and even though the war may begin as the result of a collective or national decision with complete unanimity, the release of these forces, in Thucydides' account, brings no catharsis but a multiplication of divisiveness. A set of intimidating conditions is created which fragments a society until it results in "such a war, as is of every man, against every man." The language is Hobbes', and there is a great deal in the theoretical base of Thucydides' narrative which reminds us of Hobbes (see appendix).[2] We can repeat Adam Parry's dictum: "War is the final reality" (see chapter 3, note 8).

But what happened to the greatness of Thucydides' war? Clearly, in the mean-spirited interactions of book VIII, we have descended a long way from the high-mindedness of Pericles and the beginning of the war; by this time, we have a war without a cause. But we mentioned at the beginning that Thucydides consciously inverted many of the historical conventions which he inherited; and one of his preoccupations, writing, without any buffer of nostalgia for the past, about a war which he experienced and suffered, is to strip his war of any epic pretensions. But this does not make it trivial. The greatness of the Peloponnesian war, as Thucydides records it, lies in its very inexorability; not in the greatness of its exploits, but in the greatness of the sufferings it caused, as he very clearly spelled out at the end of his introduction: "but the length of this war was greatly protracted, and suffering was involved in it on a scale unprecedented for Greece over any similar span of time" (1.23.1).

When we read Thucydides, we are impressed with the single-mindedness (so unlike Herodotus) with which he pursues his theme. His often congested and knotty prose traces every involution and extension of hostility, and involves the reader, like the actual victims of war, inexorably, almost claustrophobically. And yet for all his concentration on the war, his insistence on its destructiveness can seem impersonal, and his vantage point on its progress at times one of cold and fatalistic distance. Thucydides will not rhapsodize about the evils of war, but contents himself with the general proclamation, spoken by the herald Melisippus on the threshold of the first invasion: "This day will be the beginning of great evils for the Hellenes" (2.12.3). In his careful, factual way, Thucydides parades for us, by summers and winters, the victims of war—the countrymen of Attica evacuated into the crowded city (2.14.7), the victims of the plague, the Plataeans on their way to execution, the Melians left without an argument, the population of Mykalessus mindlessly slaughtered, the Athenian aggressors in retreat from Syracuse, the democrats in Athens silenced by the terrors of revolution. All of these victims appear in episodes of great intensity, and engage the reader's concern, though for the most part we do not know their names.

But Thucydides is more interested in the problems of public life and the movements of power, than in personal calamities. And as the war proceeds, the lesson it seems to teach him is that its principal victim is not the individual who engages in it, but the delicate fabric and organization of society as a whole, at the hands of individuals who pretend to leadership, but end up fragmenting their *polis* with their self-seeking. States are unjustly treated by their citizens rather than *vice versa*. In the next generation, Plato, who was born in 427 and came to manhood during the war, would be the first to articulate a coherent political theory to guard against the aberrations of the individual in his authoritarian republic, by defining justice, "written large" in the state, as "doing one's own proper work and not meddling" (*Republic*, 433a).

Thucydides has few explicit theories to offer; he is engaged in following the course of actual events, and is prepared to be taught by them. At the outset, he seems to take it as a natural thing that a great state would assert its power, and that another great state would fear and resent it. But the inevitable war which these assumptions produce engenders a destructive force of its own, and drives those who are involved in it to abandon the traditional codes which their countries stand for, and to carry the war into personal confrontations of their own. This is the lesson Thucydides learns, above all others. He clearly endorsed the original decision to go to war. He lived to see the final result twenty-seven years later. His intelligence and his strong concentration on the events as they happen have shown him that neither Pericles' ideals for Athens nor Nicias' personal virtue were equal to the demands made by the war itself. The real coldness of Thucydides' unfinished work is that it falls silent without telling us whether he finally found anything to take their place.[3]

APPENDIX

HUMAN NATURE IN HOBBES

At the end of chapter 2, and again in the last chapter, we suggested an affinity between Thucydides and Hobbes, and will now establish it more securely. Other authors have indicated it, but rather tentatively, and without reaching, as I see it, the essential ground of connection. One might start perhaps by noting the parallels between the lives of the two men. In both cases it is civil war that brings them to their final pessimism about man, in both cases this is observed from exile, and in both cases their skepticism has been prepared by close contact with the scientific and philosophical thought of the day—Thucydides by the sophists and Hippocrates, Hobbes by his friendship with Bacon, acquaintance with Galileo, and work with Mersenne and Gassendi.[1] The parallels can easily be extended to the writings and thought of the two authors.

David Grene, in the introduction of his edition of Hobbes' translation of Thucydides,[2] remarks that "it is very probable that the intense study of the Greek historian which this translation necessitated had great influence on Hobbes' later speculations." He goes on to say that it is "tempting" to link the discussion of *stasis* in book III, Diodotus' argument about "the invincible appetites of individual and state for power," and the three "drives to empire" (fear, honor, gain) with "much in *Leviathan*," but warns that we must also allow room for the influence of the English Civil War on Hobbes.

Richard Schlatter, in the introduction to *his* more recent edition of Hobbes' translation, is more detailed. "The idea of an unchanging human nature, . . . which enables the historian to compare one event with another and construct a formula or pattern which is intelligible and useful, was a basic assumption of the science of history as Thucydides expounded it."³ (We discussed this in chapter 1). Schlatter then goes on to offer "concrete examples of how human nature performs" in Thucydides, several of them matched with striking textual echoes and marginal notes from Hobbes. In the first example, he notes the passage in the Athenians' speech at Sparta, where they claim to be "overcome by three of the greatest things, honor, fear, and profit," to retain their empire, and then quotes (without commenting on Hobbes' rather significant gloss) a similar passage in Leviathan:⁴ "So that in the nature of man, we find three principal causes of quarrel. First, competition; secondly, diffidence; thirdly, glory" (pt. 1, ch. 13). The resemblance is clear, though Hobbes has interestingly changed "profit" to "competition," but only as a prior category—in the very next sentence he says "The first, maketh men invade for Gain"; he has also taken what Thucydides describes as general motive forces of human action, and made them essential forces for conflict, or "quarrel". Hobbes could not find this in the particular passage of Thucydides, but he makes exactly the kind of extension on that passage that I have argued is warranted by Thucydides' view of human nature in its full development. Human nature for Thucydides, as for Hobbes, is essentially in conflict. Further quotation of Hobbes will show, if only by total resonance rather than exact verbal echoes, how close the two authors' views on this point are.

The following passage from the same chapter of Leviathan calls to mind the cycle of violence, as it was sketched in Thucydides' Archaeology:

> And therefore if any two men desire the same thing, which nevertheless they cannot both enjoy, they become enemies; and in the way to their End, (which is principally their own conservation, and sometimes their delectation only,) endeavor to destroy, or subdue one another. And from hence it comes to pass, that where an Invader hath no more to fear, than another man's single power; if one plant, sow, build or possess a convenient Seat, others may probably be expected to come prepared with forces united, to dispossess, and deprive him, not only of the fruit of his labour, but also of his life, or liberty. And the Invader again is in the like danger of another. (pt. 1, ch. 13)

Later in the same chapter, we come to the definition of the state of nature—which, for all its familiarity, is still worth quoting in full:

Hereby it is manifest, that during the time men live without a common Power to keep them all in awe, they are in that condition which is called War; and such a war, as is of every man, against every man. For War, consisteth not in Battle only, or the act of fighting; but in a tract of time, wherein the Will to contend by Battle is sufficiently known: . . . So the nature of War, consisteth not in actual fighting; but in the known disposition thereto, during all the time there is no assurance to the contrary. All other time is Peace.

Whatsoever therefore there is consequent to a time of War, where every man is Enemy to every man; the same is consequent to the time, wherein men live without other security, than what their own strength, and their own invention shall furnish them withal. In such condition, there is no place for Industry; because the fruit thereof is uncertain: and consequently no Culture of the Earth; no Navigation, nor use of the commodities that may be imported by Sea; no commodious Building; no Instruments of moving, and removing such things as require much force; no Knowledge of the face of the Earth; no account of Time; no Arts; no Letters; no Society; and which is worst of all, continual fear, danger of violent death; and the life of man, solitary, poor, nasty, brutish, and short. (*Ibid.*)

A little later he describes the moral consequences of such a condition:

To this war of every man against every man, this also is consequent; that nothing can be Unjust. The notions of Right and Wrong, Justice and Injustice have there no place. Where there is no common Power, there is no Law: where no Law, no Injustice. Force, and Fraud are in war the two Cardinal virtues. (*Ibid.*)

In the next chapter, the effects of moral lawlessness are pushed to their logical conclusion:

And because the condition of Man . . . is a condition of War of every one against every one; in which case everyone is governed by his own Reason; and there is nothing he can make use of, that may not be a help unto him, in preserving his life against his enemies; It followeth, that in such a condition every man has a Right to every thing; even to one another's body. And therefore, as long as this natural Right of every man to everything endureth, there can be no security to man. (*Leviathan*, pt. 1, ch. 14)

It is interesting that when Hobbes feels the need to defend himself against charges of the artificiality of his construction of the state of nature, he points to the example of *civil war:*

It may peradventure be thought, there was never such a time, nor condition of war as this; and I believe it was never generally so, over all the world: but there are many places where they live so now. For the savage people in many places of America, except the government of small Families, the concord whereof dependeth on natural lust, have no government at all; and live at this day in that brutish manner, as I said before. Howsoever, it may be perceived what manner of life there would be, where there were no common Power to fear; by the manner of life, which men that have formerly lived under a peaceful government, use to degenerate into, in a civil war. (*Ibid.*, ch. 13)

Leviathan was published in 1651, by which time Hobbes himself and his readers would have had close experience of civil war and its effects. Later in the work, while defending monarchy as his preferred constitution, he uses the potential threat of civil war, as though it amounted to a *reductio ad chaos*, against the merits of democratic assemblies:

Fourthly, that a Monarch cannot disagree with himself, out of envy, or interest; but an Assembly may; and that to such a height, as may produce a Civil War. (*Ibid.*, pt. 2, ch. 19)

Sixthly, that it is an inconvenience in Monarchy, that the Sovereignty may descend upon an infant. . . . But to say there is inconvenience, in putting the use of the Sovereign Power, into the hand of a Man, or an Assembly of men; is to say that all Government is more Inconvenient, than Confusion, and Civil War. (*Ibid.*)

As suggested above, it is unnecessary to look for influences beyond the immediate situation for arguments about civil war written in 1651. But in fact Hobbes did not need actual experience to see civil war as the greatest social evil; in his case, his view of human nature was already formed much earlier, and with this in mind every kind of sedition and civil disturbance, as fissures in the brittle fabric of the commonwealth, would necessarily be dreaded, for all the evils of the natural man that would climb out of them. We already find the same preoccupation with civil war, in much the same passages of Hobbes' argument, in *The Citizen*, though it was completed by November, 1641,[5] before the English upheaval had begun: talking of the possibility of a "mixed monarchy" he says

But if it were possible that there could be such a state, it would no whit advantage the liberty of the subject. For as long as they all agree, each single citizen is as much subject as possibly he can be: but if they disagree, the state returns to a civil war and the right of the private sword; which certainly is much worse than any subjection whatsoever. (*The Citizen*, pt. 2, ch. 7, art. 4)

I have argued that Thucydides came to his notion of human nature essentially at war, from learning the lessons of *stasis*, moving progressively to the center of all the concentric circles of wars within wars. On chronological grounds alone, whatever the currents of sedition in the air, Hobbes did not have to experience *stasis* to form his judgments of man. But the worlds of both Thucydides and Hobbes are similarly dominated by the emotion of *fear*. The second sentence of John Aubrey's brief life of Hobbes tells us that "His mother fell in labour with him upon the fright of the Invasion of the Spaniards" (April 5, 1588);[6] and this is referred to later in the essay, as an explanation of his temperament: "His extraordinary timorousness Mr. Hobbes doth very ingeniously confess and attributes it to the influence of his Mother's dread of the Spanish Invasion in 88, she being then with child of him."

For Hobbes, it is the force of fear that drives men to make the contract, to make their society secure:

> We must therefore resolve, that the original of all great and lasting societies consisted not in the mutual good will men had towards each other, but in the mutual fear they had of each other. (*The Citizen*, pt. 1, ch. 1, art. 2)

This is then defended in a long note:

> It is objected: it is so improbable that men should grow into civil societies out of fear, that if they had been afraid, they would not have endured each other's looks. They presume, I believe, that to fear is nothing else than to be affrighted. I comprehend in this word fear, a certain foresight of future evil; neither do I conceive flight the sole property of fear, but to distrust, suspect, take heed, provide so that they may not fear, is also incident to the fearful. They who go to sleep, shut their doors; they who travel, carry their swords with them, because they fear thieves. Kingdoms guard their coasts and frontiers with forts and castles; cities are compact with walls; and all for fear of neighbouring kingdoms and towns. Even the strongest armies, and most accomplished for fight, yet sometimes parley for peace, as fearing each other's power, and lest they might be overcome. It is through fear that men secure themselves, by flight indeed, and in corners, if they think they cannot escape otherwise; but for the most part by arms and defensive weapons; whence it happens, that daring to come forth they know each other's spirits. But then if they fight, civil society ariseth from the victory; if they agree, from their agreement. (*Ibid.*, n.)

Hobbes does not acknowledge any debt to Thucydides for the formulation of his conception of human nature, either in the Dedication or Letter to the Readers, with which he prefaced his translation, or later in his verse *Autobiography*. The translation was clearly an important venture to him (his first publication), and we are told that he kept it by him for some time, and submitted it first for the criticisms of his friends, including Ben Jonson. In the dedication to the young Earl of Devonshire, he says: "I could recommend the author unto you, not impertinently, for that he had in his veins the blood of kings; but I choose rather to recommend him for his writings, as having in them profitable instructions for noble men, and such as may come to have the managing of great and weighty actions"; but in the chapter "Of the Life and History of Thucydides" he acknowledges that "Digressions for instruction's cause, and other such open conveyance of Precept (which is the Philosopher's part) he never useth." Hobbes does not probe Thucydides' conceptual framework in this chapter, but defines and defends his historical methods against other critics. When he comes to write his *Life*, in listing the classical authors he read, he mentions "many writers of histories, but Thucydides pleased me before all others." His reason, however, is disappointingly narrow: "He showed me how useless (*inepta*) a democracy is, and how one man has more sense than an assembly (*coetu*)".[7]

We need not be disconcerted by this lack of explicit acknowledgment of substantial influence. Hobbes labored for a large part of his life to refine his own thought, as the three drafts of his principal theory through the *Elements of Law*,[8] *The Citizen*, and *Leviathan* make clear beyond any doubt; even in this limited space, we have quoted enough of him to show how strongly personal and independent his expression is, whatever the timorousness of his nature. Hobbes is a major thinker, and no derivative hack. What I am suggesting by this comparison is that his close reading of Thucydides did not merely leave him with a warm impression of a kindred spirit, but could have planted, perhaps even unrecognized at the time, the seeds of specific ideas about the nature of man and war, which would reach full fruition in his political theories.[9]

When all is said, it is perhaps this major difference between political theory and history that we should insist on. Hobbes the theorist uses the systematic bleakness of "the condition of mere nature," and the fear it arouses, as the driving incentive to form the Covenant, and acknowledge the absolute authority of the Sovereign, who is to guarantee security. "Convenants entered into by fear, in the condition of mere nature, are obligatory" (*Leviathan*, pt. 1, ch. 14). As we have seen above, Thucydides the historian offers no escapes from the impasse.

NOTES

INTRODUCTION
THUCYDIDES' OWN EXPERIENCE OF THE WAR

1. This is Andrewes' argument in Gomme, *A Historical Commentary on Thucydides*, 4:12.

2. The intellectual background of Thucydides, especially the sophistic and scientific background, has by now been fairly firmly delineated. The rather sketchy compilation of a *Life*, which is attributed to Marcellinus (probably 6th century A.D.) mentions various influences on him—Anaxagoras, the philosopher and cosmologist, whose lessons "gave him the reputation of being an atheist" (*Vit. Marcellin.* 22; Plutarch describes Anaxagoras as probably the leading intellectual influence on Pericles also—*Per.* 4–6, 8; but cf. 16), Prodicus, the sophist who was interested in the precise use of words, and Gorgias the rhetorician, whose visit to Athens from Sicily in 427 created a stir and gave a great stimulus to rhetorical theory (*Vit. Marcellin.* 36 for both). W. K. C. Guthrie, in *A History of Greek Philosophy*, lists the passages of Thucydides where he distinguishes shades of meaning between near synonyms, in a manner reminiscent of Prodicus (3:223–224), and sets him in the middle of the debate on law (*nomos*) and nature (*phusis*) (3:84 ff.). The most lucid single chapter I know on this background is chapter 2 of John Finley's *Thucydides;* he strongly emphasizes the influence of Protagoras.

3. One should not assume that any of these were *purely* cultural figures. Plutarch says specifically of Damon that he hid political intrigue behind the mask of musician; he was, in fact, "the masseur and trainer of statesmen" (Plut. *Per.* 4.1). To the Greek sensibility, the worlds of politics and music could be closely associated. For interesting comments on the political influence of Damon and other musicians, see W. G. Forrest, "The Date of the Lykourgan Reforms in Sparta," *Phoenix* (1963), 17:157–79.

4. This is one passage where Thucydides seems to point to and endorse another set of moral standards than the prevalent trend he describes. Adam Parry ("Thucydides' Historical Perspective") mentions another passage, at a similar period of social disintegration—the Corcyrean revolution: ". . . and simple innocence, of which a noble nature is largely comprised, was ridiculed into oblivion" (3.83.1). There is a clear note of regret.

5. Thucydides' awareness of the accomplishments of Archelaus, king of Macedonia from 413 (2.100), may be a small confirmation of his residence in the

neighborhood for at least a part of his exile. If he visited Archelaus' court, as is quite likely, did he meet Euripides, who found refuge there for a short time and died there (406?)?

1. ACCURACY AND THE PATTERN OF EVENTS: METHODOLOGY AND POINT OF VIEW

1. For the transition from the poetic tradition to history, the most useful work I know is Felix Jacoby's *Atthis: The Local Chronicles of Ancient Athens:* "The science of historiography (if I may use this convenient term in order to distinguish from the historical interest of the epos historical literature proper with its systematic work) manifestly originates in criticism of epic poetry, the contents of which are adopted, because they are considered to be historical: even Thucydides did not doubt the reality of a Helen, a Pelops, an Agamemnon, or the Trojan War" (p. 199). See also Wilhelm Nestle, *Vom Mythos zum Logos,* especially ch. 5, "Allegorische und rationalistische Mythendeutung. Ionische Historie."

2. "Modernity" is presumably an ephemeral quality, but it is a fact that many writers in this century have been struck by Thucydides' contemporariness; a fine, dated acknowledgment of this is found in C. N. Cochrane, *Thucydides and the Science of History:* "If then, in the judgement of moderns, Herodotus is inferior to Thucydides, it is not because he is a 'romancer.' That theory should long ago have been discarded. If we praise Thucydides and decry Herodotus at the present day, it is because our spiritual affiliations are with 'science' rather than with 'philosophy'; for Thucydides is the most scientific, as Herodotus is the most philosophical of Greek historians" (p. 15).

On Thucydides' anomalous standing in the Greek historical tradition, see Ronald Syme, "Thucydides": "The doctrines so nakedly expounded in the History might have made Thucydides a name of obloquy for ever, had he been assiduously read and studied. Some learned from him, his insistence on warfare and politics was influential (notably with Polybius), but he did not create a school of historiography" (p. 53). There follows a discussion of his influence on Latin writers, and (thinly spread) on later centuries. Syme concludes: "Only in recent times and within the memory of people not old has Thucydides come into his own" (p. 54).

One can see how long the influence of epic assumptions on history lasted, and how far out of step with them Thucydides appeared, in the following passage of Dionysius of Halicarnassus, who taught at Rome from 30 to 8 B.C.:

The principal and most necessary office of any man that intendeth to write a history, is to choose a noble argument, and grateful to such as shall read it. And this Herodotus, in my opinion, hath done better than Thucydides. For Herodotus hath written the joint history both of the Greeks and barbarians, to save from oblivion, Etc. But Thucydides writeth one only war, and that neither honourable nor fortunate; which principally were to be wished never to have been; and next, never to have been remembered nor known to posterity.

The quotation comes from Dion. Hal. *Pomp*. ch. 3 (see W. Rhys Roberts, *Diony-sius of Halicarnassus, The Three Literary Letters*, p. 107); the translation is Hobbes' from the chapter "Of the Life and History of Thucydides" with which he pre-faced his translation of Thucydides (see n. 8 below). Hobbes enjoyed himself destroying this and others of Dionysius' assumptions.

3. The fact that a myth, in its primitive formulation, typically concerns an *in-dividual* god or an *individual* hero is apparently so basic that it is hard to find sources for the idea. However, it is worth discussing. Even where there are *na-tional* myths, there are a variety of epic devices that associate them with particu-lar personalities—through a genealogy (the sons of Heracles reclaiming their in-heritance in the Peloponnese) or by explicit leadership (the island of the Phaeacians settled under Nausithous, the Amazons ruled by Penthesilea); in cre-ation myths, impersonal powers like Night or Earth must be personified, and produce children. When Plato fashions the myth of Atlantis, with the help of Critias and his ancestor Solon, he conforms to the convention by talking of Poseidon's influence, and then giving a genealogy of the first inhabitants (see *Cri-tias*, 113c–114d). It is clear that for Thucydides a *mūthos*, quite apart from the question of its historical veracity, connotes something *unserious*, like the word "anecdote."

4. This point could be developed very extensively on literary grounds. On more technical grounds, both Eduard Norden, *Die antike Kunstprosa* (Stuttgart: Teubner, 1958), p. 45, and A. W. de Groot, *Der antike Prosarhythmus* (Gron-ingen: Bouma's Boekhuis, 1967), pp. 29 and 34, find strong epic rhythms in Herodotus' prose, including what is very nearly a perfect hexameter in book VII; by contrast they find Thucydides arhythmic. But W. R. M. Lamb, in *Clio Enthroned: A Study of Prose-Form in Thucydides*, makes more positive assessments of Thucydides' rhythms.

On Clio, John L. Myres, *Herodotus, Father of History:* "The name of Clio among the Pierian Muses takes us straight back to the 'deeds of man' with which Achilles beguiled his leisure, singing to his lyre, and forward to the project of Herodotus." (p. 68). The whole of Myres' chapter 4 is useful for this back-ground.

5. The first person to comment on the subordination of the individual in Thucydides' writing seems to be Marcellinus in his *Life:* "He often made his sub-ject matter the (dominant) emotions (*pathē*) and (common) action (*pragmata*) in-stead of individuals (*andrōn*), as in the case of reciprocal fear" (53). Thucydides uses the word *kleos* three times; in the Archaeology (1.10.2), where he predicts that future archaeologists, on exhuming the remains of Sparta, would infer that its power was smaller than its reputation (*pros to kleos*); at the beginning of the conflict between Corcyra and Corinth (1.25.4), where the Corcyraeans vaunt themselves on their nautical prowess because of an alleged identity with the mythical Phaeacians; and thirdly, in a very ironic use of the word, in the Funeral Oration, where the widows of the dead are consoled with the admonition that their great glory (*doxa*) will consist in their having the least possible renown (*kleos*)

among men, "whether for good or ill" (2.45.2). The tone of the last two is clearly negative, and the first, by its projection into the future, leaves Sparta as an epic relic, like the Phaeacians.

6. Longinus, *On the Sublime*, 11–15; the distinction is used to show that the *Iliad* must be the earlier work, written by genius in its prime, whereas the *Odyssey*, falling from high passion to mere character study, is a work of genius in decline.

7. Dion. Hal. *Thuc.* 336–37, edited in the Teubner text by H. Usener and L. Radermacher, reprinted 1965; the work is available in an edition by W. Kendrick Pritchett, and in the Loeb series, edited by S. Usher. Dionysius does an anatomy of book III, and argues that the system of chronology contributes nothing but fragmentariness. Taking the main divisions of the narrative, we go from the case of the Mytileneans in revolt (2–18), to the escape from Plataea (20–24), to the surrender of the Mytileneans and debate on their fate at Athens (25–50), back to Plataea for the final surrender (52–68), and then on to the revolution in Corcyra (70–85). It is not worth paying much attention to Dionysius' complaints; we find them already answered by an ancient scholiast in an early papyrus (*POxy.*, 853). But it is worth noting the *effects* of Thucydides' chronological system. The interweaving of the episodes allows us to compare at this point Athenian moderation (though strained) against Spartan ruthlessness (though reluctant); at the same time, it is good to separate the "upbeat" incident of the partial escape from Plataea from the depressing finale. It is hard to know whether Thucydides allowed for such possibilities in choosing his system; it seems likely that the greater precision of his system appealed to him, and possible that he was, as in other respects, following Hippocratic precepts: "As time and the year passes he will be able to tell what epidemic diseases will attack the city either in summer or in winter, as well as those peculiar to the individual which are likely to occur through change in mode of life. For knowing the changes of the seasons, and the risings and settings of the stars, with the circumstances of each of these phenomena, he will know beforehand the nature of the year that is coming." *Airs, Waters, Places* II (Loeb translation, *Hippocrates I*), W. H. S. Jones, ed.

8. Thomas Hobbes, *The History of the Grecian War in Eight Books, Written by Thucydides* (London, 1629). The quotation is taken from the chapter "Of the Life and History of Thucydides," which is reprinted, along with the dedicatory epistle and letter to the readers, in Richard Schlatter, *Hobbes's Thucydides;* for the quotation, pp. 22–23. The impression of unity has been able to survive to the present day, despite all the scholarship which has challenged it; Jacqueline de Romilly, in *Thucydides and Athenian Imperialism*, begins her General Introduction: "Perhaps more than any other historical work, Thucydides' description of the Peloponnesian War differs from a simple collection of raw facts: every single word in it seems to imply choice and arrangement; and this gives the reader the impression that, from beginning to end, a sure and certain hand is guiding him towards definite conclusions" (p. 3, cf. p. 370). It is worth attending to the *logic* of the long debate on the chronology of Thucydides' composition, though cer-

tainly not to all of the debate itself. We begin with Thucydides' statement that he began to write as soon as the war began (1.1.1), and that he described events as they happened by summers and winters (2.1.1; 5.26.1). But we discover 1) that Thucydides makes occasional references to the end of the war and to final Athenian defeat; and 2) that his account does not reach the end. We conclude, therefore, that although Thucydides is still engaged in writing his history at the end of the war, he has not been engaged in writing events "as they happened" over the last part. Did he instead become involved in *editing* the whole, and if so, how systematic was this process? This last question is unanswerable in principle, and the fact that it has continued to be asked and answered unsatisfactorily has weakened the spirit of Thucydidean scholarship, by presenting the text as a kind of minefield of buried charges, some of them with immediate and some with delayed fuses. Let us take the example of the summary of Pericles' career (2.65), in which Pericles is compared with his successors down to the final Athenian defeat. We could, in fact, remove the anachronisms from this assessment and make it fully contemporary with Pericles' death, by eliminating the second half of 65.6 and 7, and then sections 10–13. Having done that, we realize that historically we have deprived ourselves of Thucydides' judgment of Pericles against the test of time and the reversal of his policies by later Athenian leaders, and that *these comparisons were the purpose of the summary as a whole.* Does this mean that the summary as a whole was written after 404? But there are close connections between the summary and Pericles' last speech (the qualities which Pericles claims for himself in the speech are confirmed in the summary, the speech at 64.3 hints at the possibility of decline for Athens, and the summary says it happened). Is the speech therefore also late? By pursuing this piecemeal method, we never know how much to bracket as "late"—a sentence, a chapter, a whole episode? And what about the impression of unity with which we started?

We need, therefore, another set of principles to work the problem more fruitfully. We should realize at the outset that the virtues of contemporaneous composition are strictly limited, except to save the appearances for Thucydides' statement that he recorded events as they happened (2.1; 5.26.1). These can be saved anyway by accepting the notion of an "immediate" version of the events (whether notes, outline, rough draft) and subsequent rewriting. The fact that some notes of *some* kind would be necessary for a historian writing at the end of a twenty-seven-year war, with several theaters of operation and very complicated details of logistics and strategy to cover, is, I think, undeniable. That this was the methodology Thucydides used is asserted with absolute clarity in the *Life* of Marcellinus: "When the war began, he made notes (*esēmeiouto*) of everything that was said and done, but at first had no thought of polishing it (*kallous*), but only to fix events in his notes; but later after his exile, he spent time in Scaptē Hylē in Thrace, giving an ordered, literary shape to what initially he had noted to help his memory" (47). The question of the exact balance between early and late strands of writing is unanswerable and on the whole uninteresting, *except where judgments of hindsight produce anomalies or contradictions with previous accounts, which have been allowed to stand in the text.* We should realize that we do, in fact, have an *ordered* text, in the sense that events follow each other by summers and winters in a strict chronology which scholars respect. If events have been ordered in this way, can their descriptions not also be edited in tone and judgment, to conform to patterns of events that are seen in force elsewhere? Again, an example will clarify this: it has seemed to many scholars that the account of the Sicilian expedition (books VI and VII), because of its high polish and completeness, may have been written before book V, which, as we shall see, has much in common with book VIII (see, most recently, Virginia Hunter, "The Composition of Thucydides' *History*"). This seems to me quite likely. But there are various points at which "Sicilian" events seem to take into account, and proceed from, points made in book V. Thus the character of Nicias as defined at 5.16.1, in making the peace, seems to give us the key to his subsequent behavior in Sicily, and Euphemus, speaking at Camarina, says that the Athenians "will not use fine words (*kalliepoumetha*) to the effect that they have every reason to rule because they removed the barbarian singlehanded" (6.83.2—though he *has* used the Athenian contribution against the Persians in the previous sentence)—apparently in deference to the scorn poured on such "fair words" (*onomata kala*) by the Athenian speakers at Melos (5.89). There is nothing at all surprising about this. It is as easy for the careful writer to produce conformity working from B to A, as from A to B.

But does it follow, if there is consistency of judgment in the work, that all the judgments must be *final* judgments? And if we were to postulate that the bulk of the writing was done after 404, would we logically be entitled to trace a *development* of thought in the work? The answer to this last question, which is important for the argument of this book, is certainly "yes." It is quite possible that Thucydides started his work in 431 believing that this would be the greatest of all wars in a positive sense, that he thought it was worth fighting, sharing the enthusiasm of the young men he describes at 2.8, that his notes reflected this, that as the war proceeded he became increasingly disillusioned with it, and saw it as a squalid and destructive force, *and that he let his prior judgments emerge in the text and allowed the reader to follow the same course of disillusionment he had followed himself.* Such a progression is dramatically superior to a monochromatic account, and Thucydides had strongly developed dramatic instincts.

The most complete bibliography on this *Thukydidesfrage* is now found in O. Luschnat's Supplementband for Pauly Wissowa, *RE* Supp. 12 (1971), vol. 2, sec. 5, pp. 1183–229. The strongest work of the "divisionists" is shown by Eduard Schwartz, *Das Geschichtswerk des Thukydides*. Schwartz saw the work as a basic account written according to Thucydides' announced methodology, revised after 404 to protect Pericles' name and policies. The unity of the work, written as a piece after 404, was staunchly defended by John Finley, "The Unity of Thucydides' History," *Harvard Studies in Classical Philology*, Supp. 1 (1940), pp. 255–98, reprinted in his *Three Essays on Thucydides*, pp. 118–69. The argument of this note is an extension of one used in my doctoral dissertation, "Thucydides and Pericles" (Columbia University, 1969).

9. In her book *Thucydides, the Artful Reporter*, Virginia Hunter insists on the interaction between the speeches and the narrative. She is particularly helpful when she shows how plans and purposes announced in speeches can in fact be drawn from results—this is especially true of the *paraineseis* (speeches of encouragement) of successful generals: what they accomplish often turns out to conform to their prescient briefings of troops. (Herodotus had also used this device, to underline the wisdom of a counselor—see Artabanus' warnings to Xerxes, Hdt. 7.49–51.) Hunter also follows the pattern of events, catching frequent repetitions of action as well as word. At times she pushes this too far. It is one thing to say (p. 105) that Lamachus learned from King Archidamus' delays to insist that one should ram home the advantage of intimidation upon arrival; but to go on and say that Demosthenes' attempt to do just that upon arrival in Sicily is a sign that he, unlike Lamachus, has failed to learn from experience is clearly an attempt to have it both ways—her thought, like Thucydides', has been influenced by the result.

10. The problem with the speeches begins with Thucydides' puzzling statement of methodology about them: "As for what various people said in speeches either on the verge of war or while actually engaged in it, it has been difficult for me to recall the exact words of those I heard myself; and so, too, for those who reported speeches to me from elsewhere. As a result, in this History each one speaks in the way in which I thought he would be most likely to convey what had to be said (*ta deonta*) in the immediate situation, always clinging as closely as possible to the general drift (*gnōmēs*) of what was actually said" (1.22.1). It is clear that Thucydides, given the difficulty of setting down "the exact words," has evolved a method to give himself some license, and also that he would like it to be assumed that the license he took was small. The two Greek expressions above are genuinely ambiguous in this context: *deonta* has some connotation of "ought" in it, and could mean "what the situation called for" or just possibly "what the speaker had to say." Gomme, in his *Historical Commentary on Thucydides*, is very adamant for the latter interpretation, and paraphrases Forbes for the other: cf. W. H. Forbes, *Thucydides Book I*, Oxford 1895, p. 26: "*ta deonta*—'what was wanted,' what was appropriate to each occasion, i.e. what, to the best of Thucydides' own judgment the circumstances called for, under the limitation only of keeping to 'the general sense of what was actually said.'" As for *gnōmēs*, it could mean "sense" and it could also mean "plan" or "intention"—the latter giving the author a relatively free hand to compose arguments for any particular goal. Gomme points out that in the case of *actions*, Thucydides expressly says that he did not feel free to narrate them "as they seemed to me" (22.2), and that he was unlikely to be claiming the opposite for speeches, just because they were difficult to record accurately.

In the face of these ambiguities, it seems to me worth noting that Thucydides has brought much of the debate down on his own head, by choosing two expressions that not merely widen the scope for the speeches in his work, beyond the *ipsissima verba* of the speaker, but could be interpreted as extending it almost to their contradictory: "what ought to have been said" and "what was actually said" on any given occasion can be two very different and possibly opposite things, and so can the "general purpose" as opposed to the "actual words"—one may say "his general purpose was conciliatory, but his actual words only inflamed them further." Given the ambiguities, our only solution is to consider each debate in its context, and analyze its argument in terms of the particular situation: as we shall see, each speech or debate does serve to focus the narrative in the reader's mind, but with many of them, as we analyze further, Thucydides seems often to have broadened the argument beyond the limits of his stated methodology, so that a particular speech does not answer the particular question at issue, but rather speaks to other debates in the work, setting up connections that ask to be taken as a related body of argument. I would regard 1.22.1 as one of the few passages that really justify Collingwood's well-known asperity against Thucydides: "In reading Thucydides I ask myself, What is the matter with the man that he writes like that? I answer: he has a bad conscience" (R. G. Collingwood, *The Idea of History*, p. 29; quoted by Syme, "Thucydides," p. 44 in a more general context). If he had meant to give himself just a little rope, he could have phrased his statement far more tightly, and more accurately.

But we should not be too hard with Thucydides. He is writing not only for posterity, but for an audience that expected certain conventions to be met—and the provision of speeches was one of them (see R. C. Jebb, "The Speeches of Thucydides," pp. 359–445). The statement of methodology appears more conscientious than he could fulfill, and the signs are that in antiquity no one expected him or anyone else to meet its terms. Polybius, for example, though he has clearly been influenced by Thucydides, seems to insist, in his criticisms of Timaeus' speeches, that a historian ought to invent arguments to fit the occasion (12.25.i.4–8—cf. Gomme's *Commentary*, 3:522, and Luschnat, *Thukydides*, p. 1295). Dionysius, in his review of Thucydides' speeches, takes it for granted that they are his own composition (Dion. Hal. *Thuc.* ch. 34, 381 ff.). I do not believe that this was ever seen as a disparaging assumption: a historian, in the ancient view, is not merely a reporter of other men's actions and words, but a literary writer in touch with the important philosophical and rhetorical currents of his day—and how can he show his rhetorical power if he does not write speeches?

Such attitudes survived antiquity for a considerable period. Samuel Johnson was employed, before his fame was established, in writing parliamentary debates, constructing speeches out of notes brought to him by William Guthrie: "The debates in Parliament, which were brought home and digested by Guthrie, whose memory, though surpassed by others who have since followed him in the same department, was yet very quick and tenacious, were sent by Cave to Johnson for his revision; and after some time, when Guthrie had attained to greater variety of employment, and the speeches were more and more enriched by the accession of Johnson's genius, it was resolved that he should do the whole himself, from the scanty notes furnished by persons employed to attend in both houses of Parliament. Sometimes, however, as he himself told men [sic], he had nothing more communicated to him than the names of the several speakers, and the part which they had taken in the debate" (Boswell's *Life of Johnson*, Oxford Standard Edition 1965, p. 85). A century later, however, Dickens recorded authentic debates in the Commons, aided by improved methods of shorthand (brachygraphy).

For a complete modern bibliography on the speeches, and useful essays of discussion on various aspects of them, see *The Speeches in Thucydides*, edited by P. A. Stadter.

11. A funeral oration provides a context where it is particularly seemly for the speaker to feel the inadequacy of words; see Lincoln's "The world will little note nor long remember what we say here, but it can never forget what they did here." Aspasia's funeral oration in Plato's *Menexenus* inverts this *topos*, and makes the speaker fully adequate to the occasion: "A well-delivered speech earns as its reward from the audience a heightened memory of deeds well done" (236e). C. H. Kahn, in "Plato's Funeral Oration: The Motif of the *Menexenus*," argues that Plato had read Thucydides.

12. E. R. Dodds, *Missing Persons* (Oxford: Oxford University Press, 1977), p. 56—an epigram which seems to fit Thucydides' temperament well.

13. See H. D. Westlake, *Individuals in Thucydides*, chapters 5 and 6, for an analysis of Cleon's and Nicias' character; for the specific debate on Pylos, pp. 69 ff. and p. 88. For Nicias, see below, chapter 8.

14. For the connections between Pericles' first speech and Archidamus' and the Corinthians' last speech, see Rose Zahn, *Die erste Periklesrede*, Borna-Leipzig Diss. Kiel, Noske, 1934, pp. 38 ff.

15. This progression has been mapped out by Jacqueline de Romilly in *Thucydides and Athenian Imperialism* with many astute comments on individual passages. But her conclusions are ultimately, I think, unbalanced and confused. Her chosen theme of Athenian imperialism obscures for her (perhaps inevitably) the fact that in Thucydides' mind *both* sides behave in essentially the same manner (cf. 1.19; 1.76.2; 1.77.7; 1.144.2; the conduct of the Plataean incident; and the Ionian operations, among other passages, for Spartan uses of power). In part 3, chapter 3, "The Theory of Athenian Imperialism," she presents her conclusions with the formulation of three overlapping and competitive laws—political, psychological, and philosophical (pp. 313–43). The political law is that imperialists are hated, and must therefore maintain their empire by force. The psychological law is that imperialists are never satisfied, and proceed to the point of excess, or *hubris*. The philosophical law (pp. 336 ff.) is that the strong always rule the weak. I do not believe myself that a correct reading of Thucydides' text allows much stress to be placed on the second law—*hubris* is a moral category and one that has no very clear place in his scheme of things (see the detailed discussion below in chapter 6, on Melos); the preoccupation is rather with the physical necessities that force disintegration in wartime. But the real trouble with de Romilly's account is that it stops short; she is full of allusions to the underlying common ground of human nature, but does not conduct her argument far enough to show that human na-

ture in fact subsumes all three laws and renders their odd compartmentalization by discipline unnecessary. The regularity of all behavior, and all responses to initial behavior, on all sides has its base in the constancy of human nature and its narrow range of motives, especially fear and self-interest.

16. The notion of the *paralogos*, the incalculable stroke of chance (*tuchē*), is an important one in Thucydides' *History*. It cannot be provided for in any accurate way, but the possibility of such an event must be taken into consideration by any intelligent planner, anticipated with an additional "margin" of preparation, in case it is adverse, and with a readiness to exploit it, if it is favorable. One can see that such a concept is essentially tied to the notion of individuals not fully in control of their situation; but true intelligence knows how to live with it. The subject has been much discussed by recent authors, perhaps most fully and directly by Lowell Edmunds in *Chance and Intelligence in Thucydides*. He proceeds by separating out Spartan and Athenian attitudes to chance, and the corresponding roles of intelligence in confronting it. As Thucydides clearly establishes, Spartans are cautious and Athenians are adventurous. But, as Edmunds shows, there can be interesting inversions of type—the Athenian Nicias, for example, is clearly a Spartan by temperament. But one should beware of too schematic a treatment, and of elevating the twin concepts of chance and intelligence to any architectonic status in the work. Spartan caution does not have to proceed from a philosophical attitude to chance; an agricultural people always has sufficient reason to stay at home. I do not myself find that the Spartan King Archidamus *speculates* differently about chance from Pericles (compare 1.80.1, 82.6 and 84.4, with the introduction to Pericles' first speech, 1.140.1). And Thucydides certainly did not intend the Syracusans' defeat of the Athenians, by approximating the Athenian character (cf. 8.96.5), to constitute a kind of paradoxical "apology" for the Athenian attitude (see Edmunds, p. 142). Some involutions of theory tie their authors in knots.

17. It would be useful to make a distinction between "self-contained" or, by analogy with the philosophic term, "nominalist" passages of narrative, from which no "universals" are to be drawn, and "generic" or "archetypal" narrative, which connects to other episodes and encourages the reader to draw large implications. N. G. L. Hammond, in Stadter's *Speeches in Thucydides*, pp. 49 ff., makes a distinction between the particular and universal in *speeches*, but as we shall see, the "universal" in narrative is often packed with particularity, and other terms seem preferable.

18. Hans-Peter Stahl, in his influential work *Thukydides: Die Stellung des Menschen im Geschichtlichen Prozess*, emphasizes the negative aspects of human nature. He is skillful at detecting the elements of miscalculated action in Thucydides' narrative—human plans not only fall short of their objectives, but often end up achieving exactly the result they were intended to avoid (the Athenians remove the Corinthian magistrates from their colony Potidea, to prevent subversive activity there, and end up with a revolt of the town, which lasts two and one-half years and costs 2,000 talents worth of siege operations to put down). Everywhere

things go awry—the wind blows from the wrong direction, reinforcements miss times of assignation. All of this is an important undercurrent in Thucydides, and no one brings it to light better than Stahl. But it is not the whole *History*, and Stahl, by concentrating on the tyranny of the *paralogos* and the lowest common denominators of human inadequacy, gives the work an unnaturally flat uniformity; by this emphasis he also makes it improbable that human beings could ever accumulate power or build any solid historical achievements—which is clearly further than Thucydides is prepared to go. There are other distortions of the historian's intention. Thus in Phormio's great naval battle against superior numbers off Naupactus (2.85–92), Stahl points to the fact that the Athenian reinforcements were delayed by bad weather off Crete (85.6), that Phormio was forced to do what he had said he had no intention of doing—withdraw to narrow and shallow waters, and that he was only saved by the "accident" of the moored merchantman in the harbor: "Hier neutralisiert ein Zufall die Folgen eines anderen Zufall" (p. 92). He stresses these details at the expense of the real seamanship and discipline involved in an instantaneous and concerted response to the straggling Athenian ship's surprise maneuver. Thucydides intends the reader to gather from this incident a reinforced sense of Athenian naval superiority. Stahl's account of it is misinterpretation of a high order.

19. See Cochrane, *Thucydides and the Science of History*, especially chapters 2 and 3. Although others had noted the resemblances between Hippocrates and Thucydides earlier, Cochrane's book was the first work to explore them thoroughly.

20. Honor (*timē*) is in short supply in the second half of the *History*. For Pericles and Brasidas it was clearly a strong motive. ("From the greatest dangers, the greatest honors are won"—1.144.3; cf. 5.16.1.) After the Peace of Nicias, the noun is only used once (6.16.2), by Alcibiades of the honor that comes to the city from his activities. The city did not appreciate his efforts (6.15.4).

21. The pattern of narrative in the Corcyrean Revolution follows closely that of the Plague, where the general social disintegration is analyzed after the *akribeia* of the clinical details of the disease itself; in the Plataean episode, as we have seen, the moral implications are reserved for a final debate.

22. F. M. Cornford, *Thucydides Mythistoricus*. The work was treated as something of a pariah of scholarship for a long time, no doubt because a philosopher should not dabble in history, and it has been ignored in many bibliographies, though it has had a substantial influence. Cochrane, from his opposite point of view, is generous to it, calling it "a brilliant and powerful argument" (p. 15).

23. They are nonentities to us, and probably to Croesus, but W. W. How and J. Wells, in *A Commentary on Herodotus*, mention that the statues of Cleobis and Biton, and also the inscription which identifies them, have been recovered at Delphi; it is possible that by Herodotus' time they were already invested with philosophical significance in the Greek world, and that Herodotus had Solon refer to a well-known example. How and Wells rightly point out that the definition of happiness in such negative terms is indicative of a profound vein of pessimism that runs throughout Greek thought.

24. According to Diogenes Laertius 1.1.40, Ephorus had said that all the Seven Sages except Thales had met at the court of Croesus. In Herodotus, six of the seven (Periander, Bias, Pittacus, Solon, Chilon, and Thales) appear in various contexts in the first half of book I; but whether or not any comparisons with other sages are intended, Solon the Athenian gives the work its cornerstone of received wisdom.

25. Cochrane, *Thucydides and the Science of History*, p. 15.

26. See Introduction, n. 2.

27. Seth Benardete, in *Herodotean Inquiries* (The Hague: Martinus Nijhoff, 1969), p. 17, says that Herodotus' insertion of the intercalary months "makes the total too large by 700 days." Furthermore he uses Herodotus' later endorsement of *Egyptian* calendar calculations (Hdt. 2.4.1) to conclude that the error is deliberate. I accept the fact of the error, but do not believe it was intentional; the intention is still for *akribeia*.

2. THE PROGRESS OF PESSIMISM IN THUCYDIDES: THE SKETCH OF AN ARGUMENT

1. Felix Jacoby has discussed the ancient ritual, which is described in such detail before the Funeral Oration and gives it such a solemn prelude, in *"Patrios nomos*. State Burial in Athens and the Public Cemetery in the Kerameikos"; he questions the accuracy of Thucydides' account of the practice.

2. For a stylistic commentary on the Funeral Oration, see J. T. Kakridis, *Der Thukydideische Epitaphios*. Denys Page has pointed out the technical vocabulary in the account of the symptoms of the plague in "Thucydides' Description of the Great Plague at Athens"; he counts over forty words that are "unexampled" anywhere else in the *History* in 2.49–50 alone, and relates them to the Hippocratic corpus. But Adam Parry, in "The Language of Thucydides' Description of the Plague," denies that the language is strictly technical, and finds instances of many of the terms in regular, even conversational usage. However, he does not deny that the account of the symptoms, in its detail and precision, wears a scientific aspect. We are certainly at a time before professional terminologies have evolved fully, so I would not feel Page's case had been completely invalidated. But Parry is useful in showing how the account also contains *figurative* language: "Much of the language of the description of the Plague, in fact, suggests that it comes as a military attack" (p. 116—and he lists the words). "The Plague is a pathos, like war, and in fact it is a partner of war" (p. 115)—this is certainly the correct emphasis.

3. Dionysius of Halicarnassus, *Thuc.* 351–352, is extremely incensed that Thucydides should have wasted an oration for ten or fifteen cavalrymen, when there was the great triumph of Pylos or the great disaster of Sicily begging for a speech; but then he would have left the *akmē* of Athens uncelebrated and unlamented. Wilamowitz, in his *Griechisches Lesebuch* (Berlin 1902), 1²:137, says, of the Funeral Oration, that it was written for Athenian democracy.

4. This part of the passage runs as follows (2.52.4–53 *fin.*):

All the burial rites which they had previously observed were thrown into confusion, and everyone buried his dead as best he could. Many turned to shameless devices because of the shortage of necessary materials, caused by the large numbers of those who had died before them. They used pyres intended for others, cremating their corpse before those who had built the pyre could use it, or throwing it on top of one already lit.

(53) Then the disease first produced other kinds of lawlessness and spread it through the city. For a man who had been previously inhibited would more readily dare to act openly as he felt inclined, seeing the catastrophic change from prosperity to sudden death that befell people, with those who had had nothing inheriting their wealth at a stroke. So they thought it right to take their pleasure quickly and to act on whim, seeing that their lives might be as swiftly spent as their money. No one had any inclination to waste effort on building a good reputation, considering that it was by no means certain that he would live to enjoy it. So whatever gave pleasure or served to procure it in any way became accepted as both right and useful. No fear of the gods or human law restrained them, because in their judgment the observance of such things fared no better than neglect, since all alike, as they saw, went uniformly to the wall. Besides, no one expected to live to go on trial or give satisfaction for his crimes, but rather thought a much weightier sentence hung over him, so that it was only natural, before it finally descended, to try to find some pleasure in life.

5. The rest of the relevant passage (3.82.3–83.4) reads as follows:

So revolution spread through the cities, and later attempts, in the awareness of what had gone before, brought a spirit of excess to their initiatives, both in the ingenuity of their plans and the outlandishness of their reprisals. To do justice to their actions, they had to change the regular meaning of words. Mindless daring was considered the courage of a comrade, whereas watchful deliberation was a euphemistic phrase for cowardice; moderation was the mark of unmanliness, and a completely rounded intelligence was completely useless for anything. The art of shock tactics was added to a man's essential skills, and to plot against someone while one was still safe oneself was quite reasonably excused as a preventive measure. The man whose anger always raged was trustworthy, whereas the one who opposed him was suspect. Anyone who had a plot going was obviously intelligent, and one who suspected a plot was cleverer still; but anyone who took the necessary steps to steer clear of such things clearly disrupted his party, and deferred to its opponents. In short, the man who got his blow in first, before another could do the same, was praised, and so was the man who urged such action against someone who had no such intentions. Family relationships were more distant than party ones, because with the latter there was a greater willingness for undertaking indefensible activity; their associations did not exist within the context of the laws of the day, but in a spirit of competition against them, and they cemented their oaths of loyalty to each other not by the divine law, but by their common partnership in some crime. Decent suggestions from the opposition were greeted as something to be actively blocked, if one had the upper hand, and not with any reciprocal generosity. It counted more to take reprisals on someone than to avoid trouble oneself. As for the occasional oaths of armistice, they only exchanged them for an immediate crisis, when they had nothing to fall back on; and on the spur of the moment, a man would get his treachery in first, if he saw the other off his guard, and would relish his vengeance more for violating a trust than if he had acted openly. Survival was the prime consideration, and the one who survived by treachery won the prize for intelligence. Most people would rather be called clever for their villainy, than stupid for their honesty—the latter shames them, but they take real pride in the former. And the cause of all this was the pursuit of power by greed and ambition; and the result was that once they were established in power, their energies were spent on divisiveness. The political leaders on both sides had fine-sounding programs, with stress on democratic equality throughout the state or moderate rule by the best, as though they made the prize a matter of public service; but in fact their whole preoccupation was to get the better of each other, and they stopped at nothing in the way of terror, but took still more excessive reprisals in their stride. They had no concern for the limits which justice or the city's interests dictated, but on each side set their own according to their inclinations; their only aim was to fulfill their immediate ambition for power, whether it called for an unjust vote of condemnation against a rival, or simply for violence. Neither side had any respect for traditional pieties, but whoever managed to perform some atrocity with the semblance of rectitude was highly regarded. Those of the citizens who were neutral were killed by both sides, either because they refused to take part in the struggle, or for jealousy of their immunity.

(83) Thus every form of depravity became established in the Greek world by these revolutions, and simple innocence, of which a noble nature is largely comprised, was ridiculed into oblivion. They armored themselves in attitudes of mistrust against each other and made it pervasive, and there was no argument strong enough or oath fearful enough to dissolve it; and everyone who had the edge in strength calculated that the prospect of true security was hopeless, and took steps to avoid harm rather than relying on trust. Those with weaker intelligence on the whole fared better: they were afraid of their own inferiority and the intelligence of their opponents; they feared they might get the worse in the planning and be outmaneuvered by their enemy's versatile strategies, so they went boldly and promptly into action. Whereas those who were complacent, and saw no need for thinking ahead

and fulfilling in action the possibilities they could envisage, were destroyed with their defenses down.

6. The concept of necessity (*anagkē*) is an important one in fifth-century thought, especially as a cosmological principle. Guthrie, in *A History of Greek Philosophy*, 3:99–101, gives a brief and useful comment on its range. He shows that it had become a vogue word of philosophical jargon, as we see in the play on it in Aristophanes' *Clouds*, where the Unjust Argument says he is present for "the necessities of nature," referring to the problems occasioned by committing adultery and getting caught (1075–76). Thucydides certainly does not apply the concept with strict philosophical consistency; though history follows a pattern, "the necessities" of war work upon the passions of "most people," not of all (3.82.2). But there is clearly enough determinism in the historical process to make his projections valid for the future, and his history useful to posterity: great powers will necessarily come into conflict, and once involved in conflict, people will be forced into destructive choices and actions. These are the layers of necessity associated with war, which give this book its title.

7. It is the strong resonance of passages like this that leads to Andrewes' conclusion that "[Thucydides'] feeling that the power of Athens was somehow admirable seems to me beyond question" (Gomme, *A Historical Commentary on Thucydides*, 4:186); earlier he has commented: "Thucydides cannot be taken as merely hostile to Athenian imperialism: the rhetoric of (e.g.) ii. 64.3 is too warm, his regret (even exasperation) at Athens' eventual defeat too evident at ii.65" (*ibid.*, p. 184).

8. This kind of paradox has a long history in Greek thought, dating back at least to Hesiod, *Works and Days*, 11 ff., where he distinguishes a good and a bad Strife (*Eris*), the one making a man compete industriously with his neighbor for prosperity and the other making him lazy and prone to political contention. Isocrates, in the *Peace*, 28–35, makes a distinction between the right and wrong sort of *pleonexia* (ambition or greed), though he uses verb forms (*pleon echein* or *pleonektein*) rather than the abstract noun. For further references, see de Romilly, *Thucydides and Athenian Imperialism*, pt. 3, especially ch. 3.

9. I believe this question is properly answered only in book VIII; see Chapter 9 below.

10. In the preceding chapter (1.75.3), the three motives are put in a chronological order, in their influence on the formation of the Athenian empire: it also seems to be in order of *cogency*—fear comes first, followed by honor, with self-interest last. As we have seen, later history eliminates honor almost completely.

11. Some simple statistics will reveal the shift in technique most clearly. There are 106 named individuals in book I, 101 in book IV, and 91 in book VIII. Even with these unqualified totals, on the relative lengths of the three books there is a higher incidence of individual names in book VIII than the other two; there are 146 chapters in book I, 135 in book IV, and only 109 in book VIII. But the differences are not perhaps strong enough to be statistically significant. They

become so if we look for *actual historical agents* in the work, as opposed to names used merely for dating purposes, as a list of signatories to a document, as patronymics to other names, or mythical names. If we remove these latter categories, the final totals we arrive at are 73 for book I, 68 for book IV, and 83 for book VIII. (The three books in question provide both the highest qualified and unqualified figures.) Given the different lengths of the three books, these last totals are clearly significant. If one was to do a more sensitive evaluation, and notice where individual names were merely syntactically parenthetic, instead of being the subject or object of action, which remains collective (e.g. "the *Athenians* invaded Boeotia, *with Myronides as general*"), the balance would favor book VIII even more. I am grateful to Mr. Kenneth Rothwell for help with these and other Thucydidean statistics.

12. Thucydides clearly endorses the Spartan argument, and blames the continuation of the war on Cleon and on the insatiable Athenian appetite for further conquest. The word *oregomai* (grasp for something) is used exclusively of *unjustified* ambition by Thucydides. The crucial nature and timing of the Spartan speech were noted by Finley, *Thucydides*, pp. 193 ff.: he calls it "the dead center of the *History*."

13. Hans-Peter Stahl, among others, would resist the notion of the transition from a relatively controlled war to an uncontrolled one. Most of his work, *Thukydides: Die Stellung des Menschen im Geschichtlichen Prozess*, concentrates on the Archidamian War (431–421 B.C.), and at no point within it can human enterprise be said to control events. But I believe my argument is valid. If one begins at the middle point, the Peace of Nicias, and attends closely to what is left of book V and to book VIII, there appears an evident shift in the author's interest. He insists that war still goes on, but a higher proportion of the incidents he describes has nothing to do with attempts to win it; in both books, more time is spent on diplomatic moves, or personal moves, for security against the hostile background of the war. There are no generals in these books who take commanding initiatives and enjoy the glory of success in battle—or at least Thucydides does not highlight their efforts as he did for Phormio and Brasidas.

The Sicilian expedition is indeed a bold initiative, though it should probably be regarded as an extension of the war rather than an attempt to win it. More importantly, the focus on the defeatist spirit of Nicias transforms the account of the expedition very close to its midway point (7.6.4 is where the balance tips downwards) into precisely the kind of uncontrolled climate of helplessness that I am urging for the second half of the work as a whole. As noted in my text, books VI and VII in their organization could be considered a microcosm of the whole.

14. I have been arguing for a planned and deliberate recession through the work, down to the named individuals in book VIII. There are other examples in Thucydides of exactly this kind of controlled recession. The first is the very slow movement through book I towards the formal introduction of Pericles at 1.127.1 (we should not count the parenthetic references to him in the Pentecontaetia—the reader in those passages has no way of knowing whether he is still involved,

or even alive). That means that, although Athens has been embroiled in the action leading up to the war since 1.31, for very nearly one hundred chapters we do not have the name of an active Athenian politician. Another example would be the structure of Pericles' Funeral Oration, and the way in which *ad gentem* points are scored against Sparta, although the Spartans are not actually named until 2.39.2. Before that point is reached, we have been told that the Athenians are an autochthonous people (36.1), that they have a constitution that is their own and not an imitation of other people's (37.1), that they preserve relaxed social relations (37.2), and that they refrain from excessive regimentation and expulsion of foreigners (39.1). With all these points scored anonymously, but increasingly close to the bone, the name of the enemy finally bursts on the page. Gomme, over these passages, is wrong to discount the deliberateness of this staged progression to the particular—rhetorically it has the effect of a suspense device.

15. One should perhaps exclude Hermocrates from this group: his preoccupation is limited to getting the pay that was contracted, but for his men and not only himself (8.45.3; cf. 8.29.2). In the end, he is exiled by Syracuse, but not before he has perceived Tissaphernes' destructive tactics (8.85.2–4). For the others, see chapters 7–9.

16. The eighth book has seemed anomalous since antiquity. Marcellinus mentions that various people have dubbed it spurious altogether, or attributed it to Xenophon or Thucydides' daughter (*Vita*, 43). He rejects these possibilities himself, but while defending it as the work of Thucydides, concedes that it was written when he was "running down" (*arrōstōn*—44). Eduard Schwartz, in *Das Geschichtswerk des Thukydides*, calls it a "series of not even well-connected outlines" (p. 90), and argues for an editor. Jacqueline de Romilly, in *Histoire et raison chez Thucydide*, p. 84, notes the high incidence of personal narrative, but calls it the least elaborate of the books, and suggests that Thucydides may have been bothered by the complexity of events he had to cover. John Finley seems to see the book as something of an anticlimax: "Had Thucydides lived to complete his work he would no doubt have risen to a final climax" (*Thucydides*, pp. 246–47). For a full discussion of the differences in book VIII, and their possible explanations, see Kurt von Fritz, *Die Griechische Geschichtsschreibung*, 1:757 ff.

3. THE ARCHAEOLOGY (1.1–23)

1. Thucydides' "inflation" (*auxēsis*) of his subject matter seems at first sight particularly disingenuous, in view of what his war will degenerate into: is he being ironic with his reader? We will see that before the Archaeology is over the conception of "the greatest of all wars between the Greeks" has already been defined in terms of the suffering it caused (see 1.23.1–3, and note 3 below). The best treatment of this *auxēsis*, setting it alongside the opening of Hecataeus' and Antiochus' works, as well as Herodotus', is found in Eugen Täubler's *Die Archaeologie des Thukydides*, pp. 96 ff. See also Gomme, *A Historical Commentary on Thucydides*, ad loc. We should remember that at the outset, whatever happened

later, Thucydides based his prognosis of the greatness of the war on the fact that both sides were "at their peak," and he clearly found it impressive.

2. The convention established by the Catalogue in the *Iliad* is that the count is given just before the two sides converge. This is observed by Herodotus: although various numerical calculations have been made previously, the full count of Xerxes' force is withheld until Xerxes, with proper drumroll of patronymic, arrives at Thermopylae at the head of 5,283,220 men (7.186.2). Thucydides also delays his count of Athenian strength, deferring it to the point where the Peloponnesians are mustering at the isthmus (2.13.1); Pericles, at that point, "at the time of action," as he had promised (1.144.2), reports on Athenain resources, and includes financial assets among them. The epic effect of large numbers is not confined to the Greek tradition. The Irish writer Flan O'Brien does a fine satire on the same patterns in Celtic legends, when he has Finn MacCool make "a humorous, or quasi-humorous incursion into ancient mythology," and give the physical dimensions of the heroes in his seven companies (*At Swim-two-birds*, New York: Viking, 1967, pp. 16 ff.).

3. N. G. L. Hammond, in "The Arrangement of the Thought in the Proem and in Other Parts of Thucydides I," does a careful analysis of the logic of the argument and concludes that 1–19 of the Archaeology belongs to an early strand of writing, leaving the methodological chapters to a later stage, and thus severing the "positive" view of the greatness of the war, from the more negative aspects stressed at 1.23.1–3. I do not know whether the Archaeology was written at one or more periods, but I see no need to separate one strand of thought from another as though there were a contradiction between the two. The positive aspect proceeds from his projection (*elpisas*) of the scope of the war, based on his knowledge of the resources available to each side; the final judgment is based on the actual events of the war. Both could be left side by side. Hammond does not want the word *kinēsis* to have any negative connotation (1.1.2), but translates it simply as "movement."

4. Gomme, *ad loc.*, gives the references to this question in the *Odyssey:* Telemachus arriving at Nestor's house (*Od.* 3.71–74); Odysseus at Polyphemus' (9.251–255). When he lands at Scheria, there is a small inversion: on waking up the traveler asks himself whether he has landed among savages (6.119, and also again on arriving home in Ithaca—13.200–1); at his appearance, Nausicaa's retinue flees, leaving her to face him alone, and she might be expected to put the question to him again, but he forestalls her with misinformation and flattery (6.149 ff.).

5. It is perhaps notable that the development of thalassocracy is followed with an attention to individuals that is not matched in the account of the development of Peloponnesian land power. After Minos, we have references to Ameinocles of Corinth, the first shipbuilder (1.13.3), Polycrates of Samos (1.13.6), and Themistocles (1.14.3). We shall find Themistocles closely associated with Pericles, who strongly insists on the uses of sea power, and takes his place in this line of development as the builder of a maritime empire—as it turns out, the last in the line.

6. Tyranny at its first appearance has a quietist character, and Thucydides is always insistent on the gentleness of the tyrant regime at Athens, which he uses as an example of the errors of popular opinion (1.20.2; cf. 6.53–59: the latter passage is sensitively analyzed by Hans-Peter Stahl, *Thukydides*, in his first chapter).

7. The phenomenon of polarity in Thucydides' world is discussed in Peter J. Fliess' *Thucydides and the Politics of Bipolarity*. Although he has brief sections on bipolarity "as a psychological reality" (pp. 22 ff.) and on the inevitability of the war (pp. 66 ff.), he does not really grapple with Thucydides' text, or put such considerations in the full context of his theory of history. But the notion of complete, "exclusive" polarity is an important and neglected one.

8. Much of this progression is noted, though briefly, in Adam Parry's "Thucydides' Historical Perspective," though he does not comment on the importance of *stasis*. But overall, of all the writing in this area, I find this article comes closest to my own position. Parry was certainly not afraid of the large idea: "War is the final reality. There can be no civilization, no complex of power without war, because the one word implies the other" (p. 58).

9. The fact that the Archaeology traces the development of *Greece*, for the most part, as a whole, and puts some weight on the notion of *stasis*, raises the question of whether or not Thucydides looks on the war as a *civil* war, from a Panhellenist perspective. This might give special point to the sad incident at Plataea—the last place where most of the Greeks had fought on the same side, and to Melesippus' prediction at the moment of the Spartan invasion of Attica: "This day will be the beginning of great evils for the Hellenes" (2.12.2). One could also point to the various appeals to Hellenic customs (e.g. the discussion about propriety of occupying sacred places in wartime, and the universal right to retrieve one's dead—4.98.2 and 8). But this path will not take us very far. Panhellenism did not really gain currency as an idea until the very end of the fifth century (see Klaus Bringman, *Studien zu den politischen Ideen des Isokrates*, Hypomnemata [1965], 14:19–27 for its early history), and Thucydides cannot have entertained it seriously. He is too impressed with the fragility of the structure of the individual *polis* to consider it plausible that the whole of Greece should preserve a harmonious unity. Larger ethnic loyalties (Ionian and Dorian) may be appealed to in rhetorical contexts (e.g. 5.9.1), but they may also be discounted: at the Battle of Miletus in 412, Ionian Milesians and Dorian Peloponnesians fought against Dorian Argives and Ionian Athenians, and Thucydides notes the unusual conjunction and also that the action went against form, with soft Ionians winning both encounters (8.25.3–5). The fact is that Thucydides has seen beyond all accidental identities or differences to the common roots of human nature, and he clearly considers that the two blocs which Athens and Sparta assembled are as large as humanity can contrive, before it sets about destroying them. In the last analysis, the common human nature that we share is what can be relied on to keep us apart.

4. COLLECTIVE ACTION TO THE POINT OF WAR

1. Mabel Lang, in "Thucydides and the Epidamnian Affair," *Classical World* (1968), 61:173–76, goes into the details of these interactions, and finds some anomalies in the Corinthian behavior, which make her ask whether Thucydides has not slanted his account to put them in a bad light.

2. Donald Kagan, in *The Outbreak of the Peloponnesian War*, pp. 208–9, argues that Corcyra was *democratic* at the time of this dispute, because she certainly was at the time of its revolution in 427 B.C. I reject the argument. It is quite possible that the fact of the alliance with Athens produced an unrecorded, perhaps peaceful, swing to democracy; Athens would certainly have aided such a move, and might have urged it as proof of good will to herself. The argument from silence speaks fairly strongly for an oligarchy in 435: if Corcyra had been democratic surely she would have used the fact in her appeal to Athens for help against oligarchic Corinth, playing on ideological sympathy and the need for solidarity. But the speakers do nothing of the sort.

3. The debate that is given us between the Cocrcyreans and the Corinthians, the first in the work (1.32–43), brings into focus this pivotal point in Greek international relations, at which Athens, confident that war is inevitable, feels compelled to extend her influence by an alliance, but the alliance itself deepens the tensions and makes the prospect of war likelier. We may see some deliberate irony in the fact that, although the war will be seen as proceeding from Athens' treatment of her allies, and will in fact pose on one side as a crusade of liberation from that treatment, the first scene that explores the relationship between metropolis and "dependent" colony is one that involves Athens only as an outsider being appealed to for help (which was the way she built her empire—see Alcibiades at 6.18.2). Corinth is shown in this episode as having the same imperial instincts as Athens herself, and casts her speech in the debate as one ruling power to another: "We say in return that we never settled them as colonists to be insulted by them, but to remain their leaders and receive a reasonable respect from them" (1.38.2).

4. The shift in the spectrum of advantage (*ōphelia*) from altruism to self-interest in this speech was explored in my "Thucydides and Pericles" (Ph.D. diss., Columbia University, 1969).

5. There is also another progression worth noting in the speech, in the concept of "worthiness"—the Athenians become more assertive as they proceed. Having stated at the outset rather mildly that their city is "worthy of note" (*axia logou*—1.73.1), they enter the main body of their argument and claim first negatively that they "do not deserve to be so unpopular" (*axioi . . . mē houtōs agan epiphthonōs diakeisthai*—1.75.1); they next say that they inherited their empire and consider themselves "worthy" of it (1.76.2); and finally they say they actually deserve *praise* for the manner in which they conduct themselves (*epaineisthai te axioi*—1.76.3).

6. The exact legal point at issue between Athens and Sparta does not receive much attention: the Athenians base their indictment of Sparta on the fact that

she has refused arbitration on the outstanding differences as specified by the treaty (see Pericles, at 1.140.2). The Spartan position is that Athens has committed a substantial violation of the terms of the treaty (she actually engaged in battle with Corinthian ships during the Corcyrean incident—1.49.7), that this is technically an *adikia*, and that such violation nullifies (*luein* is the technical word, "to loose") the terms of the treaty. All of this was argued, with examples from other treaties, in my "Thucydides and Pericles." The terms of the original thirty-year truce have been reconstructed, and can be found in H. Bengtson, *Die Staats-verträge der Altertums* (Munich/Berlin: 1962 Beck), no. 139 (IG I² 19). Thucydides says at 7.18.2 that the Spartans felt they had been in the wrong to reject arbitration: I am not sure they were.

7. The causality of the Peloponnesian War, and Thucydides' account of it, have been endlessly debated in this century. Thucydides himself distinguishes between the *aitiai* (causes of complaint) and the *prophasis* (the root cause, which is called "the truest but least evident"). Attempts have been made to link this distinction to Hippocratic usage, and it is true that the Hippocratic works use *prophasis*, at least, in the sense of "cause" (see Cochrane, *Thucydides and the Science of History*, p. 17). The essential point for us is that whether one agrees with Thucydides' account or not, there is no formal contradiction in it. The *aitiai* are not causes in any *effective* sense: after he has given his account of the affairs at Epidamnus and Potidea, he says, "The war did not yet break out" (1.66). The latest extensive additions to the long bibliography on the subject are Donald Kagan's *The Outbreak of the Peloponnesian War*, especially chapter 19, and G. E. M. de Ste Croix's *The Origins of the Peloponnesian War*, chapters 2 and 7.

5. PERICLES

1. Gomme, *Commentary* 1:446–47, finds most of this material out of place: "The whole excursus on Themistokles is irrelevant to the narrative, and so is the greater part of those on Kylon and Pausanias." He thinks Thucycides here "betrays a strong biographical interest," which elsewhere he "sternly represses."

2. Herodotus does mention in passing the removal of the hegemony from Sparta, following Pausanias' arrogance (*hubris*), at 8.3.2, but he does not mention his subsequent disgrace: his great triumph at Plataea still lies far ahead of us in the text.

3. For the demagogic phase of Pericles' career, Plutarch is the best source. In Plutarch's *Life*, a combination of factors—his unfortunate resemblance to the tyrant Pisistratus, the aloofness of his temperament, and the need to protect himself from the consequences of these traits—and the fact that the conservative Cimon dominates the political scene—induce Pericles to enter public life on the far left (Plut. *Per.* ch. 7). He stays there through Cimon's life and through the opposition of Thucydides, son of Melesias, who is finally eliminated in a contest for ostracism (*ibid.* 14), and who by his departure leaves Pericles room to move to the center. Thucydides' (the historian's) portrait of him has him consistently

there from the start, and allows nothing to obscure the image of him as a responsible moderate.

4. Many authors have noted Athenian interest in the West, which finds no mention in Thucydides, apart from the casual statement that they made their defensive alliance with Corcyra because it lay on the route to Italy and Sicily, among other reasons (1.44.3). Plutarch refers to "that sick passion and ill-fated craving" for Sicily, which seized the Athenian people (*Per.* 20.3) and dates it early (in the sequence of events it must appear about 450 B.C.), and though he says that Pericles resisted such urges, as the people's man he must have been vulnerable to them, and his past record would keep him vulnerable through his career. The first sign of Athenian interest in the West must on any chronology be the treaty with Egesta in Sicily, which Russell Meiggs and David Lewis, *A Selection of Greek Historical Inscriptions* (Oxford: Oxford University Press, 1969), now date tentatively to 458/7. For a discussion of this and other events in the trend, see Donald Kagan, *The Outbreak of the Peloponnesian War*, pp. 154 ff.

5. In my dissertation I was troubled, like others, by Cleon's plagiarism of Pericles. The use of such a phrase as "I am the same as I always was" (3.38.1; cf. 2.61.2), the comparison of the empire to a tyranny (3.37.2; 2.63.2), and the remarkable verb *andragathizesthai* (3.40.4; 2.63.2—"to play the philanthropist") clearly catch the reader's attention and are intended to. These duplications seemed to me possibly a cynical device of the author's, leading us to draw the conclusion that if Pericles and Cleon can use the same language, then anybody can say anything, and under pressure is quite likely to. But I now think that this underestimates the author's respect for his readers. It is precisely because he is confident that the readers will perceive that Pericles and Cleon are totally opposite types in their character and priorities (differences that are established at least in part by the speeches themselves), that he can count on them not to see these echoes as disparaging to Pericles, or to the nature of speech itself, but merely to Cleon.

6. Eduard Schwartz, in *Das Geschichtswerk des Thukydides*, saw a strong polemical strain of writing, designed to protect Pericles' name, superimposed by Thucydides over an earlier draft. In my "Thucydides and Pericles" I also found the polemical intention dominant, though I did not see any inconsistencies with other parts of the work. It is still clear to me that Pericles is a very protected character in the work, but having widened my horizons to embrace the rest of Thucydides' text, I no longer believe that protecting Pericles' name is the only, or even the major, preoccupation in his mind.

7. Plutarch's *Life* is extremely useful in its frequent citation of the comic poets, now lost, who give us the flavor of the political climate of the day. Thus from one point of view, the "Olympian," who thundered, stayed remote, but monopolized the government, is a conservative figure, perhaps with pretensions to tyranny: trading on his resemblance to the tyrant, the comedians refer to his party as "the new Pisistratidae" (Plut. *Per.*, 16.1). On the other hand, the spendthrift, crowd-pleasing demagogue, whom Thucydides son of Melesias had campaigned

against, is the Pericles we find in Plato's *Gorgias* 515e: "For I hear that Pericles made the Athenians lazy and cowardly, garrulous and mercenary, by putting them first on the dole." The demagogic title of *prostates*, which Thucydides withholds from him, is given to him by Aristotle (*Politics* 1274a4). Thucydides' own title of "First Man" is stressed by E. Bayer, "Thukydides und Perikles," *Würzburger Jahrbücher* (1948) 3:1–57. Bayer, though he does not mention Cornford, is impressed with the tragic influence on the portrayal of Pericles, and sees him as Ajax.

8. Herodotus is unfriendly to Themistocles. He says that he was bribed by the Euboeans with thirty talents to make a stand at Artemisium, after the Greeks showed signs of being intimidated by the size of the Persian force (Hdt. 8.4.2), and that after the victory at Salamis he dissuaded the Greeks from pursuing the Persian king, to store up Persian credit for himself in the future (8.109–110).

9. H. T. Wade-Gery, in the article "Thucydides," *Oxford Classical Dictionary* (Oxford University Press, 1949), p. 902.

6. MELOS

1. It seems possible that the relationship between *character* and *power* in this argument plays upon a pair of correlative Hippocratic terms. W. H. S. Jones, in *Philosophy and Medicine in Ancient Greece*, defines the terms thus:

> The word *dunamis*, besides its ordinary meaning of "strength" or "force" and its Aristotelian meaning of "potentiality" as opposed to "actuality," has in the writings of the fifth century B.C. a special and technical signification, which for modern minds at least is not easy to understand.
>
> A really existent entity, any truly real thing, manifests its nature (*phusis*) to our perceptive faculties through its *dunamis*, or perhaps its *dunameis*. A *dunamis* is a property of a body considered as having the power to act or be acted upon, or, as Plato puts it in the *Phaedrus* (270c,d), the *phusis* of a thing may be discovered by examining its power of *poiein* (acting) and *paschein* (being acted upon). (pp. 93–96)

See also H. W. Miller, "Dynamis and Physis in *On Ancient Medicine*," *Transactions of the American Philological Association* (1952), 83:184–97. Thucydides connects the two terms in the phrase "by the power of his nature" at 1.138.3, speaking of Themistocles.

2. A. W. Gomme, *A Historical Commentary on Thucydides*, 4:187.

3. The compound form of *exēgeito*, and the balance of two verbs in the sentence, make it likely that Thucydides is talking of an *aggressive* policy in the one (*exēgeito*—he led them *out*), and a *defensive* or domestic one in the other (*diephulaxen*—he protected them).

4. F. M. Cornford, *Thucydides Mythistoricus*, pp. 182–83: "As we read the dialogue, the impression deepens that the speaker is out of his right mind. We can, moreover, put a name to the special form of his madness, which shows the peculiar symptoms of a state classed, perhaps rightly, by the Greeks as patholog-

ical. The two notes in it are Insolence (*hubris*) and Blindness (*atē*, in the subjective sense)."

5. Gomme in his note at 3.82.2 insists on "teacher of violence," and adds "so that violence within a state is a natural consequence of war between states." But in his translation of the whole passage, book 1, 383–86, he translates the phrase as "violent taskmaster." John H. Finley, in his *Thucydides*, also goes both ways: at p. 160, in citing the particular passage, he uses "teacher of violence," but in his translation at p. 183 he uses "harsh teacher," which I have used myself. Striking though the phrase "teacher of violence" is, and close to Thucydides' thinking overall, I don't believe it is a philologically correct translation of the present phrase: in Greek, disciplines are not conveyed by adjectives modifying "teacher."

6. In Priam's plea to Hector, women are dragged off to slavery, but small children have their brains dashed out. Andromache, in her lament, *Il.* 24.725 ff., sees slavery for wives and children, with danger to Astyanax from some Greek whose family was bereaved by Hector.

7. This argument was explored by A. Andrewes, in "The Melian Dialogue and Perikles' Last Speech."

8. Donald Lateiner, in "Heralds and Corpses in Thucydides," comments in detail on this passage and relates Thucydides' agnosticism to it.

9. *Apragmosunē* (noninterference) and its obverse *polupragmosunē* (meddlesomeness, or a policy of intervention or imperialism) are political slogans, taken from the debates of the day. The Spartan equivalent of *apragmosunē* is *hēsuchia* (literally "quietness"), which is treated as a set policy by the Corinthians in their first speech at Sparta (1.71.1). But immediately before this, they have spoken of the inadequacy of Sparta's reactions in the face of the Athenians who regard *apragmona hēsuchian* ("an idle quiet," or "noninterfering laissez faire") as a misfortune no less than "the most laborious toil" (1.70.8 and 9). For *apragmosunē*, see W. Nestle's article on it in *Philologus* (1925), NF 35:129–40: he tends to limit it to a philosophical circle, which seems excessively narrow. Leo Strauss, in *The City and Man*, pp. 139 ff., sees Thucydides' *History* as favorable to the Spartan notion of *hēsuchia*. For *polupragmosunē*, see Victor Ehrenberg, "Polypragmosyne: A Study in Greek Politics."

10. For the popularity of Athens with her empire, see G. E. M. de Ste Croix, "The Character of the Athenian Empire," and more recently his book, *The Origins of the Peloponnesian War*; for a view corresponding more closely to Thucydides' own, see D. W. Bradeen, "The Popularity of the Athenian Empire."

7. ALCIBIADES: A PATRIOT FOR HIMSELF

1. Gomme, *Commentary*, 4:242–45.

2. Alcibiades leaves Sparta with the Spartan admiral Chalcideus and only five ships (8.12.3). They are successful in buttressing their forces by persuading first Chios and Erythrae to revolt from Athens (8.14.2), and then Clazomenae (14.3); soon afterwards Alcibiades' influence is instrumental in getting Miletus to revolt

(8.17.2–3). Miletus is where he first comes in contact with Tissaphernes (8.26.3): from that point he is on his way.

3. With the Oxford text I read *prōton* and not *prōtos;* the latter would have a more favorable sense for Alcibiades: "Alcibiades was the first at that time to perform . . ."

4. Gomme, Commentary, 4:366. The language at the end of this quotation is erotic, though not perhaps with the explicit connotation of Pericles' *erastai* in the Funeral Oration (2.43.1), but it serves to remind us that Pericles is the only other person in the work who uses the word *philopolis* (2.60.5). It does not so remind N. M. Pusey ("Alcibiades and *to philopoli*"), however, though he does manage a few gnomic remarks: "And finally Pericles. It is not easy to know what to say of him in view of the great success the Greek genius for idealizing achieved in his portrait. . . . For the rest can it not perhaps be said that patriotism is clearly inconsistent with divinity" (p. 228).

5. The instability of Alcibiades is the characteristic most stressed by Jean Hatzfeld in his book *Alcibiade*—"un personnage aussi inégal et aussi variable" (p. 356).

6. Dionysus explains the situation for Aeschylus and Euripides, who are to answer the question, and seems to suggest that the majority at Athens want Alcibiades to return: "She (the city) longs for him and hates him, and wants to have him (back)" (Aristophanes, *Frogs,* 1425). Euripides' judgment seems to conform to our hypothesis 1 above; he finds Alcibiades "resourceful for himself but impossible for the city" (1429).

8. INDIVIDUALS IN THE TOILS OF WAR: NICIAS AND PHRYNICHUS

1. Nicias' career is followed by H. D. Westlake, *Individuals in Thucydides*, in two stages, in chapters 6 and 11. Westlake's methodology proceeds from his assumptions concerning the *History's* composition, before the Peace of Nicias and after; I don't believe his premises are sound.

2. Lowell Edmunds, commenting on this passage in his *Chance and Intelligence in Thucydides*, calls Nicias' action "a characteristically negative daring" (p. 111). Edmunds also sees Nicias' character as "Spartan," but does not make much use of Thucydides' contrast of him with Brasidas, as an inversion of national types. For the whole treatment, see pp. 109–42.

3. Dover praises Nicias' technical competence in retreat in Gomme, *Commentary* 4:462.

4. Phrynichus' career is followed in part by Westlake, *Individuals in Thucydides*, pp. 242–47.

9. HUMAN NATURE AT WAR IN THUCYDIDES

1. The source of the trouble in the human individual is most apparent at 3.82.8, where the evils are traced to the leaders' ambition and greed, exactly as

they are in the summary of Pericles' career, and in the oligarchic revolution (8.89.3).

2. In his elevation of war to an essential tendency of nature, Thucydides could draw on a long philosophical tradition. We might single out Heraclitus for his stress on the cosmic principle of War or Strife. Fragment 53 says "War is the father of all and king of all," and the same line seems to be maintained in fragment 80: "One should know that war is common, and justice is strife. . . ." For a discussion of these fragments, see W. K. C. Guthrie, *A History of Greek Philosophy*, 1:446–49. Guthrie sees a strong reaction by Heraclitus against Pythagoras and others: "The kernel of Heraclitus' quarrel with other thinkers seems to lie in his revolt against their ideal of a peaceful and harmonious world. This was in particular the ideal of Pythagoras" (p. 448). The philosophy of Empedocles also makes use of the principle of Strife (*Neikos*), balancing and counteracting the work of Love, as a principle of differentiation in the formation of the cosmos. His stress on the concepts of Necessity and Chance also finds Thucydidean echoes (see chapter 2, note 6). We should emphasize that with the philosophers these principles are *cosmic* forces; Thucydides as a historian reduces them in scope to principles governing *human action*. The notion of a principle of alienation inherent in nature recurs at intervals in the history of philosophy, including the age of Hobbes. One example from Jacob Boehme, *Mysterium Pansophicum*, 6.1: "When we consider and take cognizance of ourselves, we find the opposition of all essences, each being the loathing of the other, and enemy to the other." Boehme dates his revelation May 8, 1620. (See Jacob Boehme, *Six Theosophic Points* [Ann Arbor, Mich.: University of Michigan Press], p. 150.)

3. The Peloponnesian War did eventually reach an end, and Thucydides lived to see it, though he evidently did not live to record it. It is perhaps worth asking what sort of finish he intended to give his account, and what sort of moral he intended to suggest, if any. The war finally had a winner, and it is possible that we have the hint of a final judgment, in his aside that "the Chians, *next to the Spartans*, combined success with moderation better than anyone else" (8.24.4). In that case, the traditional Spartan virtue of *sōphrosunē* would have reasserted itself at the end. While indulging such veins of speculation, we could go further, and consider whether Thucydides intended to find in the character of Lysander a new embodiment of that virtue, balancing the moderate King Archidamus at the beginning. Plutarch, in the comparison of Lysander with Sulla, finds him "*sōphrōn* and Spartan" (*Comparatio*, 3.1; cf. 5.5), but in the *Life* itself, we see cruelty and arrogance and no "measure" (*metron*) to his vengeance (Plut. *Lys.* 19.1). However Thucydides intended to proceed, it would have required considerable ascent from the nadir we reach on all sides in book VIII, to give his work a positive ending.

APPENDIX: HUMAN NATURE IN HOBBES

1. As one would expect, we have better documentation for the intellectual background of Hobbes than Thucydides, including the verse autobiography and

his friend John Aubrey's *Life* (see notes 6 and 7 below). In some ways he was a late starter, his career only finding its direction after he was forty (1628—the year his translation of Thucydides was published). Before that he had been the favored secretary of Francis Bacon, in the latter's final years (c. 1621–26). He was extremely excited and strongly influenced by geometry, after first lighting upon Euclid's theorems apparently while he was tutor to the son of Sir Gervase Clifton in Paris (1629–31). But unquestionably the most intense period of personal formation was a later visit to the continent (1634–37), during which he worked closely with Mersenne, was exposed to Descartes' philosophy, and visited Galileo in his forced retirement outside Florence. By the end of this period, his own political theories were taking shape.

2. David Grene, ed., Hobbes' translation of Thucydides (Ann Arbor, Mich.: University of Michigan Press, 1959); the edition does not include Hobbes' introductory letters or chapter.

3. R. Schlatter, *Hobbes' Thucydides*, p. xxi.

4. All references to Hobbes will be to book and chapter heading and to article, where it is given. I have used C. B. Macpherson's edition of *Leviathan* (Baltimore, Md.: Pelican Books, 1968), taking the liberty of modernizing the spelling, but leaving the punctuation intact.

5. Hobbes wrote his dedicatory epistle of *De Cive* in November 1641. I have used the Doubleday Anchor edition, *Man and Citizen*, edited by Bernard Gert (Garden City, N.Y., 1972).

6. Aubrey's *Brief Lives*, written over a tumultuous career, are available edited by Oliver Lawson Dick (Ann Arbor, Mich.: University of Michigan Press, 1962, or Baltimore, Md.: Penguin Books, 1972); Aubrey knew Hobbes and corresponded with him. The story of the Armada is noted in Hobbes' own *Vita* in Latin elegiacs, first published at the end of 1679, and followed by an English verse translation at the beginning of 1680:

> For Fame had rumor'd that a Fleet at Sea
> Would cause our Nation's Catastrophe:
> And hereupon it was my Mother dear
> Did bring forth Twins at once, both me, and Fear.

7. The relevant lines on Thucydides read as follows in the verse translation:

> . . . but of all these
> There's none that pleas'd me like Thucydides.
> He says Democracy's a foolish thing,
> Than a Republic wiser is one King.
> This Author I taught English, that even he
> A guide to Rhetoricians might be.

8. *The Elements of Law*, edited by Ferdinand Tönnies (Cambridge: Cambridge University Press, 1929), was first published in 1650, but it is the earliest in composition of the three works: the dedicatory epistle is dated May 9, 1640. The no-

tion of the state of nature as war is already fully elaborated—see part 1, chapters 14–19. Tönnies prints as an appendix to the *Elements* "A short tract on first principles," which he discovered among Hobbes' papers and dates "as early as the year 1630." The influence of Hobbes' geometrical and scientific work is very evident in this list of principles, but there is no trace of Thucydides.

9. Leo Strauss, *The Political Philosophy of Hobbes* (Oxford: Oxford University Press, 1936, reprinted Chicago: University of Chicago Press, 1963), interestingly minimizes the scientific influence on Hobbes, and says that the formation of his political theories drew more heavily on his personal observations and experience and his readings of history: "Political philosophy is independent of natural science because its principles are not borrowed from any science, but are provided by experience, by the actual experience which everyone has of himself, or, to put it more accurately, are discovered by the efforts of self-knowledge and the self-examination of everyone" (ch. 2, p. 7). In chapter 6 Strauss comes to the influence of *history*. He uses Hobbes' Introduction to his Thucydides translation heavily (see Michael Oakeshott, *Hobbes on Civil Association* [Berkeley, Calif.: University of California Press, 1975, p. 140]: "He extracts all, and perhaps more than all, that can be got from the introduction"), but he does not comment on the formation of the concept of the state of nature.

SELECT BIBLIOGRAPHY

Adcock, F. E. *Thucydides and his History*. Cambridge: Cambridge University Press, 1963.

Andrewes, A. "The Melian Dialogue and Perikles' Last Speech." *Proceedings of the Cambridge Philological Society* (1960), NS 6:1–10.

Bradeen, D. W. "The Popularity of the Athenian Empire." *Historia* (1940), 9:257–69.

Cochrane, C. N. *Thucydides and the Science of History*. Oxford: Oxford University Press, 1929.

Collingwood, R. G. *The Idea of History*. Oxford: Oxford University Press, 1946.

Cornford, F. M. *Thucydides Mythistoricus*. London: Edward Arnold, 1907. Reprint London: Routledge & Kegan Paul, 1965.

Dover, K. J. "Thucydides." *Greece and Rome*, New Surveys in the Classics, No. 7 (1973).

Edmunds, Lowell. *Chance and Intelligence in Thucydides*. Cambridge, Mass.: Harvard University Press, 1975.

Ehrenberg, Victor. "Polypragmosyne: A Study in Greek Politics." *Journal of Hellenic Studies* (1947), 67:46–67.

Finley, John H., Jr. *Thucydides*. Cambridge, Mass.: Harvard University Press, 1942.

—— *Three Essays on Thucydides*. Cambridge, Mass.: Harvard University Press, 1967.

Fliess, Peter J. *Thucydides and the Politics of Bipolarity*. Baton Rouge: Louisiana State University Press, 1966.

Fritz, Kurt von. *Die Greichische Geschichtsschreibung*, vols. 1 and 2. Berlin: Walter de Gruyter, 1967.

Gomme, A. W. *A Historical Commentary on Thucydides*. Oxford: Oxford University Press, vol. 1², 1950; vols. 2–3, 1956; vol. 4 (continued by A. Andrewes and K. J. Dover), 1970.

—— "Speeches in Thucydides." In *Essays in Greek History and Literature*. Oxford: Oxford University Press, 1937.

Guthrie, W. K. C. *A History of Greek Philosophy*. Vols. 1–3. Cambridge: Cambridge University Press, 1962, 1965, 1969.

Hammond, N. G. L. "The Arrangement of the Thought in the Proem and in Other Parts of Thucydides 1." *Classical Quarterly* (1952), NS 2:127–41.

—— "The Particular and the Universal in the Speeches in Thucydides with Special Reference to that of Hemocrates at Gela." In P. A. Stadter, ed., *The Speeches in Thucydides*, pp. 49–59. Chapel Hill, N.C.: University of North Carolina Press, 1973.

Hatzfeld, J. *Alcibiade*. Paris: Presses Universitaires de France, 1940.

Hobbes, Thomas. *The History of the Grecian War in Eight Books, Written by Thucydides*. London, 1629.

How, W. W. and J. Wells. *A Commentary on Herodotus*. Vol. 1. Oxford: Oxford University Press, 1912.

Hunter, Virginia. "The Composition of Thucydides' *History:* A New Answer to the Problem." *Historia* (1977), 26:269–94.

—— *Thucydides, the Artful Reporter*. Toronto: Hakkert, 1973.

Jacoby, Felix. *Atthis. The Local Chronicles of Ancient Athens*. Oxford: Oxford University Press, 1949.

—— "*Patrios nomos*. State Burial in Athens and the Public Cemetery in the Kerameikos." *Journal of Hellenic Studies* (1944), 65:37–66.

Jebb, R. C. "The Speeches of Thucydides." In *Essays and Addresses*, pp. 359–45. Cambridge: Cambridge University Press, 1907.

Jones, W. H. S. *Philosophy and Medicine in Ancient Greece*. (Supplement to the Bulletin of the History of Medicine, no. 8). Baltimore, Md.: Johns Hopkins University Press, 1946.

Jones, W. H. S., ed. *Hippocrates*. Vol. 1 (Loeb series). Cambridge, Mass.: Harvard University Press, 1923.

Kagan, Donald. *The Archidamian War*. Ithaca, N.Y.: Cornell University Press, 1974.

—— *The Outbreak of the Peloponnesian War*. Ithaca, N.Y.: Cornell University Press, 1969.

Kakridis, J. T. *Der Thukydideische Epitaphios (Zetemata* Heft 26). Munich: Verlag C. H. Beck, 1961.

Kahn, C. F. "Plato's Funeral Oration: the Motif of the *Menexenus*." *Classical Philology* (1963), 58:220–34.

Lamb, W. R. M. *Clio Enthroned: A Study of Prose-Form in Thucydides*. Cambridge: Cambridge University Press, 1914.

Lateiner, Donald. "Heralds and Corpses in Thucydides." *Classical World* (1977), 71:97–106.

Luschnat, O. *Thukydides, der Historiker*. (Paulyschen *Realencyclopädie*, supp. 12, 1086–1354). Stuttgart: Alfred Druckenmüller, 1971.

Myres, John L. *Herodotus, Father of History*. Oxford: Oxford University Press, 1953.

Nestle, Wilhelm. *Von Mythos zum Logos*. Stuttgart: Kröner, 1942. Reprint Aalen: Scientia Verlag, 1966.

Page, Denys. "Thucydides' Description of the Great Plague at Athens." *Classical Quarterly* (1953), NS 3:97–119.

Parry, Adam. "The Language of Thucydides' Description of the Plague." *Bulletin of the Institute of Classical Studies* (London) (1969), 16:106–18.

—— "Thucydides' Historical Perspective." *Yale Classical Studies* (1972), 22:47–61.

Pritchett, W. Kendrick. *Dionysius of Halicarnassus, On Thucydides*. Berkeley, Calif.: University of California Press, 1975.

Pusey, N. M. "Alcibiades and *to philopoli*." *Harvard Studies in Classical Philology* (1940), 51:215–32.

Roberts, W. Rhys. *Dionysius of Halicarnassus, The Three Literary Letters*. Cambridge: Cambridge University Press, 1901.

Romilly, Jacqueline de. *Histoire et raison chez Thucydide*. Paris: Société d'édition "Les Belles Lettres," 1967.

—— *Thucydides and Athenian Imperialism*. Translated by P. Thody. Oxford: Blackwell, 1963.

Schlatter, Richard. *Hobbes' Thucydides*. New Brunswick, N.J.: Rutgers University Press, 1975.

Schwartz, Eduard. *Das Geschichtswerk des Thukydides*. Bonn, 1919 (2d ed. 1929). Reprint Hildesheim: Georg Olm, 1960.

Stadter, P. A., ed. *The Speeches in Thucydides*. Chapel Hill: University of North Carolina Press, 1973.

Stahl, Hans-Peter. *Thukydides: Die Stellung des Menschen im Geschichtlichen Prozess (Zetemata* Heft 40). Munich: Verlag C. H. Beck, 1966.

Ste Croix, G.E.M. de. "The Character of the Athenian Empire." *Historia* (1954) 3:1–41.

—— *The Origins of the Peloponnesian War*. London: Duckworth, 1972.

Strauss, Leo. *The City and Man*. Chicago: University of Chicago Press, 1964.

Syme, Ronald. "Thucydides." *Proceedings of the British Academy* (1960), 48:39–56.

Täubler, Eugen. *Die Archaeologie des Thukydides*. Leipzig: Teubner, 1927.

Usher, S., ed. *Dionysius of Halicarnassus, The Critical Essays.* Vol. 1 (Loeb series). Cambridge, Mass.: Harvard University Press, 1974.
Westlake, H. D. *Individuals in Thucydides.* Cambridge: Cambridge University Press, 1968.
Woodhead, A. G. *Thucydides on the Nature of Power.* (Martin Classical Lectures 24.) Cambridge, Mass.: Harvard University Press, 1970.

INDEX